Open Systems and IBM

Further Titles in the IBM McGraw-Hill Series

OS/2 Presentation Manager Programming: Hints and Tips
Bryan Goodyer   ISBN 0-07-707776-8

Introduction to MVS Systems Programming
David Elder-Vass   ISBN 0-07-707767-9

IBM RISC System/6000 User Guide
Mike Leaver and Hardev Sanghera   ISBN 0-07-707687-7

PC User's Guide: Simple Steps to Powerful Personal Computing
Peter Turner   ISBN 0-07-707421-1

Dynamic Factory Automation: Creating Flexible Systems for Competitive
Manufacturing
Alastair Ross   ISBN 0-07-707440-8

IBM RISC System 6000
Clive Harris   ISBN 0-07-707668-0

Details of these and other titles in the series are available from:

The Product Manager, Professional Books
McGraw-Hill Book Company Europe
Shoppenhangers Road, Maidenhead, Berkshire, SL6 2QL
Telephone: 0628 23422 Fax: 0628 770224

Pamela Gray

Open Systems and IBM

Integration and convergence

McGRAW-HILL BOOK COMPANY

London · New York · St Louis · San Francisco · Auckland
Bogotá · Caracas · Hamburg · Lisbon · Madrid · Mexico
Milan · Montreal · New Delhi · Panama · Paris · San Juan
São Paulo · Singapore · Sydney · Tokyo · Toronto

Published by
McGRAW-HILL Book Company Europe
Shoppenhangers Road, Maidenhead, Berkshire, SL6 2QL, England
Tel 0628 23432; Fax 0628 770224

British Library Cataloguing in Publication Data

Gray, Pamela A.
  Open Systems and IBM: Integration and
  Convergence.—(IBM McGraw-Hill Series)
  I. Title II. Series
  004.6

ISBN 0-07-707750-4

Library of Congress Cataloging-in-Publication Data

Gray, Pamela A. (Pamela Anne)
    Open systems and IBM: integration and convergence / Pamela Gray.
      p. cm.—(IBM McGraw-Hill series)
    Includes bibliographical references and index.
    ISBN 0-07-707750-4
    1. Computer architecture. 2. IBM computers. 3. Computer
networks. I. Title. II. Series
QA76.9.A73G72 1993
004.6–dc20
                                                                      92-41541
                                                                           CIP

1234 CUP 9543

Typeset by Alden Multimedia
and printed and bound in Great Britain at the University Press, Cambridge

Contents

This book is dedicated to the memory of Winifred Gray,
who proved it possible to handle conflicting demands with
commonsense, humor and love.

Foreword

The IBM McGraw-Hill Series

IBM UK and McGraw-Hill Europe have worked together to publish this series of books about information technology and its use in business, industry and the public sector.

The series provides an up-to-date and authoritative insight into the wide range of products and services available, and offers strategic business advice. Some of the books have a technical bias, others are written from a broader business perspective. What they have in common is that their authors—some from IBM, some independent consultants—are experts in their field.

Apart from assisting where possible with the accuracy of the writing, IBM UK has not sought to inhibit the editorial freedom of the series, and therefore the views expressed in the books are those of the authors, and not necessarily those of IBM.

Where IBM has lent its expertise is in assisting McGraw-Hill to identify potential titles whose publication would help advance knowledge and increase awareness of computing topics. Hopefully these titles will also serve to widen the debate about the important information technology issues of today and of the future—such as open systems, networking, and the use of technology to give companies a competitive edge in their market.

IBM UK is pleased to be associated with McGraw-Hill in this series.

Sir Anthony Cleaver
Chairman
IBM United Kingdom Limited

Acknowledgements

Grateful acknowledgements are due to IBM as the source of data for Figures 2.9, 5.5, 5.12, 5.15, 6.7, 6.8, 6.10, 6.11, 7.4–7.6, 8.6–8.12, 9.7–9.9, 9.14, 9.15, 9.19–9.21, 9.25, 10.1–10.6, 10.9, 10.12, 11.4–11.9, 11.15, 12.3.

IBM coordinator Stephen Lockey

Preface

This book was written specifically to help interested parties understand IBM's position within the rapidly evolving international open systems marketplace.

IBM has declared that it will be a world leader in open systems, and it is moving rapidly into that position. Based on in-depth studies of the needs of its customers, it is making extensive enhancements to its products and services and dramatically changing the way in which it conducts its business.

In the early stages of the open systems movement, IBM was not perceived as a strong advocate of the concepts. The huge investments which had been made in IBM proprietary technologies, and the size of the installed base of its customers' systems made it difficult for IBM to change fast in response to market demands for increased openness. In order to satisfy its own and its customers' needs, an evolutionary rather than revolutionary strategy had to be defined and followed.

The IBM open systems strategy is based on the principle of providing maximum protection of investment, both for its customers and for itself, while moving to new technologies. It covers many migration and integration issues that are important to the installed base, and in this sense provides an incremental approach to the opening up of components required for integrated systems.

There are wide-ranging and subtle implications of IBM's strategy, relating to business issues as much as to technology. These need to be communicated to the marketplace both outside and inside IBM, for the overall strategy is as complex as the changes IBM is making in order to implement it.

To help interpret IBM's strategy for as wide an audience as possible, the first part of this book (Chapters 1–4) reviews the background to the open systems movement, indicating how IBM's position has evolved within it. The second part (Chapters 5–7) provides an overview of IBM's open systems strategy, while the final part (Chapters 8–12) discusses the most important parts of the strategy in more detail, including looking into the future.

Chapters 1–4 describe the evolution of the open systems movement by outlining historical and technical developments in the computer industry from both the user and the vendor standpoint. Those particular forces which have led to open systems are discussed, and the role played by IBM highlighted. The objective is to show how and why IBM is in its current position and to indicate the changes that open systems forces it and its customers to make if they are to exploit the advantages.

At the end of the first four chapters, the conclusion can be drawn that since IBM has by far the largest installed customer base of any vendor, it carries the greatest responsibility for preserving as much as possible the investments made to date by its customers. This forces it into a complex transitional strategy.

Chapters 5–7 cover matters specific to IBM. Chapter 5 focuses on the issues of supporting the installed base and describes the relationship between the IBM proprietary (SAA) and UNIX (AIX) product lines. It explains why both are presented as 'open' by IBM and describes the steps being taken to provide inter-operability between the two families. Chapter 6 is an overview of the open enterprise concept and provides a complete summary of IBM's open systems strategy. Chapter 7 describes the many relationships which IBM is developing with other companies in order to implement the strategy faster and better than it could alone.

Chapters 8–11 contain more detail on the strategy and its implementation. Chapters 8 and 9 present the view that the demand for integrated information systems, distributed over networks, is driving the uptake of open systems and considers the consequences. Chapter 8 discusses open integrated information architectures, and describes the approach that IBM is taking to the development of products and services for implementation through the Information Warehouse. Chapter 9 covers developments in distributed computing, highlights some of the problems in implementation and references the Open Software Foundation's Distributed Computing Environment, to which IBM is committed.

Chapter 10 presents some applications of open systems concepts and technologies, and describes IBM's approach to providing solutions. It looks forward to some of the new technologies that will be embedded in applications of the future. Indications are given as to where these fit within open systems specifications and some products under development within IBM are described. Chapter 11 considers the practical issues of implementation of an open systems strategy across the enterprise and presents some of the services provided by IBM and its partners. Chapter 12 summarizes the book as a whole and presents some conclusions.

Appendix 1 contains a brief summary of the activities of some of the standards organizations that are referenced in the main text. The deliverables of the Open Software Foundation are described in some detail, since these are particularly relevant to IBM's strategy. Appendix 2 is a glossary of terms and Appendix 3 a list of addresses for some key standards organizations; the book concludes with a short bibliography and an index.

Detailed information on standards and the standards-setting process, other than what seemed essential for the understanding of the points to be made, has not been provided in this book. This is first because there is enough to say without including it, and second because my previous book *Open Systems—A Business Strategy for the 1990s*, also published by McGraw-Hill, is written from the open systems standards-setting perspective.

The accuracy of the technical information contained within the book has been checked by others, but any opinions expressed or implied within it are mine.

Although I am grateful to IBM and many of its staff for the help which they have unfailingly given me whenever I have requested it, there has been no intention to present the issues in any way other than how I personally see them, based on as much information as possible. IBM has supplied a great deal of the material on which the presentation is based, but it has had no editorial control over the content of the book, nor has it ever expressed a wish for it.

I would like to express my thanks to all the people who have contributed to the contents. Many of these go unacknowledged by name, being the friends, colleagues and acquaintances who continually input ideas and information to me. I would like to mention in particular: Pauline Brand of Dyadic Systems Limited, who has helped me to understand some of the problems of real customers; Brian Jeffreys of the International Technology Group, expert on AIX, RISC and many other subjects, and who has passed some of his knowledge on to me; Michael Milliken of Gunstock Hill Associates, who knows more about client/server computing than seems possible; and Esther Dyson of EdVenture Holdings Inc., whose analysis of technological trends always gives me food for thought.

Within IBM, I would like to thank all the many people who shared with me their time, information and insight. I would like particularly to thank Dave Larsen for providing much of the background material and for painstakingly reading the draft text. Special thanks go also to Debra Thomson, who was my anchor point within that complex organization. Her enthusiasm for the company for which she works was infectious and her energy sometimes kept me going when mine failed.

Finally, I would like to express my appreciation for the help of Janet Wass, whose efficient organization and administration left me free to think with an easy mind. She checked the manuscript in detail from my original input and coordinated the final production process. Without her encouragement I would not have completed the work.

Open systems is about integrating and providing access to information. McGraw-Hill is clearly a company that understands the value of information, and it demonstrates this through the breadth and depth of its activities and products. These are supplied primarily on paper today, but undoubtedly will be on many new electronic technologies tomorrow. McGraw-Hill therefore remains my publisher of choice and I am proud to be associated with it.

Pamela Gray

1
The information age

1.1 Introduction

The integration of today's technologies into information systems able to support worldwide needs for the 1990s and beyond offers major new business and management opportunities to both vendor and user organizations. But there are a number of fundamental problems that must be overcome before the full potential of integrated information systems can be realized. Many of these are at the strategic planning level and arise from the difficulty of integrating business and information technology (IT) strategies. Practical difficulties also occur at the implementation level, caused by incompatibilities in the hardware and software components of today's real-world information systems.

In this chapter we consider this situation in a general way. We will see that information systems are extending their reach within, between and across organizations, and across departmental, divisional and international boundaries. As a result, the design, implementation and management of such systems is becoming extremely complicated, and using appropriate planning methodologies is critically important.

As we proceed through the discussion, we will find that designing an information architecture for the enterprise as a whole, in which the business strategy is closely integrated with the IT design and implementation methodology, is a crucial step that must be taken by any organization looking to its long-term future. This architecture is dependent on the structure of the enterprise as a whole, and will change as the organization changes.

We will also see that to successfully design and use an information architecture that will take an organization into the twenty-first century requires taking a new approach to the acquisition of technology—one which turns out to be at the heart of open systems concepts. We will show that IBM has recognized the importance of this, and that its 'open enterprise' strategy is based upon it. As a consequence, IBM is changing its internal structure and its product offerings to be ready to support its customers as they start to move in the direction of integrated information systems.

In this chapter, we will be laying important groundwork for the material that is to follow. Once this chapter is read and understood, everything that follows is backup material, designed to show how we got to where we are today, and what needs to be done to get to where we want to be tomorrow.

1.2   The information age

Information has become as critical to most organizations today as land, machines and labor were in the Industrial Revolution of the 1800s. The 1990s have become known as 'the Information Age', and technologies to integrate, present and ease the assimilation of information are the focus of huge amounts of activity in the IT industry.

The means by which an organization exploits information will be a major competitive differentiator in the 1990s. We can already see this happening. As examples of the trends, consider the following leading-edge applications:

- Airline reservation systems have become a major competitive tool in the airline industry and are a significant revenue generator for the companies that own them. While providing a huge amount of market data, these systems also allow the carriers to market to their frequent travellers, price each seat by flight and date, link to a passenger's hotel and rental car preferences, and track luggage from destination to destination around the globe.
- Traditional banks pioneered local branch offices to which their customers went for banking services. More recently established electronic branch offices use automatic teller machines, debit cards and bank-by-mail, and are able to operate without the heavy personnel and real-estate overheads associated with traditional local bank sites. Strong competitive pressure forced all banks to change fast in order to compete.
- Telemarketing has grown very rapidly in the USA and in other countries. Firms have been able to cover wide areas electronically as a supplement to the physical coverage provided by the territorial salesmen. They have been able to do this by building up sophisticated computer databases that reflect a customer's buying and credit histories. Since the data usually reflects other account specifics, they are able to add a personal touch to an otherwise impersonal telephone call or direct mail piece. As costs of direct selling have escalated, telemarketing has grown rapidly as an alternative.

The well-known futurist Alvin Toffler views data (information) as a key ingredient to making wealth in the next century. In his book *Powershift* he writes: 'The new system for making wealth is totally dependent on the instant communication and dissemination of data....' This cannot possibly happen without the backing of appropriately designed information technology systems.

1.3   Information as a strategic weapon

Information is the lifeblood of an organization. It is the single most important asset, and yet it exists in, and flows around, most organizations in an almost totally undisciplined and unstructured way. Much of it resides in the heads of the key people within the enterprise, and consequently is often lost when such people leave. Communication of information in a timely and efficient way is one of the most difficult and frustrating management tasks.

Nevertheless, it is increasingly universally recognized that information can be used for the betterment of a business in many different ways:

- By supplying information automatically to those who need to respond to it quickly—for example, when a salesman needs to check a credit rating for a particular client—it can help to improve an organization's internal productivity and performance.
- Information can support new ways of managing and organizing a business —for example, two departments linked electronically, perhaps the design office and production, can work together on projects easily and interactively, cutting down the time to go from approved design to manufacturing, and ensuring that products are designed to production requirements.
- Information can be used as the basis for new applications to be developed, perhaps leading to new businesses—for example, specially designed new products might be designed for particular customers, based on their past buying habits.
- Relevant information at the fingertips of those who need to respond fast to competitive threats or to changes in the external market can help a company gain competitive advantage—for example, by alerting the sales force imme- diately to a move taken by a competitor, and suggesting the compensatory moves to take, or by adjusting prices in an international market as soon as currency exchange rates change.

1.4   The basis of competitive advantage

Until recently, competitive advantage was sought and found mainly on the basis of cost control. Systems monitored and controlled costs tightly, producing, for example, 'just-in-time' ordering and inventory control systems that reduced man- ufacturing costs considerably. Automated manufacturing, sometimes without the involvement of any human operators, is now common in many industries. Factories can work around the clock, and human labor costs can be minimized.

In Chapter 2 we will see that most of today's existing IT systems were designed to monitor and control costs, particularly in manufacturing applications, and to manage assets and other financial matters in all industries. Consequently the most common use for computers until recently has been for accounting, manufacturing and engineering applications.

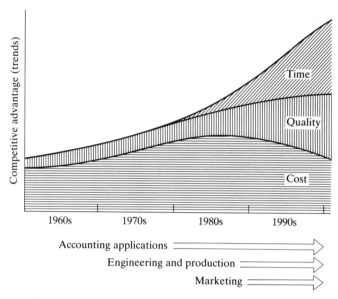

Figure 1.1.   The basis for competitive advantage.

In the late 1980s the emphasis for competitive advantage shifted to quality of products, and computer systems were concentrated on resolving engineering and production problems. Adherence to internationally defined quality standards is now a requirement in most industries, and prestigious awards for quality are given. The demand for quality is not just applied to products—it extends to services and to internal structures and procedures too.

Today, response time is becoming the differentiating factor (Fig. 1.1). Financial institutions are the obvious example of this, where a financial trader's business succeeds or fails on the basis of responding faster than a competitor to an opportunity in the market. Other examples are the international delivery companies, such as Federal Express and DHL, where speed and reliability of delivery are the products. Competitive pricing is assumed to follow automatically from the already tightly controlled cost structures that are in place.

1.5   Knowledge workers

Almost all businesses need to respond quickly and efficiently to new product introductions, customer service queries, and changes in the external environment. To be able to do this cost-effectively requires a system which provides the right information to the right people at the right place and time. If the old systems cannot be suitably adapted to do this, then new processes and systems must be developed.

These newer applications increasingly involve people whose jobs primarily involve managing information in some form. This group of 'knowledge workers' is growing rapidly, and will soon be the largest single category of workers in the developed countries. To quote management guru Peter Drucker, 'The center of gravity of the business has shifted to the knowledge worker.'

1.6 Integrating information systems with business

As the nature of work changes, the information systems must change with it. They must be able to deal with rapid organizational, business and technological changes in a cost-effective manner. For this to be done, the information systems must be designed and implemented in a new way—with adaptability built in.

In the 1960s and 1970s information systems structures were driven by the technology, and highly specialized skills were required for their design, implementation and use. The systems could be characterized as centralized, specialized and controlled (Fig. 1.2).

By the early 1980s functional management began to be involved in the decisions regarding purchases of minicomputers for departmental and divisional use. These often required the development of turnkey vertical solutions, with software written for a particular use. Later, individuals installed many thousands of personal computers (PCs), growing them into networks as the technology developed that allowed them to do so easily. The systems at this time could be described as distributed (throughout the organization) and uncontrolled, although they were often centrally supported by the IT 'experts'.

Today, the information system extends both within and outside the enterprise. Departments and divisions work together, and organizations increasingly communicate with each other, for example, when trading electronically. The information

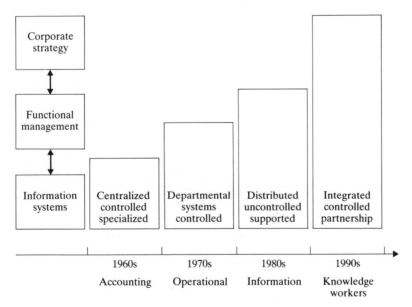

Figure 1.2. Integrating information systems with business.

system has become an integral part of the business, and is heavily embedded within the corporate strategy. As a result, functional management and information systems management must now work closely together, defining and solving business problems in a controlled partnership.

The experience of many organizations in developing and using time-critical information-based applications shows that the greatest level of success is achieved when a company's business plan is tightly integrated with, and closely reflected in, its information systems plan. Unfortunately this integration is very difficult to achieve, particularly given the starting positions in which many companies today find themselves.

1.7   Information infrastructures

The proper design and subsequent implementation of an 'integrated information infrastructure' is the key to achieving flexibility in the business as the environment changes. The business must put the mechanisms in place which transport information from its source to wherever the decisions are to be made, and must make sure that these mechanisms can change quickly in response to business needs (Fig. 1.3).

An information infrastructure is a full support structure of interfaces, standards and architectures—for communications, data, user access, applications development tools, operating system interfaces, systems management—chosen so as to provide the information flow that the business requires across the enterprise and between enterprises. It provides the basic facilities and architectures to allow the movement and management of information. Properly designed it will help to safeguard the existing investments made in IT while defining the path for the future. The objective in building an information infrastructure for the business is to enhance the effectiveness of all the system users, from one end of the company to the other.

There are several basic components to the infrastructure, but the most obvious, the most important and the most difficult to deal with in a practical sense is the raw data itself. At present few organizations have enterprise-wide standards for the cataloging, retrieving or storing of data. In fact, getting everyone to agree on

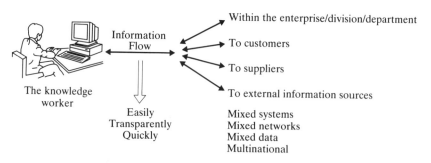

Figure 1.3.   The information infrastructure.

standards for describing the common entities used within an organization is sometimes the most difficult task of all in the practical implementation of an integrated information system. We will return to this problem later.

1.8   The evolution of computer use

In the past, the use of technology was focused on improving the efficiency in an individual, workgroup or application area. Now, this focus has extended to involve all of the operation, as well as outside parties.

As an example, consider the feedback provided to retail distributors from automated point of sale devices in stores (Fig. 1.4). These devices allow the store's inventory database to be updated automatically. When this information is passed to the company-wide electronic ordering systems, merchandise might only be reordered at those stores that are below a certain prespecified level of stock. Furthermore, if the purchasing information is linked to the customer data, as is the case when a credit card is used, then information can be accumulated on customers' buying habits, allowing special targeted marketing campaigns to take place.

Today's computing systems can grow from personal computers used by individuals, to departmental solutions on networks or minicomputers, through divisional lines of business applications on networks of machines, extending out to enterprise-wide data-intensive programs, and encompassing suppliers, business partners, and customers. As we move to a global economy, we must focus not only on the intra-enterprise capabilities, but also on the inter-enterprise communications, data access and applications issues.

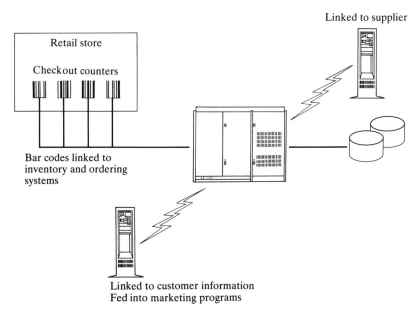

Figure 1.4.   Integrated information systems in retail stores.

As an example, an automobile manufacturer may be electronically linked with its suppliers, perhaps a subcontractor making a particular component for just-in-time assembly line delivery. It may also be linked with its dealers, who might wish to order special options for particular models when, and only when, customers want them. If the two pieces of information can be dealt with together in one system then the manufacturer can keep its inventory to a minimum, provide rapid delivery to the dealers, and help the dealers to reduce their inventory also. In addition, if the dealer keeps electronic records of customers, and these are accessible to the manufacturer, then cars can easily be identified and recalled directly by the manufacturer, if there is a need to do so.

Today's computing systems can provide a broad range of services, from simple electronic mail messages to accessing the corporate databases. They are able to serve many users and to incorporate diverse functions. In theory, they are able to integrate all users in all applications needed by the business.

In practice, the lack of control at earlier stages of development has resulted in systems used within one part of the enterprise often being technically incompatible with those used elsewhere. As a result, for the sake of being able to link efficiently with other systems, valuable and scarce technical resources must be used to modify the incompatible products. When new technology appears, this process of modification must be repeated, or else, and too often, valuable investments made earlier must be discarded.

The aim of open systems advocates from the start has been to change this situation. The dream is to have information accessible to any authorized person from anywhere in the organization. Systems should be designed in a modular way so that components can be replaced as appropriate, while the investment made in the rest of the system is retained as much as possible. The question is—how can this be achieved in practice? The answer lies in choosing the technology appropriately.

1.9   The technical framework, or architectural design

In the technical implementation of integrated information systems, there are a number of elements that have to be considered (Fig. 1.5). The most important of these are:

- The computers themselves, which process and present the information to the user
- The methods by which the computers communicate one with another
- The means by which the various computers may cooperate to work on problems (this will be a combination of their internal technologies and the communication methodologies)
- The manner in which the data is stored, accessed, presented, controlled and used
- The function of the applications, the relationships between them, and the methodology used for their development.

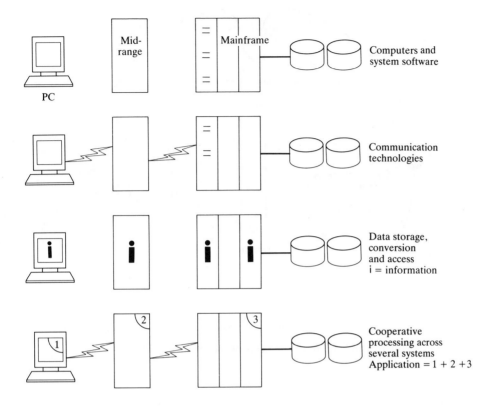

Figure 1.5. Architectural design considerations.

It is important to note the clear separation made here between the data—i.e., the facts—and the applications that use the data—i.e., the interpretations made of the facts.

Data should be regarded as a corporate asset. Huge investments are made in the collection and maintenance of it, on a par with that of many other corporate assets. An important difference is that accountants do not normally track the corporate data assets carefully, nor do they yet appear on the corporate balance sheet, other than under the general heading of 'goodwill'. This must change eventually, when the true value of information is formally recognized.

In the logical design of an information infrastructure, it is essential that data is separated from applications. Different applications should be able to use the same data, even if for very different purposes. Today, very few organizations have managed to make this separation, although many are known to be working towards it. As we shall see later, the concepts of the consolidation of data and the separation of data from applications are fundamental to IBM's long-term enterprise data management strategy.

Although each element in the architectural design (Fig. 1.6) must be tackled to some extent separately, they are all interdependent. For example, the needs of the

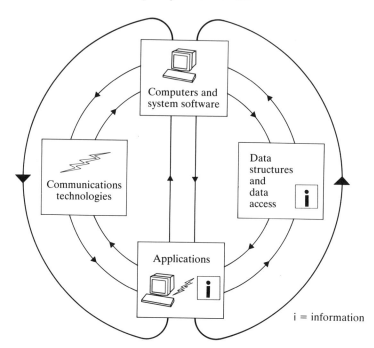

i = information

Figure 1.6.   Interdependence of components of the architecture.

application may determine the network technology to be used, or the computer operating system may put constraints on the way that data is presented to the user.

1.10   Why is an architecture necessary?

The task of designing an overall information architecture for an organization of any size has proved to be very difficult. Nevertheless, it has also proved to be very helpful to the understanding and successful implementation of the systems, and to their ultimate use within the business.

According to Michael Earl's definition (Earl, 1989), an information architecture is defined as 'the technology which guides the organization in satisfying business and management information systems needs'. He gives the main reasons for requiring such an architecture as:

1   When IT becomes embedded in the business, the need for systems integration increases. An agreed and well-defined architecture provides a framework for, and a mechanism to, consider and agree the necessary interfaces and compatibilities which will allow the integration to take place easily.

2   Organizational structures evolve and change, business needs change, and technology advances rapidly. An architecture provides the framework for reviewing technological choices over time.

Elements	Parameters	Policy	Plans
Computers and system software	Minimum number of variants	PCs, UNIX, IBM mainframe	Common office automation software across group
Communications	All computers must be linked	OSI, TCP/IP, SNA and bridges	Complete voice and data network
Data	Data must be compatible and accessible	Data definitions agreed, SQL access	Implement universal access with security
Applications	Business priorities determine development program	Buy in packages wherever possible	Develop new applications

Figure 1.7. Defining the architecture.

3 Once the information strategy is formulated, the architecture provides a structure for implementation.

4 As the business and IT strategies converge, a technological model of the organization itself is required. This will be a part of the architecture.

An example of how the architecture might start to be defined is shown in Fig. 1.7, based on Earl's approach.

IBM's open systems enterprise strategy is based on the concepts of information architectures, frameworks and information modelling. In IBM's terminology, the information model of the enterprise itself is known as the 'Repository', and the information framework is called the 'Information Warehouse'. These are discussed in detail in Chapter 8.

1.11   Modelling the enterprise

Enterprise information modelling allows an enterprise to understand and communicate the basic functions and goals of the business. To some extent, it can also protect the organization from important information being lost to the company should key employees leave. Some of the questions that the enterprise model should be able to answer are shown in Fig. 1.8, based on Earl.

Although enterprise models exist for all businesses, they are most commonly only in the minds of the senior executives. When a model is put down on paper, it can be out of date within a few months if it has not been properly constructed to take account of the changes which are constantly occurring in the business.

Today, there are no generally accepted standard methodologies for formally producing enterprise models. The few proprietary methods which do exist are not widely used or well understood.

The enterprise model defines the characteristics of the business at a conceptual

- The business vision
- Organizational structure
- Management style
- Accountability
- Human resource policies
- Business strategies
- Critical success factors
- Attitude to risks
- Cost constraints
- Regulatory factors
- Effects of external environment
- Dependence on IT
- Requirements for IT
- Measurements of success

Figure 1.8.   Factors in the enterprise model.

level—what the business does (the processes), what data is needed by the processes (information flow), how the business is run (guidelines, procedures, policies and goals), and how the current information systems support the work done by the business. The model will usually reside in a central access point, to be used by various applications as required.

Completing the model and validating it against the actual business is critical. Once this has been done it can be used as a planning tool to identify important requirements, suggest projects to undertake, and evaluate their possible impact. This is discussed further in Chapter 11.

1.12   The enterprise data

In order to produce an integrated information system in which different applications are able to access the corporate data for specific purposes, it is first necessary to consolidate the data that is scattered around the enterprise. There are a number of issues that must be addressed (Fig. 1.9):

- Where the data is stored now, and where and how it is to be stored in the future
- How the data is to be accessed within the enterprise, across geographical locations and across systems from different vendors
- How the data is to be managed, who is to have access to it, and how it is to be protected and updated
- How the data is to be used and what it means in the business context.

IBM is addressing these issues through its 'Information Warehouse' concept. This consists of products, standards, processes, program tools, interface specifications, and information for the use and management of a company's data assets. It is designed to address long-standing problems in access to data, management of data, and use of data.

The Information Warehouse is much more than a single product from IBM. It is a framework in which many products from IBM and from other vendors are designed to work together in harmony. Starting with today's products, standards

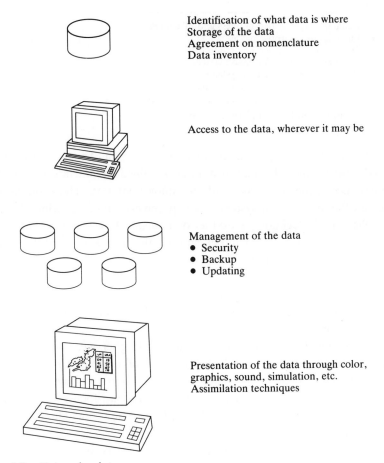

Identification of what data is where
Storage of the data
Agreement on nomenclature
Data inventory

Access to the data, wherever it may be

Management of the data
• Security
• Backup
• Updating

Presentation of the data through color,
graphics, sound, simulation, etc.
Assimilation techniques

Figure 1.9. Enterprise data.

and processes, it will evolve over time as new products, standards, interfaces, processes and business information are added. It will provide access to data across both IBM and non-IBM platforms, using products from IBM and other vendors.

As we will see in Chapter 7, IBM is working with a number of partners and other vendors to plan the evolution of the Information Warehouse and related concepts over time. Chapter 8 contains detailed information on the Information Warehouse.

1.13   Implementing an information architecture

The integration and subsequent use of information resources can mean increased flexibility and productivity for an enterprise, but implementation of integrated information systems is not easy. Designing the enterprise model takes skill and experience; in-depth knowledge is needed of the available technology as well as of the business in which the enterprise is engaged.

The business and IT strategies need to be closely interwoven, and the enterprise

---

- Defining the integrated business and IT strategy
- Building the enterprise model
- Designing the information architecture
- Implementing the information systems
- Operating the information systems
- Maintaining, updating and developing the system

Figure 1.10.   Implementing an information architecture.

model will embody the important characteristics of each of them. Only after the integrated business and information strategy is defined and the information architecture designed is the enterprise ready for implementation. The planning phase then defines the information system (IS) requirements in detail, while the design phase applies specific technologies to the components of the solution. The solution can then be implemented, tested and integrated into the business and IS processes, and managed as necessary thereafter (Fig. 1.10).

An information systems supplier that wishes to implement an information architecture for an enterprise as a whole will necessarily need to be very close to the thinking embodied in its enterprise model, and have a full appreciation for the needs of the information architecture.

Recognizing this, IBM is increasingly concentrating services and support in all of the areas indicated in Fig. 1.10. It now offers a full range of services, including strategy, planning, design, implementation and operation for IT systems for enterprises of all sizes. The strategy consultancy services are focused on helping to translate business requirements into technical IS directions, including defining the enterprise model.

In other words IBM is taking steps to ensure that it has strong service offerings for all the steps that an organization must go through when designing and managing an integrated information system for now and the future. Its plan is based on being able to implement and manage any or all of the implementation processes that its customers wish to subcontract to it.

Most of these services have in fact been offered by IBM to its customers for implementations based on its own proprietary products for many years. But in the open systems world there are three important changes to note:

- First there is IBM's public recognition of the importance of the enterprise model to the implementation decisions that follow. This has resulted in the subsequent gearing up of its consultancy services to offer help in an area previously very much the domain of the big management consultancies.
- Second there is the fact that the frameworks which it is defining and implementing are very much cooperative efforts across the industry as a whole, involving both software companies and other vendors. More on this can be found in Chapter 7.
- Third and most radical, none of the services which IBM is now offering are restricted to IBM products. IBM has announced that it will supply and support

products from other vendors, depending on what is already at the customer's site, and what products provide the best solution to the customer's future requirements.

The implementation services offered by IBM range from designing, building and running a data center, regardless of the vendor mix of hardware and software products, to providing business recovery backup in case of an unexpected breakdown or data loss; from customized turnkey network management of multi-vendor networks to customized systems integration; from end-user support help desks for IBM and non-IBM hardware and software to international value-added networking services; from maintenance services for IBM and non-IBM equipment to the supply of software products in a heterogeneous environment.

As time goes on, IBM can be expected to expand these services to cover as much as possible of the total enterprise requirements, using both its own developed and other vendors' products, as required. It can also be expected to open up many of its own technologies to its competitors. As it does so, it will continually be forced to decide where to draw the line between cooperation and competition. Cooperation may grow the market faster, but in the end IBM, like any other vendor, wants as much of the business for itself as it can get.

1.14   Multivendor support

In theory, IBM could implement a well-designed enterprise information infrastructure based entirely upon its own current and very comprehensive range of systems, software and service products. But to do so in practice, the enterprise would be required to start with a clean slate of entirely IBM or compatible systems, and have no need to communicate with external organizations.

Few organizations are in that position. Most have evolved through a period of decentralized or uncontrolled purchasing strategies, or have seen the business grow through acquisitions or mergers. As a result, they now have multivendor networks of considerable complexity, on which many different types of systems are linked. Even if an enterprise adopts a single vendor policy for itself, it is unlikely that the same will apply for the external organizations with which it needs to communicate.

Enterprises today are trying to build integrated information systems on top of the mixture of multivendor and multi-protocol systems that they already have installed and in which they have invested vast amounts. IBM systems may dominate on many sites, particularly at the mainframe end, but many other manufacturers are well represented on the networks overall.

Some enterprises have taken a positive decision to build heterogeneous systems for the future from hardware and software components supplied by a number of different vendors. They have recognized the long-term advantages that could accrue from an 'open' procurement policy based on standard technologies supported by a number of vendors.

All vendors of information technology products must consider and respond to the issues raised by an increasingly multivendor-installed base of hardware and software components. This has implications for requiring products to be designed to work more easily together, as well as for services that cross vendor boundaries. IBM is increasingly providing multivendor support across its full range of products and services; this is an integral part of its 'open' strategy, as we will see in later chapters.

CASE STUDY

We finish this chapter with a case history that graphically illustrates the points made in it. It is reproduced here by kind permission of the Connecticut Mutual Life Insurance Company.

Presented at Executive INTEROP, 1991, and updated by Janice L. Scites, Connecticut Mutual Life Insurance Company.

To re-invent the business, re-engineer the business systems

There are certain facts about Connecticut Mutual that will help you better understand the business issues and problems we are facing.

Connecticut Mutual Life Insurance Company was founded in 1846 and ranks among the top 25 US life insurers, with assets of $11.75 billion and more than $79 billion of life insurance in force. There are approximately 1900 home office staff. The company has 1.2 million life policyholders, and distributes products and services in all 50 US states, Puerto Rico, and the District of Columbia, through a network of general agents and more than 3000 career agents and brokers. We also sell and manufacture mutual funds, annuities, disability income, and pension products.

Life insurance is a business in which commitments last 10, 20, or even 50 years. Long-term financial strength, and world-class, outstanding quality service are essential to survival through the nineties and beyond.

Historically, the insurance industry has been characterized by paper-driven, clerically based, sequential, factory-like workflows. These workflows, which are labor-intensive and inefficient, no longer meet our service and financial objectives.

In the fall of 1990, we embarked on a project to create 'One Image' of Connecticut Mutual. This project is pulling together our fragmented systems, eliminating paper, restructuring and compressing our complex business work process.

One Image, which is now a registered Service Mark, was and is endorsed as a vision by Connecticut Mutual's senior management and enterprise-wide by all division heads.

In addition to a vision, we agreed to adhere to the following management watchwords:

- Manageable increments of change
- Implementation of technology tools
- Orderly, planned development of services and systems
- Action orientation with defined deliverables
- Cost and benefit justification of capital outlays.

Armed with these watchwords, we agreed to the following tactical approaches:

- Cooperative vendor solutions
- Maximization and absorption of technology change
- World-class service as benchmarked against companies like American Express
- Clients being treated as important and special, having affinity with Connecticut Mutual
- Location-independent services
- Enterprise-wide shared service tools called utilities.

The 'command center', or integrated workstation, is our focal point to pull together clients, systems, service and products into a single customer view. The One Image vision, the management watchwords and the tactical approaches are the business drivers. The systems and people implications of this initiative are formidable when put into practice.

Our business and technical teams began by taking a serious look at our business processes. We asked some very basic workflow/re-engineering questions—not technology questions:

- What are we doing? (The business activities)
- Why are we doing them? (Are there legal, service, product, systems, or financial reasons)
- Do we really need to do them?
- If we don't need to do them, will we stop? (Do we have the courage to stop?)
- Of the balance of activities that are left, which must we do for legitimate reasons, what is the current workflow or business area analysis?
- How do these activities translate into job functions, such as underwriting or claims?

Each job function was then defined as related to the command center and we created business process views or fields of view. The command center had to allow employees to be fully accountable for doing their jobs from start to finish with minimal or no handoffs—we wanted to empower each employee.

These business process views or 'fields of view' include:

- Underwriters
- Customer service representatives (which includes phone reps, premium payments, check service)
- Claims examiners
- Agents and/or other field staff
- Technicians (by technicians we mean programmers, business analysts, technical operating staff)
- Executives.

In this phase, we discovered that our use of software and hardware had been fairly random. Enormous amounts of software had been placed on various PCs, but no hard questions had been asked about use and cost-effectiveness. We brought to a halt this unfocused approach to the purchase and use of technology tools to solve business problems.

Instead we embraced the disciplined, command-center-driven fields of view, and began in September 1990 the vendor review for selecting the tool set for the command center.

We completed vendor review by November 1990, sent the proposal to our Board in December and embarked on implementation in January 1991.

The tool set on the command center includes, and is now functioning with, the following:

- Image processing, storage and retrieval
- Image management with queuing and prefetching
- Workflow management or scripting
- Systems masking (icon-driven)
- Automated forms handling, with no printed forms
- Expert systems and rule-based files
- Central document preparation
- Client relational database (DB2-based)
- Management statistical reporting
- Pending/tracking for every transaction with appendage to the client file on the mainframe and the image file.

In addition to these tools we have installed other client-driven utilities such as:

- Voice response for agent data, for policyholder data, and teleservicing
- Bar coding for forms, routing and marketing insertion
- Common print engine creating a common bill, letter and annual statement format
- Fax as a communications device into the PC and as a scanner for image

- Delivery to our field locations of inquiry access to the direct file and transaction activity detail.

We will continue to take advantage of all available technologies as they reach acceptable maturity at reasonable expense.

The basic technical environment we have chosen to support the command center is:

- IBM PS/2s, running Windows 3.0
- Campus token-ring LAN
- FileNet imaging hardware and background software
- IBM mainframe host computer services.

We are testing PC clones for data entry and rendezvous work. This configuration allows us to provide our tools as utilities company-wide.

We have installed 300 workstations in the life division since January 1991. By the end of 1992 150 will be installed in my area and potentially many more in the rest of the company, depending on capital and our ability to absorb the charge. Disability Income has installed claims workstations and will follow our initiative in the underwriting area. The mutual fund area and annuity division started their rollout in September 1992.

As part of the project plan we implemented workflow scripting in our check service operation. As part of that rollout we converted, scanned and indexed 300 000 pieces of paper, eliminating 120 file cabinets containing over 400 drawers. By creating our first paperless business process, we increased productivity by 60 per cent.

For the client relational database we have developed a corporate indexing scheme for all paper and data, the index supported in the image system and in the mainframe.

In our customer service division we have masked 26 old but functional systems allowing:

- One-time system entry for reps
- On-line client consolidation statement with production in seconds versus days
- On-line super inquiry of a client's product holdings in seconds versus days
- On-line death claims payment in 4 days versus 21.

Programmers each received a technician's command center, which boosted productivity by 20 per cent. We required that maintenance and development cycles decrease on a step basis over 1991 and 1992. We are now moving to object-oriented programming.

My purpose in reviewing at least a few of the deliverables is to emphasize the speed of implementation plus the power of the configuration of tools.

As we have dealt with the new work world certain re-engineering philosophies have emerged. First, no vendor had or has the full package. We believe that in the blended world our business requires a distributed client/server systems architecture providing access to mainframe data. No vendor for the foreseeable future, if ever, will have the total solution. We have broken the internal and external vendor monopoly attitude.

This approach means that we require vendors to deliver functionality, not promises. Vendors have agreed to work closely with other vendors to solve Connecticut Mutual's business problems. To this end we will continue to strive for equipment, software and location independence.

Second, to accomplish what we have to date, our management has adopted a cross-divisional team technique which ignores hierarchy, turfdom, rank and serial number. We share resources between areas and rotate project leaders. Teams are required to be equally business plus technical with access on an *ad hoc* basis to expert consultants, if warranted.

Next, on integrating the new and old, we are committed to maximizing the skills of our existing staff and the power of old but functional systems. Masking has allowed us to leverage off the old while moving data into the new world.

Interoperability ties with a cooperative vendor solution. We are setting standards for software and hardware which vendors must meet. For internal teams it requires phasing out vertical systems if they cannot be connected and developing horizontal tools. As an example, a product engine with modules of reusable code for product development with administration modules was designed to shorten our time to market cycle.

This brings me to the close with a summary of our One Image goals and the business benefits we have so far achieved:

- Speed customer response. Business result: the beneficiary change process previously required 22 human interventions, taking days. This has been reduced to two human interventions, taking seconds.
- Improve operating productivity for all areas with 35 per cent as target. Business result: 20 per cent to 60 per cent achieved so far, with staff count reduced by 12 per cent.
- Produce significant return on investment. Business result: in the individual life area, the $6.5 million investment is being paid back in 24 months. Other areas follow a similar pattern, but will complete faster with a higher return because they can leverage off the platform that has been developed.
- Shorten and streamline the business process through disciplined review of what we do and then apply the best tools to compress the process. Solve business requirements not technology requirements.

- Eliminate paper dependence. Business result: changing from sequential to a parallel simultaneous environment. Image processing with workflow scripting allows this. Keeping images by client and by business function helps us provide quality service to our customers.

Finally, the One Image goal to which we are all committed is that we will continuously improve our business process, accepting change and managing to change for world class service while meeting pricing and revenue targets.

The change process, or re-engineering, whether with or without technology, involves planning communications with employees on a continuous basis. We announced re-engineering at the start in memo form and at meetings throughout the division. We had a PR strategy internally with videos, newsnotes, and a hands-on demo and wired the cafeteria to show the command center. We committed our management teams to a posture of openness, information flow and providing training to all employees affected. In 1991 we completed 15 000 hours of training ranging from programmers to clerical staff.

Connecticut Mutual intends to continue to be an innovator in re-engineering the business process for the decade of the nineties and beyond. By providing one integrated view of our data, we have laid the foundation for providing outstanding quality products and services to our customers.

1.15   Summary

In this chapter we have taken a general look at the business environment today and related that to a need for efficient and integrated information systems that allow an organization to respond fast to changes in the internal and external environments.

We have seen that at the heart of such systems should be a model of the enterprise as a whole, describing the interrelation between the business and IT strategies. Once built, this model should allow controlled management of change over time.

An essential part of the model is the integration of data and the separation of data from the applications that use it. This is difficult to achieve, particularly when so much of today's available data exists in many different environments, intimately tied to the application that uses it.

IBM has taken a top-down view of enterprise systems and information architectures. Through cooperative partnerships, it is developing the required data and information management technologies. Recognizing the various steps that the enterprise must go through in order to implement an integrated information system, it is strengthening its service offerings, and extending these to the supply and support of products from other non-IBM vendors. A key part of its strategy is to protect investments that have already been made by customers.

In the following chapters we will see how the situation described has evolved over time, and how IBM evolved with it. We will track the development of the open systems movement, relating it to IBM's own actions and reactions. In this way we will lead up to a full description of IBM's open systems strategy, which we will see closely mirrors the expressed needs of its largest customers.

2
The evolution of enterprise computing

2.1   Introduction

As computer technology evolved, specific applications were computerized at different times, in alignment with technical developments. As a result, the 'heritage' systems in most organizations are made up of many different and incompatible components that have been supplied by several vendors. The accumulated investment in hardware in these systems is huge, but is small compared with that made in software, training and the buildup of expertise.

Bringing these diverse systems together into an integrated information system that can serve an organization's overall interests is one of the greatest challenges facing the computer industry today.

In this chapter, we consider the circumstances that have produced the many independent and incompatible 'islands of computing' in enterprises. In the process, we should reach an understanding of the practical issues now facing internal management when trying to rationalize the current configurations. We will conclude that, if integrated information systems are to be built that will serve the needs for the medium to long term, some fundamental changes are required.

We will see that the industry is in fact moving to address this issue through the adoption of internationally agreed standards for at least some of the system components. Without this, it is impossible to predict where the solution to many of today's inherited problems will otherwise be found.

2.2   The stages of computer application development

Technical developments within the computer industry are generally considered to have taken place in distinct 'waves'. As a result, the uptake of computers in commercial and other organizations has progressed in a parallel fashion (Fig. 2.1).

The applications that have emerged have usually been associated with the kinds of machines that originally made them possible. For example, a corporation's accounting system probably runs on the central mainframe computer, initially supplied by IBM, and appropriate to the situation that applied 10 to 15 years ago. The software has most often been written in the Cobol language, and continually

Stage 1	Stage 2	Stage 3	Stage 4
Mainframe	Mainframe Minicomputers	Mainframe Minicomputers PCs PC LANs	Interconnected Integrated Information

1960s	1970s	1980s	1990s
Centralized controlled	Central and departmental controlled	Distributed uncontrolled	Distributed controlled

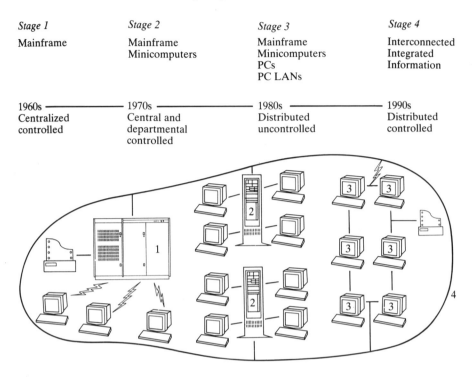

Figure 2.1.   Evolution of enterprise computing.

added to over time. It may well run in association with the IBM Customer Information Communication System (CICS) software, designed to manage high-volume transaction processing applications. Such systems have been in active use within many companies for the past 10 to 20 years.

Because of the history, the connection between the application and the size and nature of the machine still persists in many people's minds, and it is hard for them to separate the two. However, it should be remembered that the applications found on certain machines today are not there necessarily because that is the best place on which they should now be running. Rather, it is often because that is where they were first developed, and the economics of the situation dictates that it is not yet time to move them, even if new technologies have emerged which seem to offer advantages.

2.3   The first stage—data processing

In the first stage of computerization (Fig. 2.2), enterprises invested huge amounts of resources to build applications software systems to automate common processes hitherto performed by teams of people manually, with paper systems. These jobs were already systematically defined, involving large numbers of routine tasks, and were natural candidates to be performed by machines. Known as 'core' applica-

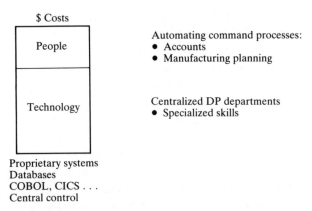

Figure 2.2.   Stage 1: data processing.

tions, these computerized what were then the clerical activities of single departments, dealing with payroll, accounts receivable, manufacturing planning and
similar tasks.

Data from reams of paper was transferred onto punched cards and then input
to the machines by specialized operators. This was eventually processed in 'batch'
mode, as one continual, large job which, in the absence of technical problems,
proceeded from start to finish, with no interruption, or possibility of interaction,
from the operator.

These applications were gradually moved away from card input to 'on-line'
implementations. This meant that they could be driven from terminals on
operators' desks. Users could then input information to them, or access information from them, by using screens connected to the main computer, though often at
some distance from it. The application itself, producing the statement of accounts
from the input data perhaps, was still run in batch mode, often at off-peak times.

These screens were 'dumb' (and many still are), in the sense that they contain no
inbuilt intelligence other than that required for the communication process. The
necessary processing power is contained within, and the application software runs
on, the large, usually centralized, most often IBM-supplied, mainframe machine.

2.4   The centralized DP department

The organizations that emerged to manage the functions on these centralized
machines comprised groups of specially trained operators, engineers and
managers. Such groups of experts were needed to facilitate the interface between
the machines and the people using them—it was not possible for untrained people
to use the technology directly.

In the centralized data-processing (DP) departments that grew continually in the
1960s and 1970s, great emphasis was placed on protection of the corporate data,
security of access to it, and on techniques to manage the administration and
maintenance of the systems. Today the most sophisticated software for such

management and control is still tied to these machines, and knowledge has been accumulated by the people who manage them.

It requires special skills to implement solutions on the centralized mainframe machines, and the supply of people with these has always been exceeded by the demand. Over time, as the needs of a business expand, new applications are continually required. The time that users have to wait for new applications to be developed starts to grow. Today the backlog time, defined as the time at which the development team is free to start a new application that is sitting in the queue, averages several years in most organizations in most countries.

Specialized computer languages were developed for business applications to be run on the large mainframe machines. The most popular of these is Cobol, which first appeared in 1958. Cobol is still the most widely used language in commercial applications. Again, this is not necessarily because it is the best or most suitable tool now available, but because there is a huge investment in software written in it, and a vast army of programmers and support staff who are familiar with it.

2.5   The emergence of the independent software industry

To facilitate management of the vast amounts of data that often needed to be processed, data management techniques were developed both by the computer hardware manufacturers and by independent software companies. In the latter case, development necessarily took place in close cooperation with the hardware manufacturer, but, since the software was intimately tied to the hardware environment, the software company often ended up selling its software products in competition with the computer manufacturer.

Examples of companies that specialized in database software for the mainframe environment were ADR and Cullinet, both now part of Computer Automation (CA), and Software AG. The former were founded in the USA, while Software AG has headquarters in Germany.

Other large application software companies grew in the 1970s and 1980s, most often specializing in the development and support of core applications for business. Examples of companies predominantly dealing with financial and accounting needs were Management Sciences of America (MSA), now part of Dun and Bradstreet, and SAP AG in Germany. Others such as Morino, Dequesne and BST (all now part of Legent) and Pansophic (now part of CA) specialized in system administration tools.

The mainframe part of the computer industry, covering both hardware and software products, has always been dominated by IBM. As a result, IBM has built up a vast army of specialists in mainframe technologies, and has developed a wide set of software and services designed specifically to support its commercial customers.

Mainframe customers are often using applications on which their businesses depend completely. To support them IBM built up the service side of its business, in the process and over many years developing sophisticated tools to handle the management and security of the systems and the data contained within them. The importance of this will become clear when we discuss those issues in the open systems world that are of greatest importance to commercial users.

2.6   Proprietary systems

In the early development of the computer market, systems were always proprietary, meaning that software written for one manufacturer's machine was intimately tied to the hardware and operating system software (which manages the hardware) of the particular machine. Software could not therefore be easily moved from one manufacturer's system to another's.

As a result, customers for a particular manufacturer's machines gradually become tied in to that manufacturer through the investments which they made in applications software and skill development. This is referred to as becoming 'locked in' to a particular manufacturer or product. It is considered dangerous for the user, in that there is no longer any control that he can exert on his supplier if, for example, prices become uncompetitive, or updates to products are not delivered. Changing suppliers is not easy, and converting software is likely to be very expensive.

When proprietary systems were sold, it was usually as a 'bundle' of hardware, software and associated services. The overall high margins that could be achieved resulted from the mixture of product and services sold, able to be compounded by the locked-in, non-competitive situation.

Some hardware manufacturers, such as Unisys (then Sperry and Burroughs, separately), NCR and Honeywell, developed mainframe computer designs of their own, selling in competition with IBM. They also achieved comparable high margins through a combination of bundling products and services, and exploitation of the proprietary lock-in.

Others such as Amdahl and Hitachi chose to develop IBM-compatible mainframe systems. These were based on specifications published by IBM. Manufacturers of these 'plug-compatibles' also licensed the operating system from IBM, and then were able to compete head-on with it.

2.7   The compatible market

With the emergence of the compatible systems market, the independent software companies flourished. Now, for the first time, they could develop software for one company's machine, and yet be able to sell it for competitive systems. This not only increased the market for their products, but reduced their development and support costs substantially.

IBM developed its own software products in the generalized areas of database management, transaction processing, systems management and software development tools, often competing with the independent software companies. In general, and continuing to this day, it left the core business applications and vertical software solutions to be developed and supplied by other software developers.

IBM has often published product specifications and has sometimes licensed its software technologies to other suppliers, particularly when this could clearly help to grow the market. It has also supplied various pieces of its own technology to the bodies responsible for the formal definition of standards. The data access language, SQL, originally developed within IBM, has in this way become a standard, as have the communications protocols, SNA.

As a result of the standards work and its various licensing agreements, IBM has both cooperated and competed with other hardware suppliers and with the independent software suppliers in many areas and for many years. As we will see, the ability to form and manage strategic partnerships with the characteristic of 'cooperating while competing' is fundamental in the open systems world. In Chapter 6 we will look specifically at some of IBM's more recent and strategically important alliances.

2.8   Today's view of Stage 1

Core applications were initially developed when processing power was expensive and programmers relatively cheap. Over time, developers of software used imaginative techniques to squeeze the maximum possible performance out of the hardware systems with little regard for the problems of maintaining and updating the software that resulted. Twenty years or more later much of that software is still in use, and the costs of maintaining it are enormous.

Today these applications remain at the core of enterprise computing. They continue to perform their prime function of automating the clerical activities of the company. They have evolved from their 1960s and 1970s prototypes by a process of piecemeal replacement, and have often shaped themselves in the process to reflect the way in which the enterprise conducts its business. Huge amounts of money have been spent, and continue to be spent, maintaining the software. It is not a simple task to consider changing these systems dramatically in any short time frame, for without them the business could not continue to operate.

2.9   The second stage—management information and departmental systems

In the 1970s a new class of applications started to emerge (Fig. 2.3), initially still designed to run on the mainframe computers in the central location. These were based on management requirements for better and more timely information. Examples are: financial planning applications that allow the examination of 'what if' scenarios to be built from models based on core accounting information;

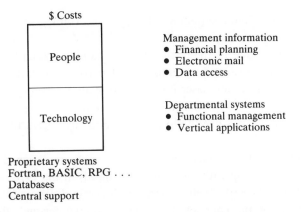

$ Costs

People

Technology

Management information
- Financial planning
- Electronic mail
- Data access

Departmental systems
- Functional management
- Vertical applications

Proprietary systems
Fortran, BASIC, RPG . . .
Databases
Central support

Figure 2.3. Stage 2: management information and departmental systems.

electronic mail systems that allow rapid communication of information between groups of individuals; and data access systems that allow data from a number of systems to be consolidated and examined in a single location.

Most of these applications involve turning raw data into intelligent information which can then be used by management in support of the operations of the enterprise. As a result, these systems became known as 'management information systems' (MIS), and the person in charge became the 'MIS director'. The more far-seeing organizations began to realize that information technology could no longer be considered simply a service to the business. If it was to be of optimal use, it had to be fully integrated with the business objectives.

Development of the new applications, and often their day-to-day use, still required help from experts trained in the technology. These were now referred to as the 'MIS department', in place of the previous 'DP department', and control of them was still centralized.

Today these management information systems exist in many departments of most companies, providing very useful support to a wide variety of functions. They run on machines of various price and performance levels, and are supplied by very many manufacturers. Most are based on the particular manufacturer's proprietary technology and an active third-party distribution network, together with a strong third-party software and associated services industry built up worldwide to support them.

2.10   The rise of the minicomputer

In the same time frame (Fig. 2.3), while the concept of information systems was growing, smaller and less expensive hardware systems were appearing in the market. Since these could handle many of the jobs previously thought to require the mainframe, serious competition for IBM and the other mainframe manufacturers emerged. This came from some new players specializing in minicomputer technologies, and included Digital Equipment Corporation (DEC), Data General and Wang.

In the 1970s IBM responded to the challenge with its own System/3X series, which did much to help establish and legitimize the 'departmental market'. These were sold not to the corporate purchaser but rather directly to the departmental users via a separate marketing organization (more akin to that used to sell typewriters). The System/3X has been followed by the highly successful AS/400 series.

There was also a parallel development of IBM minicomputers designed for the central MIS purchasers, starting with the 3790 (specialized) in the 1970s and the 8100 (general purpose) in the early 1980s. These developed in different directions, probably more because of the channel they were marketed through than for technical reasons.

Minicomputers were considerably lower in price than mainframes. Consequently they could often be purchased by departments or divisions from within their own budgets. These departmental systems were often bought without any central planning or control, and were chosen by each department purely to suit its own needs. Departments were able to have software applications built for their own specific requirements, if they could find the technical expertise necessary internally with the time available to do so, or if they had the budget to subcontract from outside.

Building departmental applications is a skilled task, requiring detailed technical knowledge of the (usually proprietary) systems environment as well as knowledge of the particular department's specialization. Many of the applications developed are classified as 'vertical', meaning that they are specific to a particular industry or industry segment.

In order to fuel their own growth, the suppliers of the new minicomputers had to find ways to satisfy the demand for a wide variety of software applications. They also had to find a way to grow a large salesforce quickly.

They achieved both these objectives by concentrating their sales activities on developing 'third-party' channels—a set of agents who would buy their computers, develop specific software on them, and sell the resulting 'complete solutions' to the specialized customers who wanted them. To satisfy the common desire for 'one-stop shopping', the agents usually supplied a range of support services with the machines—pre-sales consultancy, installation, training and post-sales technical support.

These third parties often concentrated on specific vertical markets, and over time have come to be known under the generic name of 'VARS', standing for 'value-added resellers'. They exist today as a network of companies in every country in the world, and all the hardware manufacturers, including IBM, try to earn their allegiance. They are extremely important constituents of the computer industry, not least because they form a repository for vast amounts of industry-specific software.

2.11   Today's view of Stage 2

Until recently few companies had central and controlled purchasing policies across the enterprise as a whole. Consequently, it is common for large companies to have incompatible computer systems which have been supplied by competing manufacturers to various parts of the organization. These systems have produced isolated 'islands of computing' within organizations. Today these companies face the problem of finding ways to integrate and use the information that the systems contain individually.

Nevertheless, the very largest of the mainframe IBM customers—the so-called 'Blue Chip' or 'Fortune 500' companies—have generally stayed loyal to IBM for most of their major procurements and throughout most of the enterprise. This is partly because IBM offers an extensive collection of services designed to provide as complete a service as possible, and partly because such customers tend to be conservative in their purchasing policies, particularly as regards new technologies and untested suppliers.

2.12   Stage 3: personal computing

With the advent of the microprocessor in the late 1970s, the world of computer applications changed dramatically and irreversibly. For the first time, it was possible to produce machines that were cheap enough to put into the hands of individual users, and many manufacturers started to do so (Fig. 2.4).

In 1983 IBM launched its own entry into this field. To do so at the speed that it felt necessary, IBM used a number of components supplied by third parties, including the operating system software known as MS-DOS from a then very small company, Microsoft Inc. This was the first time in its history that IBM went outside its own organization for such a vital piece of software.

When IBM subsequently published the specification of its Personal Computer (PC), it opened the doors for every other manufacturer in the world to build

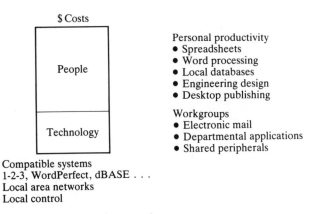

Figure 2.4.   Stage 3: personal computing.

computers which were totally compatible with it. This then spawned an enormous third-party software industry able to build applications for a vast number of users, confident that the population of machines would be large enough to justify the development costs.

Today there are more than 90 million IBM PC and compatible machines in use, and many thousands of software products available in every country in the world that can be run on them. Millions of individuals in organizations around the globe have taken advantage of these to automate some part of the job for which they are responsible.

Applications running on PCs cover almost every activity taking place within organizations, from personal productivity tools, such as spreadsheets, word processors, and project management, to specialized tasks in the engineering design areas, printing and production, and control systems. Almost all of these are supplied by independent software vendors who specialize in particular parts of the market. Leading players are: Lotus Development Corporation, with its now standard spreadsheet, 1-2-3; Ashton Tate, now part of Borland International, a prominent supplier of database management software; and WordPerfect Corporation, the leader in word-processing packages for general use.

While many of the packaged software products are in widespread use, until very recently few corporations laid down any corporate-wide guidelines relating to their purchase. Consequently, although an organization may be a major user of word-processing software on PCs throughout its activities, it is quite possible that a large number of different word-processing packages have been purchased and are used by different departments. This means that a person trained on one such package is not necessarily able to use another in a different department, if that department has made an alternative choice of product.

Departmental and enterprise systems will generally manipulate data in the way that the central MIS group defines and wants. In the absence of any rules to the contrary, personal applications will manipulate it in the way that individual users want. Furthermore, the data used in personal applications is often specific to that application and is not usually intended to be shared with other people or other applications. Although it may be imported from elsewhere and stored for future reference, it is not often designed or set up so as to be easily consolidated with data residing on other machines. Until very recently, data contained on PCs has been regarded as part of the personal application, and therefore the property, of the particular individual.

2.13   Today's view of Stage 3

Purchase of most of the millions of PC systems in use today has been by individuals or departments for their particular use. As a result, data has been accumulating within these systems steadily, with little or no regard for the needs of the organization as a whole.

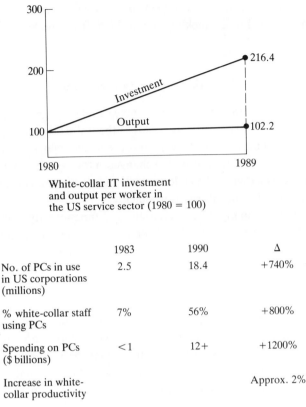

White-collar IT investment
and output per worker in
the US service sector (1980 = 100)

	1983	1990	Δ
No. of PCs in use in US corporations (millions)	2.5	18.4	+740%
% white-collar staff using PCs	7%	56%	+800%
Spending on PCs ($ billions)	<1	12+	+1200%
Increase in white-collar productivity		Approx. 2%	

Figure 2.5.   IT investments and productivity gains. (*Source*: Morgan Stanley and ITG)

Many of these personal computers are linked up on networks designed to allow sets of users to share expensive peripherals, such as high-speed laser printers. The network systems now perform the same functions as the minicomputers of Stage 2, and, when the applications software is available, can sometimes be used as replacements for them.

In theory, data could be shared on these networks of personal computers and work managed for the group as a whole. Such a concept is behind the development of software known as 'groupware'—specifically targeted to the handling of tasks which are carried out by groups of people. This integration cannot be achieved without a return to some form of centralized control, particularly for the definition of the standards for data and data-handling.

In spite of the fact that millions of personal computers have been purchased by organizations trying to improve productivity, there is no concrete evidence that this has been achieved. Over the last 10 years, investments per worker have increased by more than 200 per cent, while productivity gains have been measured at less than 3 per cent (Fig. 2.5). These figures are averages over a cross-section of organizations; a more detailed analysis indicates that the larger is the organization, the worse are the results. Clearly, if the objective of the IT systems is to improve the productivity of the workforce, tackling the problem from the PC end alone is the wrong approach.

2.14   Stage 4: the network as the corporate computer

The value of information to the enterprise was increasingly recognized during the 1980s, and led many people to describe the 1990s as the 'Information Age'. Access to information is recognized as the key to more efficient management of the enterprise internally, and to rapid response to changes in the external environment. Competitive advantage is based on the ability to accumulate, disseminate, assimilate, interpret and act upon relevant information quickly.

Over time, computers of many different designs and functionality have become distributed throughout the enterprise. Hardware, software and communications technologies have evolved continually. Data has accumulated on a number of different systems from various manufacturers. A mixture of hardware and software technologies has been used to collect, store and manipulate the data in its raw state, and many different applications software systems have been used to turn it into useful information. The result in a typical customer site is indicated in Fig. 2.6.

Much of the information potentially useful to the corporation now resides on departmental or personal systems. Although these may be connected to other machines in the department or division in which they are located, and some may be connected to the corporate mainframe, it is rare to find them part of a com-

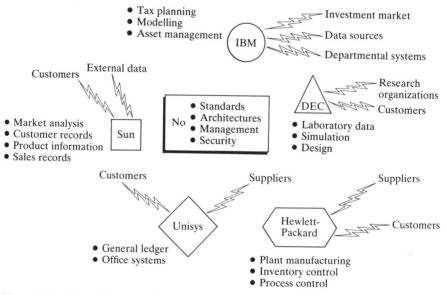

Figure 2.6.   Stage 4: islands of computing.

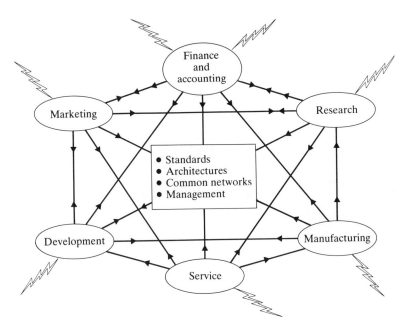

Figure 2.7.   The integrated infrastructure.

prehensive information management system designed for the needs of the corporation as a whole.

Departments, groups of people and even individuals, have developed their own
terminologies and descriptions for the items and their characteristics that make up
the data. If standards for such data descriptions were not imposed early on, any
organization wishing to integrate the various systems that exist now faces the
fundamental problem of first getting everyone to agree on data description
standards. This can be the most difficult issue of all to resolve.

When the reintegration of systems into a heterogeneous network takes place
within an enterprise, the situation which emerges is that shown in Fig. 2.7. In
contrast to the 'islands of computing' of Fig. 2.6, each system is now connected to
every other, and a common architecture based on standard technologies is at the
heart. The major components are compatible, and applications are distributed
around the network, as appropriate. Users connected to the network at any point
are able to access any system that is also connected, provided that they have the
appropriate authority. Most organizations are a long way from this situation.

Ideally the information system should serve the users by making all the facilities
that they want to use available to them easily from the systems that sit on their
desks (Fig. 2.8). It should not be necessary for users to know where the data resides
or the application runs. Instead they should be free to concentrate on the particular
job in hand, helped, not hindered, by the technology they are using.

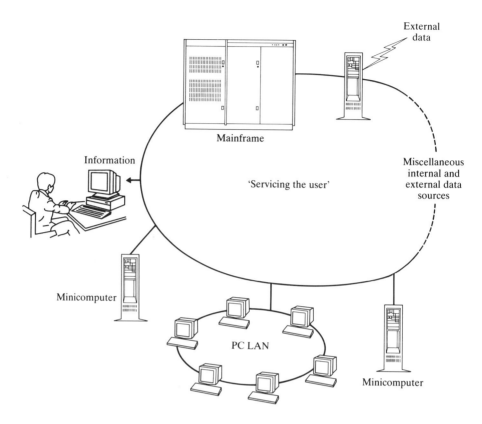

Figure 2.8.   The ideal situation.

2.15   IBM's view of today's commercial requirements

In presentations to corporate executives in which the presenter's objective is to introduce IBM's position on open systems and standards, the first slide used is very often a variation on Fig. 2.9—the 'Business requirements for IT'.

The first point made in Fig. 2.9 is that companies all over the world are trying to integrate business processes in order to improve internal efficiency and quality. For example, many manufacturing companies now have direct electronic links

- Enable integration of business processes
- Provide location independence
- Provide organizational flexibility
- Provide sustained competitive advantage
- Able to exploit new evolving technologies quickly
- Enable maximum alliance opportunities
- Have true global reach
- Be manageable and controllable

Figure 2.9.   Business requirements for IT.

between the design team and those responsible for manufacturing, so that rapid iteration of design and immediate response to practical problems with production becomes possible. Distribution companies link order entry with inventory control, which is often directly linked to dispatchers. Telesales departments are integrated with credit control systems and inventory, and can pull a customer's history from the corporate database on demand.

Throughout most large companies, the integration of hitherto isolated 'islands of information' is happening at an ever-accelerating rate. But because the systems have previously evolved in the separate units, the job of integrating them is far from easy.

The second point of Fig. 2.9 refers to a demand for location independence for both systems and people. Here, the practical need is to be able to transfer people from one location to another, possibly into another department, perhaps even into another country, and yet minimize the training or retraining that must take place before the person becomes fully operational.

If the systems used were highly compatible, this would not be difficult to achieve. Since this is not the case in general, again because the systems have evolved over time with few corporate standards imposed, it is something to be aimed for rather than something which many companies have so far achieved.

The third point emphasizes the previous two. Organizational flexibility can be achieved when systems are compatible across the enterprise, are connected together, and information can be obtained from them easily and from any location. People can then be moved around without needing to learn to use a completely new system. Departments can share expertise developed on a common base. Change can be effected fast.

The 1990s have already shown themselves to be the age for cooperation, mergers, electronic trading and many other forms of corporate alliances. More and more companies are learning how to cooperate while at the same time competing. Even companies as large as IBM have learned that they cannot supply all their customers' needs on their own, and have developed ways of working with others for the common good.

Alliance opportunities are made easier when the cooperation and sharing of information can be done electronically. But this can be achieved only when the systems are connected and when they can share data and information intelligently. This means that the concept of common data descriptions and standards must be extended across as well as within corporate boundaries. Thus we find groups of companies, for example the Petrochemical Open Systems Corporation (POSC), forming in order to agree standards to be used across the group to facilitate inter-group trading, as well as the development of third-party software tools useful to each of the members.

Competitive advantage for a company comes from the efficiency and quality of its internal organization, and its ability to respond quickly to changes in the internal and external environments. This requires good information sources and rapid access to it across the company. All relevant information must be contained within the corporate network in such a way that anyone who needs to can access it quickly and easily. This means that the individual computer systems must be connected, and the data contained on them integrated into a cohesive whole.

The fifth point on the chart expresses the need to be able to exploit new and emerging technologies as fast as possible while not disrupting the working systems of the present. This can be done most easily when systems have a modular design in which hardware and software components are built to standard interfaces. When this is the case, it is possible to replace one component with another of higher performance or greater functionality, while maintaining the basic properties of the original system.

Many companies today operate in the world market. Computer systems are linked up on networks that span the globe. International trading by electronic means is common in some industries—it is an essential part of the financial markets, for example. Global trading requires that information systems allow for the characteristics of the international market. Any standards which are agreed and used must be acceptable to the whole of the international user community.

While the computer industry struggles to find the technologies to meet the commercial needs of its users, there is an important practical requirement within all organizations: whatever the technologies that eventually dominate, the resulting international, multivendor networked systems must be internally manageable and controllable. This applies in both the technical and financial senses. For example, methods for managing corporate assets that reside on the network or agreement on charges to be imposed for usage on international networks, are as important as defining standards for security of access to confidential information.

2.16   IT requirements for business

The business requirements of Fig. 2.9 can be satisfied in the main if the information systems are defined with the following characteristics (Fig. 2.10):

- *Portability*—the ability for software, people and data to be moved easily from one system to another—provides location independence and organizational flexibility. Software developed in one department, division or company can be made available to another, even if it uses a different but compatible system on

Portability:	Software, people and data can be moved easily from one system to another
Scalability:	Software runs well on systems of varying size and performance, PC to mainframe
Interconnection:	Systems can communicate efficiently and easily, independent of the internal environment
Interoperability:	Hardware and software components are designed to work together easily, i.e., 'plug-and play'

Figure 2.10. IT requirements for business.

which to run the software. If the user interface to the application software remains the same regardless of the system environment, people can also be moved from one location to another without the need for retraining.

- *Scalability*—the ability to run the same software efficiently on systems of very different size and performance—facilitates organizational flexibility and the movement of people, particularly in companies made up of many departments or distributed branch offices of various sizes.
- *Interconnection*—the ability for systems to communicate efficiently and easily, independent of the internal environment (operating system) that exists in the separate machines—allows the integration of business processes, enables business alliances (with portability and scalability) and facilitates global reach.
- *Interoperability*—the ability of hardware and software components to work together easily, regardless of the manufacturer—is the fundamental characteristic required, and, in its most general interpretation, encompasses the previous three. With full interoperability, new technologies can be exploited easily. If the old component is replaced by the new, while the standard interfaces are protected, the system can continue without interruption, but with increased functionality.

When systems are built from hardware and software parts that conform to standard interface definitions, their components can 'plug and play' together. With professional management tools available, it remains only to build new applications tied closely to the business objectives. Technical resources can then be concentrated on these, rather than on resolving problems caused by incompatibilities in components not designed to work together. The totality of such interfaces is the user-driven definition of 'open systems'.

2.17   A famous case: McDonald's Inc.

McDonald's Inc. is a company famous worldwide as the number-one supplier of hamburgers and other fast foods, to a very high level of quality and service. Headquartered in the United States, it supplies its products through a vast chain of restaurants, some company owned, others franchised.

McDonald's competitive advantage is acknowledged to lie in the quality of its products and the speed and quality of service provided in the individual restaurants. Its information systems are a vital factor in its continuing success.

The central organization, using mainframe computers, closely monitors the performance of the company owned restaurants and constantly analyses what products sell best in which locations. It manages the supply and quality of the raw materials, and watches the activities of competitors.

Individual restaurants use a mixture of IBM PC/compatible machines, running either the MS-DOS or UNIX operating system. Most of these computers are connected to the corporate mainframes, either directly or indirectly, and data can be pulled off them from a number of locations.

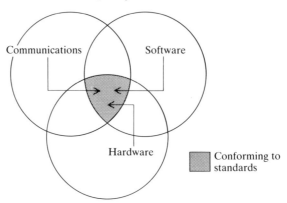

'We are forever buying products that do not quite conform
to standards and using valuable, and scarce, resources to
modify them until they do.
We must stop wasting energy on this'.

John Ozsvath, McDonald's Inc.

Figure 2.11.   The need for standards conformance. (*Source*: McDonald's Inc.)

A presentation by John Ozsvath, Assistant VP for McDonald's Inc., given at the
Uniforum Conference in 1990, commenced with the statement: 'We seem to be
continually buying products that do not quite conform to the requirements of our
corporate information network. As a result, we must continually use increasingly
scarce and very expensive resources to overcome incompatibilities over and over
again, everywhere. It is essential for us to purchase products that will work
together from the start, so that we can stop wasting our energies this way.' (Fig.
2.11.)

When Mr Ozsvath went on to describe the aims for the McDonald's enterprise
network, it contained no surprises. The overall objective is to provide connectivity
to all the entities within the corporation, so that every system can communicate
with every other. The preference is to provide a common user interface to all the
systems that are on the network, so any user anywhere can use the software in the
same way as any other. It would be desirable to provide simple tools so that users
can generate those applications, reports and views of the information that suit their
particular needs. Thus, the data must be integrated and available to all users with
the appropriate access permits (Fig. 2.12).

The software systems should be such as to allow shorter development cycles, so
that the software backlog on all systems can be reduced. Since the skill shortage
is almost universal, and expected to get worse over time, training requirements
must be minimal, with little or no retraining required if people are moved to a
different location. Above all, the emphasis must be on the development of new
applications which will allow the company to continue its outstanding growth and
performance in an increasingly competitive environment.

In all respects, McDonald's can be considered a typical, albeit very large, user
of information technology products. It has a mixture of machines and software

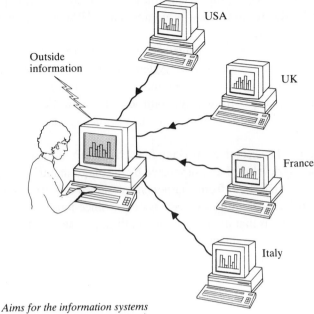

Aims for the information systems

- Connectivity to all entities within the corporation
- Common user interface throughout
- Tools for users to create own applications
- Data and data analysis for all users
- Modular, new business applications
- Shorter development cycles
- Reduction of backlogs
- Overcoming of skill shortages

Figure 2.12. Example: McDonald's Inc. (*Source*: McDonald's Inc.)

running on them, it operates in a very large number of geographical areas, so that the software it uses must be international in nature, and it has data collected in many formats through many software technologies. Its desire is to integrate the systems into an enterprise-wide information system that can then be used for maximum benefit to the company.

Mr Ozsvath summarized by saying that a move to standard technologies, supplied and fully supported by the whole of the IT industry, is the key to achieving his company's requirements.

2.18   Summary

In this chapter we have seen that the evolution of the use of computer technology in organizations has resulted in a fragmented situation where a wide variety of systems are now in common use. The high end is dominated by IBM mainframes, on which the corporate data normally resides, and the low end by the millions of IBM PCs and compatible machines that sit on the desks of individual workers.

In the middle range are a wide variety of systems performing the tasks needed by the department or division. Until recently these were predominately of proprietary design in both hardware and software components. IBM is one of the many suppliers to this segment.

For the overall information management needs of organizations, it is now accepted that these hitherto incompatible systems must work together. At the least, this means that they must be able to communicate, and that data residing on any one of them be accessible from any point on the network. It also implies that the resulting multivendor mixed networks are manageable from within the enterprise.

The conclusion of IT executives working in such organizations is that standard technologies must be developed and supported by the major manufacturers, so that distributed systems can be built from components designed to work easily together. This is the user-driven definition of open systems. Since huge investments have been made in the systems that are already in use, these standard technologies must develop and evolve so as to integrate with the so-called 'inheritance' systems. As will be shown in later chapters, it is on this conclusion that the IBM open systems strategy is based.

3
The emergence of open systems

3.1 Introduction

In the previous chapter we discussed the evolution of the use of computers in
enterprises. We found that user needs can be satisfied if system components, both
hardware and software, are designed to work together, independent of the vendor.
Vendors must design products that can be integrated easily with those of other
vendors, if they are to satisfy the long-term business requirements for integrated
information systems.

To enable the implementation of the level of interoperability required, vendors
should supply components which support standard interfaces or standard technologies. From the user point of view this is the basic concept behind 'open
systems'.

In this chapter we will continue to examine the evolution of the computing
industry by reviewing developments in technology. We will see that the demand for
software portability has been growing steadily for many years, and has led to the
rapid takeup of systems using the DOS and UNIX operating systems. As organizations moved to multivendor purchasing, this has been accompanied by a demand
for communications standards to be embedded in the operating systems.

By the end of this chapter we will have shown that the groundwork for the open
systems movement was laid a long time ago. The move to integrated systems made
up of interoperable components designed with standard interfaces is a logical
consequence of the technological, as well as the business, developments of the last
few decades.

3.2 Proprietary systems

In the 1960s IBM and other manufacturers supplied their mainframe computers to
the marketplace 'bundled' with their own operating system software.

On such 'proprietary' machines (Fig. 3.1) the hardware is intimately tied to the
operating system software. Traditionally, both of these were designed and owned

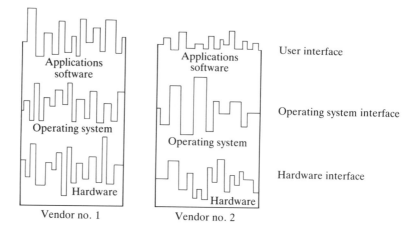

Figure 3.1.   Computer system interfaces.

- Application software cannot be moved across systems from different vendors without major changes to the software *unless* the operating system interface is the same for both (source code portability).

- Software cannot run completely unchanged on two systems unless the operating system interface *and* the hardware configuration is the same for both (binary compatibility).

- Two pieces of software will operate in different ways unless the user interface is the same for both (people portability).

- 'Proprietary' systems usually refer to those where the operating system interface is 'owned' by the particular vendor.

by the computer vendor, and application software written to run on the systems had to be designed specifically to fit with a particular operating system interface.

Since each hardware manufacturer provided a different operating system interface, it was not possible to move an application easily from one manufacturer's system to another without major changes in the software. This typically took several man-years of development work, and cost in the millions of dollars.

There were some exceptions to this. For example, applications written in a standard high-level language such as Cobol, Fortran or RPG could be compiled to different IBM (or sometimes other) operating environments if attention had been given to the differences that needed to be taken into account.

As a consequence of the proprietary operating system interfaces, applications software written for these machines, whether developed by the manufacturer or by the independent software companies, was inherently tied to a particular manufacturer's machines. IBM's mainframe computers were typical of this—applications software developed for IBM machines was generally unable to run on those from any other manufacturer, and vice versa.

3.3   Proprietary lock-in

Over the years, user investments made in software slowly but surely built up to very high levels. Once the software had been developed for a particular machine design, it was no longer economically feasible to change hardware suppliers, even if cheaper or higher performance systems became available from another manufacturer.

This led to the concept of being 'locked in' to a particular hardware manufacturer, and the beginnings of a desire in the user base to escape into a freer environment, if that could be made technically possible and economically practical.

3.4   High margins

Up until the early 1980s, hardware manufacturers were able to operate with very high margins. This is sometimes attributed to the locked-in nature of the customer base, which gave the customer no choice but to pay whatever price was set. However, systems were usually sold with operating and management software included, and with a very high level of customized services. Since these were 'bundled' into the total system price, it is not easy to analyse on what specific components the high margins were built.

It is generally accepted that in a competitive environment high margins can be achieved only by adding considerable value to products. As computer hardware becomes commoditized and hardware sold 'unbundled' from software and services, competition will not allow a manufacturer to price high on raw hardware alone. Suppliers must add value through unbundled software and services, and price for these separately. Since the market perception until recently has been that these come 'free' with the hardware, a certain amount of education of the customers will have to take place before the vendors can reap the benefits of the potential margins on these (see Fig. 3.2 overleaf).

3.5   The plug-compatible market

IBM first experienced the problem of competitive pricing after it published the interfaces to components of its mainframe systems. This allowed other manufacturers to build hardware components, such as high-capacity storage systems, that could replace those supplied by IBM but at a lower price. When IBM licensed its mainframe operating system software to manufacturers such as Amdahl and Fujitsu, serious competition also emerged for complete systems.

The emergence of compatible systems and system components had two other effects. First, it enabled the market to grow very much faster than it could with only one vendor present, even if that one was as big as IBM. Second, it allowed the

	Costs (%)	Margin (%)
Services	20	90
Software	20	80
Hardware	60	30

Total cost = 100%   Overall margin = 52%

If products are 'bundled', with high-margin elements perceived
as 'free', margins will drop dramatically when products are
unbundled, unless services are sold at high margins.

Figure 3.2.   Effect of 'bundling' on margins.

independent application software developers to produce a single product which ran
unchanged on several manufacturers' machines. This increased the application
software market and reduced software development costs, giving the software
companies the economic advantages of scale.

The result was a larger marketplace in total, with more choice of hardware
components and application software available to IBM's customers. Increased
competition meant that IBM had to maintain its competitive edge through the
quality of its products and services. IBM had one very big advantage at this time.
It controlled the basic technology within its own development laboratories, and so
controlled the timing of releases of new versions of the products. To some extent
it was also able to control pricing through its licensing policies. Thus it was able
to retain a certain advantage in the marketplace, based on the fact that it owned
the technology.

3.6   Developments in the late 1970s and early 1980s

In the late 1970s the first commercial microprocessors appeared. These were
incorporated into the designs of smaller and more powerful machines than had
ever previously existed.

Many of the first manufacturers of these microcomputers were new players in the
computer industry—startup companies that began life on a shoestring. Unfortunately, over time, many disappeared. Significant exceptions are Apple, Compaq
and Tandy.

Because many of the early entrants were poorly funded, they were driven to use
common technologies wherever possible. Many standardized on the Z80 microprocessor from Zilog, and built machines incorporating it. However, they needed
the availability of both an operating system and applications before they could sell
the machines.

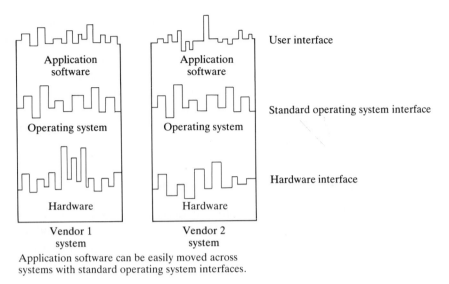

Application software can be easily moved across
systems with standard operating system interfaces.

Figure 3.3.   Standard operating system interface.

Faced with the refusal of Zilog to license its proprietary operating system
software to them, they were forced to look elsewhere. In the early 1980s, most
licensed the CP/M operating system from a then small company, Digital Research,
which had built a primitive operating system for the Intel 8080 processor. The
instruction set for the Zilog chip was a superset of the 8080, and so software written
for the 8080 also ran on the Z80. Digital Research is now part of Novell, the
leading PC network operating system company.

There were at one time more than a hundred microcomputer manufacturers
shipping machines using the Z80 microprocessor and able to run CP/M. A high
degree of compatibility existed across these machines, and so software written for
one machine could be modified easily to run on others in the group (Fig. 3.3). As
a result, many software startup companies which developed software to run on top
of CP/M were able to grow fast, independently of the success of any particular
hardware manufacturer.

Early significant high-volume software products were Wordstar, a popular
word-processing package, and Visicalc, the predecessor to the now standard
spreadsheet 1-2-3 from Lotus Development Corporation.

Once the microcomputer market started to grow rapidly, the established
computer manufacturers took notice. In particular, IBM decided to enter with a
machine of its own design, although many of the components were purchased
externally. Needing a microprocessor and operating system quickly, IBM took the
decision to purchase the first from Intel—the 8080—and the second—DOS—from
Microsoft Corporation. These decisions changed the entire balance of the emerging
microcomputer industry, and altered the computer market forever.

Eventually, almost every other hardware manufacturer switched technologies away from the combination of the Zilog Z80 and Digital Research's CP/M to the Intel 8080 and Microsoft's DOS. Thus was the IBM PC compatible market born.

New software companies such as Lotus and WordPerfect were quick to develop spreadsheet and word-processing software for these new machines, paralleling the previous successes of Wordstar and Visicalc on CP/M. Eventually, the IBM PC and compatibles became the market standard, and the non-compatible hardware and software products gradually disappeared. As so often, being first into the market was not necessarily best.

3.7   Software portability and compatible systems

Portability of software and compatibility of hardware were (and still are) vital in the PC world. Software developers wanted to develop a single product that ran without change on all the PCs, regardless of the manufacturer. This was even more important for the software distributors that emerged in the early 1980s. They certainly did not want to hold any more inventory than was necessary.

Initially, many manufacturers supplied machines that were based on the IBM design but were not completely compatible with it. It was, and still is, very difficult for computer companies to accept that advantages can come from being 100 per cent compatible with their competitors. In any case, their engineers could not resist adding special features of their own.

The computer industry had become so accustomed to establishing competitive advantage on technological grounds that it was, and still is, difficult for vendors to see how otherwise they might differentiate themselves. In particular, when a sales force has been trained to convince potential customers of the innate superiority of its company's hardware, it is a revolutionary concept to persuade it to switch to a sales strategy that relies on being totally compatible with its major competitors.

3.8   Testing for compatibility

To force the issue of compatibility, software developers tested and guaranteed their software to run on the IBM PC. If the software did not work properly on a machine from another supplier, the machine was assumed to be incompatible with the IBM PC.

Internally, Microsoft had developed a piece of software known as the 'Flight Simulator'. As the name implies, this was effectively a game that allowed the operator to pretend to be flying an aeroplane under various conditions. Because of the complexity of the software, it tested the DOS implementation almost to its limits. Thus, running the Flight Simulator on a machine became a good test of compatibility with the IBM PC (Fig. 3.4), and was used as such by many of the software suppliers.

As we will see later, the issue of testing for compatibility, albeit by more formal methods, is an increasingly important issue in the standards-based, open systems

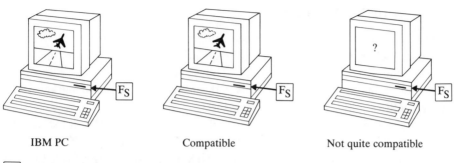

IBM PC   Compatible   Not quite compatible

$\boxed{F_S}$ Microsoft's Flight Simulator programme

Figure 3.4.   Testing PCs for compatibility.

world. It is not enough for a manufacturer to claim to conform to a standard; users want independently obtained proof.

3.9   The emergence of UNIX

In the early 1980s microprocessor manufacturers such as Zilog and Motorola started to test their 16- and 32-bit chips. It was clear that these were going to be the basis for a whole new generation of machines, and would need appropriate operating system software. Whereas the PCs were single-user machines, used to improve the productivity of individuals, machines incorporating the new and more powerful processors would be able to support many users at once. These would compete with the established minicomputers, and eventually the mainframes themselves.

The new, more powerful machines, initially called supermicros, would no longer be peripheral to the mainstream business requirements. If they replaced the mini-computers and mainframes, they would run the core business applications for the enterprise. They would need the professional support services that were already common in the proprietary operating systems.

In this environment, no one could afford to take risks. If the core systems were not running, the business would be in trouble. Learning from experiences in the PC market, the first manufacturers of these new machines looked for a suitable operating system. There were a number of candidates—most from small software development companies. The exception was the already mature operating system known as 'UNIX', developed within AT & T for internal purposes, based on a need for software that could be moved across several vendors' computers.

UNIX was the only candidate that met the practical requirements for this situation. Although at the time it lacked some of the commercial requirements for a multi-user operating system, it was clear that, given sufficient support from the computer industry as a whole, whatever was needed to support its role in the commercial world would eventually be added.

3.10   Early UNIX systems

A number of new companies developed computer systems based on UNIX. Some of these, such as Onyx and Plexus, subsequently disappeared. Others, most particularly Sun Microsystems, flourished. Today, Sun provides serious competition to the traditional suppliers, particularly in the technical workstation markets where it has, until recently, concentrated its efforts.

IBM chose not to enter the UNIX market early. It eventually did so in 1985 with a machine—the RT or 6150—very much of its own design, and utilizing a proprietary microprocessor. The RT ran UNIX as licensed from AT & T but with some IBM features added. It was aimed at the technical market and intended to compete with companies such as Sun. Unfortunately, it was not considered competitive in the technical marketplace in price/performance terms.

In spite of this, IBM sold significant numbers of the RT in both the US and Europe. These went mainly into commercial markets, where IBM reached a position near the top for shipments in every country where it was sold. The reason it was so successful despite its perceived lack of performance was the number of software applications available for it and the support services that IBM provided.

The independent software companies with commercial application products moved them to the IBM RT without paying much regard to performance issues; the volumes they expected IBM to sell were sufficient motivation for them to do the work required. To help the process, IBM offered a high level of support services, including machines on loan and technical help.

In general, the early users of UNIX systems from IBM were companies that wanted to achieve the advantages of using standard software environments, but also wanted the level of service they were accustomed to receiving from IBM.

3.11   The fragmentation of the UNIX market

In the early 1980s, AT & T licensed its UNIX operating system to almost all the hardware manufacturers, and to many software companies. However, it did not allow the licensees to use the name UNIX on their products; instead, it retained the name for its own use. As a result, each of the UNIX licensees was forced to invent a name for its UNIX implementation. IBM named its version 'AIX'.

Each manufacturer that licensed UNIX added those facilities to the operating system that it felt to be important and which were not yet supplied in the standard product from AT & T. Many of these already existed in their proprietary operating system products and were known from past experience to be essential in the commercial world in which their UNIX systems were beginning to be sold. Others were added by the engineers on the basis of 'improving' the product, often according to their own definitions.

These additional facilities are usually described by the vendors as their 'added value', and used by them as competitive differentiating factors. Others refer to the variants as 'proprietary' UNIX, since they bring back the incompatibilities and lock-in features that advocates of the use of standard technologies are trying to remove.

As a result of the many names used, and the many different 'enhancements' made, the early UNIX market became highly fragmented. By 1985 there were several hundred different versions of UNIX being actively sold on various systems in the market. This meant that few of the advantages that came from systems compatibility in the PC market were achieved for the applications software market in the UNIX world.

3.12   Portability of UNIX software

In order to achieve acceptable sales volumes, software developers targeting to UNIX systems in the early to mid-1980s were forced to modify their products over and over again to fit the many, slightly different, environments (Fig. 3.5). In one sense, this was not regarded as a problem. The work involved in moving the software—referred to as 'porting'—was not difficult. Typically, moving a sophisticated database from one UNIX system to another was the work of a few days, with testing taking perhaps a few days more. This compared with the several man-years that it took to move the same software from one manufacturer's proprietary environment to another.

However, the problems in the software distribution channels were considerable. Inventory had to be held for all the different machines. Support problems after sale

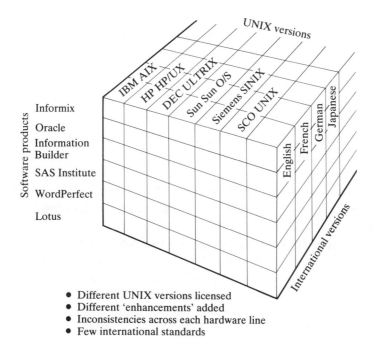

- Different UNIX versions licensed
- Different 'enhancements' added
- Inconsistencies across each hardware line
- Few international standards

Figure 3.5.   The UNIX software porting problem.

were magnified by the number of variations that existed, both in the operating system and in the application software itself. For some software developers, supporting the many hundreds of different versions of their products eventually became too heavy a burden to carry.

Internationally, the problem was further compounded by the need to repeat the porting work for every foreign language translation that was needed. The incompatibility of UNIX versions, more than any other factor, caused the UNIX market to grow very slowly well into the mid-1980s.

In spite of much work by AT & T (now moved into the UNIX System Laboratories, USL), Sun Microsystems, the Santa Cruz Operation (SCO) and many others, the incompatibilities in UNIX versions still exist today. Some of these are defensible, when they are driven by the needs of the customer or the application; others, appearing to be variations for variation's sake, are not.

3.13   Binary compatibility

UNIX is conceivably the universal operating system. It is scalable to a high degree, and can run well on machines of very different size and performance, from the PC to the mainframe. More particularly, it can run well on microprocessors of very different designs from a number of manufacturers. This is in contrast to DOS, which was designed specifically for Intel-based machines and runs only on them.

When a family of systems uses the same basic hardware design, including the same microprocessor, it is possible to provide a high level of software portability across it (Fig. 3.6). This is not the case when machines use different processors. At best, the software can be only 'source code compatible', meaning that it must be recompiled for each microprocessor family. If the manufacturers of systems within a particular microprocessor group all agree to use the same basic design of machine, software can made to be completely (binary) portable. This happened with the PC when all the manufacturers copied the IBM design (although that was not necessarily with IBM's agreement).

Groups of manufacturers are working towards providing binary portability in the UNIX market in several ways. The first, which originated within AT & T, is through the definition of 'application binary interfaces' (ABI) for each of the major licensable processor groups—Intel, Sparc and Motorola. Conformance to these by the manufacturers will ensure binary portability of software across their systems (Fig. 3.6).

Another approach has been taken by the Open Software Foundation (OSF). It has announced a technology—the 'Architecture Neutral Distribution Format' (ANDF)—that is designed to allow a single version of an application to be shipped. When installed in a UNIX system containing the ANDF technology, the software effectively recognizes the environment and adjusts itself accordingly (Fig. 3.7). More detail on the Open Software Foundation and its deliverables is contained in Appendix 1.

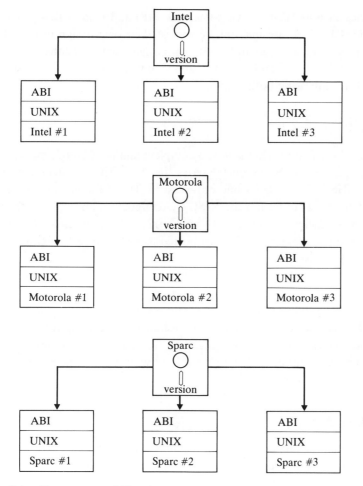

Figure 3.6.   Binary compatibility through ABIs.

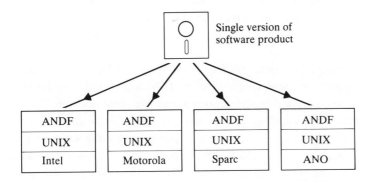

Figure 3.7.   Compatibility through the OSF's ANDF.

Companies such as IBM, Hewlett-Packard (HP) and Digital Equipment Corporation (DEC), which use microprocessors of their own design in their UNIX systems, can provide binary compatibility with other machines, either by licensing their technology to other vendors or by supplying them with complete systems for resale. All three are using both routes.

3.14 IBM's approach

IBM launched the first of what is now a complete family of UNIX machines, the highly acclaimed RISC System/6000 series, in 1989. These systems use IBM's proprietary RISC System/6000 microprocessors. The definition of an ABI will appear as IBM starts to license the RISC System/6000 technology to others.

In spite of its lack of compatibility with other UNIX systems, almost every UNIX application software vendor has ported its software to the RISC System/6000 family. As a result, the AIX software catalog produced by IBM as a service to its customers currently lists more than 3500 software products in the US edition. Similar catalogs are growing for other countries.

The number of products listed in the catalogs is not the total number available in the marketplace as a whole, in spite of best efforts to catalog these. There are many vertical market products, for example, that have not been listed directly. These often appear indirectly, having been built with tools, principally databases and 4GLs, that are themselves listed.

3.15 IBM's AIX

Although containing many proprietary enhancements, IBM's AIX implementation of UNIX is highly regarded by both software developers and sophisticated commercial users.

Many of the IBM additions to 'standard' UNIX have been made in order to support the needs of IBM's commercial customers, many of whom are already using IBM proprietary products. As we will discuss further in Chapter 5, an essential requirement of many of these users is that the IBM UNIX systems coexist happily with the already installed base of IBM and other vendor supplied hardware and software.

AIX is not completely compatible with any other UNIX version in the market, nor is it likely to be in the immediate future. IBM is not unique in this respect; all the other major computer manufacturers are in the same position.

In spite of the incompatibilities, the independent software companies generally believe that the sales volume of a UNIX machine from IBM will be high enough to warrant individualized porting and supporting work. Only a few manufacturers are large enough to enjoy such a position. The software vendors are increasingly basing their porting schedules on anticipated hardware sales volumes. In future a small manufacturer will be able to have a large number of software products available on its machines only if it can demonstrate compatibility with other suppliers.

IBM is rapidly increasing the population of binary compatible RISC System/ 6000 systems by licensing the machine for resale to other vendors, for example, Bull and Wang (see Chapter 7). The number of such licensing arrangements can be expected to increase over time.

3.16   Licensing agreements

As the shakeout in the computer industry continues, more vendors are expected to become systems integrators, rather than designers and manufacturers of information technology products. Others will certainly follow Bull's example and become value-added resellers of IBM systems, buying under specially defined terms and conditions. The agreements may go as far as to allow the manufacturing of complete systems under licence.

Licensing AIX could be an attractive proposition for other vendors, particularly if they could achieve binary compatibility with IBM systems without restricting their ability to make some innovations of their own. Under IBM's new and aggressive open systems strategy (Chapter 6) and particularly as the relationship between IBM, Apple and Motorola develops (Chapter 7), this should be expected.

3.17   Growth in the UNIX market

Market research studies show that the total IT market can be divided into four segments of approximately equal value based on operating system use (Fig. 3.8). One quarter of the value lies with systems using variants of MS-DOS and Windows on IBM PCs and compatibles. Another quarter is with IBM proprietary technology—mainframe and mid-range. A third quarter refers to a mixture of proprietary

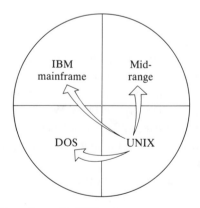

Overall growth <10% p.a.
UNIX system growth ≃ 30% p.a. on average

Figure 3.8.   Movements in the computer market.

technologies from a vast number of manufacturers of many nationalities. The fourth quarter relates to UNIX systems supplied by many vendors.

The UNIX quarter is by far the fastest growing segment. While total IT spend worldwide is growing at a rate below 10 per cent per annum, the spend on UNIX systems is growing at an average rate close to 30 per cent per annum. UNIX is penetrating all three of the other segments, but affecting the proprietary mid-range systems the most. This trend is expected to continue for the foreseeable future. Strong growth in UNIX systems is found in all geographical regions, and is taking place on three fronts—the mid-range, desktop and mainframe.

3.18   Mid-range UNIX systems

UNIX systems from almost every manufacturer in the world are rapidly replacing minicomputers of proprietary design.

IBM's proprietary AS/400 systems, which have been outstandingly successful, are exceptions to this statement. Market studies show an overall decrease in the numbers of proprietary systems in the mid-range, so the conclusion is that the AS/400 systems are replacing other minicomputers of proprietary design. These might be from IBM or from other manufacturers.

In the mid-range, IBM is the leading supplier of commercial UNIX systems. It is believed to have sold $1 billion worth of RISC System/6000s in 1990, $1.6 billion in 1991, and $2.4 billion in 1992 (*IBM System User*, February 1992). IBM has an easily accessible installed base of predominantly loyal customers, and an in-depth experience of the requirements of the commercial markets. It can therefore be expected to maintain this leadership status through the 1990s and has publicly stated its intention of doing so.

3.19   Desktop systems

While the distinction between PCs and workstations is beginning to blur, UNIX systems represent an increasing percentage of desktop installations of both designations.

According to the Santa Cruz Operation (SCO), which supplies the most popular of the packaged UNIX products for PCs, approximately 10 per cent of PCs apparently purchased with the DOS operating system are actually running UNIX.

IBM supplies a version of AIX as an alternative to DOS, Windows or OS/2 for the PS/2 family of commercial desktop systems. This is attractive to companies which have a comprehensive AIX strategy and want to maintain a high degree of compatibility across all their systems.

UNIX systems on the desktop are usually in a networked environment, running applications which may be technical or commercial. UNIX is an attractive choice for many situations because of the networking facilities built into it, the ease with which PC systems can be integrated and the graphical user interface provided in most implementations.

Desktop systems called 'workstations' rather than 'PCs' almost always run UNIX. This is the market pioneered and dominated by Sun Microsystems. With a compound annual growth rate of 44 per cent (Fig. 3.9 overleaf), it is the fastest growing of the UNIX sectors.

Hewlett-Packard and IBM are fighting for second place in UNIX workstations shipments. Both are slowly but surely gaining market share from Sun. IBM's announced intention is to become the leading supplier of UNIX workstations by 1995.

For many commercial applications, particularly those that require graphics, color, multimedia support, high performance and good communications, the cost of a suitably configured UNIX system is comparable to that of a PC (or Apple) of equal functionality. As the most popular personal productivity software becomes directly available in the UNIX environment, the move to UNIX at the desktop can be expected to accelerate unless and until an alternative with greater functionality emerges.

3.20   Windows onto information

The desktop machine of the future must provide the user with a window onto the integrated information system to which he or she will be connected. It will have an interface that uses not only graphics and color, but also interactive multimedia technologies such as sound and video. This desktop system will be linked to external sources of information, and will have built-in communications facilities, incorporating electronic mail, fax and telephone (Fig. 3.10).

The DOS/Windows operating environment of the PC cannot provide a suitable base for these new technologies. Instead, its pervasive use is probably restricting their takeup.

To take advantage of new applications incorporating emerging technologies, users must move to a more powerful operating system on the desktop. What this will be is not yet clear. It may be a variant of UNIX specifically designed for the desktop, it might be IBM's OS/2 or Microsoft's NT, or it could be a new operating system, perhaps emerging from IBM's partnership with Apple (see Chapter 7). UNIX has a time advantage—it is already in use in many organizations and the installed base is growing steadily. As a rule, an installed base represents considerable investment, resists change and exerts considerable power.

3.21   UNIX on the mainframe

Although representing only a small part of the UNIX systems market, the mainframe segment is growing—at approximately 10 per cent per annum according to Dataquest (Fig. 3.9). This is partly because UNIX is appearing on big systems, and partly because some of the older mainframes are being replaced by newer high-performance yet smaller systems built to run UNIX.

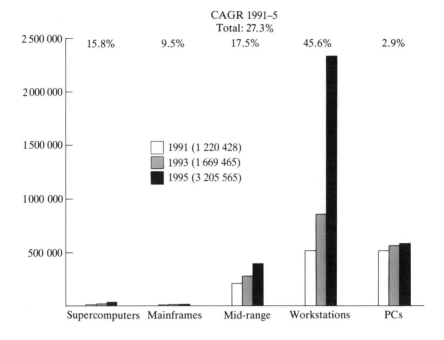

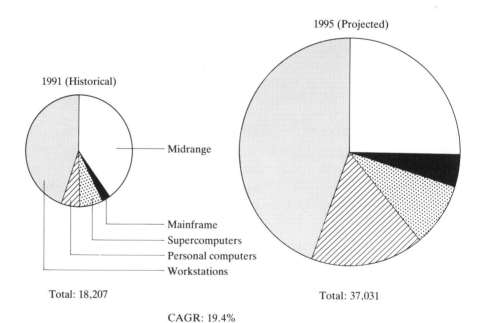

Figure 3.9.   Market forecasts in millions of dollars. (*Source*: Dataquest.)

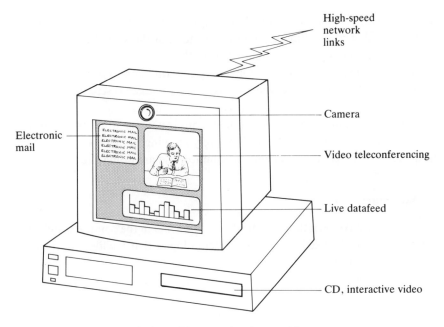

High-speed
network
links

Camera

Electronic
mail

Video teleconferencing

Live datafeed

CD, interactive video

- Multimedia technologies – video, sound, color, graphics . . .
- Electronic mail
- Video teleconferencing

Figure 3.10.   The information window.

Amdahl has been selling mainframes running UNIX directly (in native mode) for some time, as have Cray and Fujitsu. IBM supplies AIX native for its mainframe ESA/370 family, and so is able to supply UNIX on any size of machine from the PC to the mainframe. With AIX available for the PS/2, RISC System/6000 and ESA systems, together with full communications support both across the family and for many other environments, the IBM AIX family is as strong an offering as its proprietary Systems Applications Architecture (SAA) family. A discussion of the relationship between the IBM SAA and AIX families can be found in Chapter 5.

3.22   Communications

In the 1970s computer manufacturers developed and marketed products that facilitated communications between computers. Although these were technologically sound, they suffered from the fundamental flaw that they were generally appropriate only for connecting together machines from a single manufacturer.

As enterprises moved to multivendor purchasing, the need grew for machines from different vendors to communicate efficiently. Vendors provided products that enabled their systems to communicate with those from competitors and licensed their technology to others. IBM was particularly active in this regard, for example, by licensing the Systems Network Architecture (SNA) technology widely.

In the late 1970s pressure in Europe built for a set of standard communications protocols that allowed machines to communicate regardless of the internal environment. The technologies that emerged from this activity became a collection of international standards known as 'Open Systems Interconnection' (OSI).

Although UNIX and OSI developments were initially treated separately, by the late 1980s communications technologies were an integral component of the development of standard systems. Communications is now regarded as part of the operating system, and UNIX is slowly but surely growing to incorporate the OSI standards. All other operating systems in common use are doing the same.

3.23   Summary

In this chapter we have seen that technical developments in the computer industry led to acceptance of the need for standard technologies that facilitate portability of software and communications between machines.

'Open systems' implies a collection of technologies which enables software to be easily ported across machines, and machines from many vendors to communicate efficiently. The most common method of implementation of these requirements today is through the use of the UNIX operating system, with inbuilt communications protocols that will eventually conform to the international OSI standards. As a consequence, the installed base of UNIX systems is growing fast in all segments.

IBM provides a complete family of UNIX machines ranging from personal systems to mainframe configurations. It has stated its intention to become the leader in UNIX shipments based on its own version of UNIX, AIX.

PCs running DOS/Windows are binary-compatible and are considered 'open' to some degree. However, they do not provide a sufficiently powerful environment to support the functionality required in the 'window onto the information network'. A new desktop system must emerge in the next few years.

In the next chapter we will follow the development of the definition of open systems. We will see that it has moved from the concept of 'standard products' to one of 'standard interfaces'. In particular, the definition has gradually been generalized to encompass proprietary systems, allowing them also to be considered 'open' under certain circumstances.

Achieving acceptance of the most general interpretation is fundamental to IBM's open systems strategy, which is based on protecting investments made in proprietary systems as much and for as long as possible.

4
UNIX, open systems and standards

4.1   Introduction

In previous chapters we have described the evolution of the open systems movement from its beginnings in the IBM plug-compatible market. In the process, we have found that there are many different interpretations of 'open systems', driven by the particular problem which a set of users are trying to solve. Nevertheless, they all have in common the desire to achieve the ability of hardware and software components from different vendors to work together.

In this chapter we examine the formal definition and the standards required for open systems. We examine the processes by which standards are set, and the key organizations which define and control them.

We will see that IBM is devoting a huge amount of energy and resources to standardization work. Recognizing that the industry is moving to consensus standards in many areas, IBM is well represented in the relevant organizations. IBM has declared that its future technologies will conform to mainstream standards specifications.

4.2   Setting standards

An indication of the way in which the standards-setting process works in general is given in Fig. 4.1. There it can be seen that the requirement for a standard in a certain area can arise from the marketplace, through uptake of a product, or from work by a particular group of industry representatives.

When the need for the standard has been identified, the task of defining it in detail is passed to a formal standards-setting body. These exist in all countries, with regional groups coordinating their activities. The International Standards Organization (ISO) coordinates work for the world as a whole.

After the specification of a standard has been agreed, work in the particular committee is finished. But even though the standard may be accepted by the international community, it is often too general for practical use. The process of defining 'profiles' hardens the official standard into a definition which is appropriate

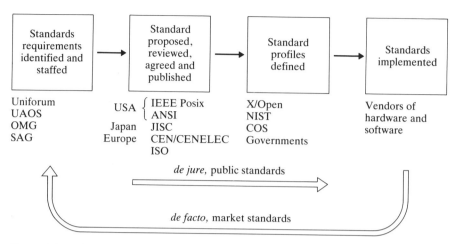

Figure 4.1. The standards process.

for use in a particular segment. Government procurement agencies are most active in this area.

To ensure that the resulting standards meet international requirements, local standards committees work closely with their counterparts in other parts of the world in a process known as 'harmonization' of the standards.

Once the standards have been agreed and profiles set, the specifications are freely available in sufficient detail to enable conformant products to be built. Over time, an iterative process may take place, where the standard is refined, based on experiences of products in the marketplace.

4.3   Conformance testing

The final and increasingly important part of the standards process concerns the definition and availability of conformance tests. These check that conformance to the standard is actually achieved in a particular product. Although producing these tests is very difficult, users still often demand independent 'proof' that a product meets their stated requirements.

4.4   The POSIX standards

The UNIX operating system is a *de facto* standard through its widespread use in the marketplace, but it is not an official standard. Though often based on a product that exists in the marketplace, publicly defined international standards never demand the use of a particular product.

The constitutional process requires a standard to be defined in such a way that any company that wishes to can build products that conform to the standard. It was therefore only ever possible to standardize officially on an interface to an operating system *based* on UNIX, and never possible to standardize on the UNIX operating system itself.

Members	Professionals	
Mission	Develop open systems specifications for ANSI	
Workgroups	1003.0	Overall workplan
	1003.1	System interface
	1003.2	Shell/utilities
	1003.3	Test methods
	1003.4	Real-time extensions
	1003.5	ADA language bindings
	1003.6	Security
	1003.7	System management
	1003.8	Networking
	1003.9	Fortran language bindings
	1003.10	Supercomputing
	1003.11	Transaction processing
	1003.12	Protocols
	1003.13	Real-time applications environments
	1003.14	Multiprocessing
	1003.15	Batch processing
	1003.16	C bindings
	1003.17	Directory
	1003.18	Profiles

Figure 4.2.   IEEE POSIX committees.

The international UNIX User Group, Uniforum (previously known as '/usr/ group'), initiated work to define standards for portability of software in 1981. Working closely with AT&T, the group produced a definition of a 'portable operating system standard based on UNIX', which was subsequently passed on to the formal standards-setting process. The USA-based Institute of Electrical and Electronic Engineers (IEEE) was charged by the American National Standards Institute (ANSI) with formalizing agreement on the standard. The IEEE called the standard for the interface POSIX (from 'Portable Operating System based on UNIX'), and this is the name by which it, and the related standards-setting committees within the IEEE, are now known worldwide.

The Technical Committee on Open Systems (TCOS) is the IEEE Committee involved in developing the set of open specifications for the operating system environment. While these have evolved from the UNIX environment, UNIX is not mandatory for their implementation.

POSIX is now used to describe a set of workgroups which are defining interfaces for many components of open systems. As well as working directly on the interface to what was traditionally known as the operating system, there are POSIX committees working on communications, security, transaction processing, computer languages, database access and many others (Fig. 4.2). A more complete description of the POSIX work and how it ties into the international standardization work can be found in Gray (1991).

The POSIX standards are developed in an open forum by technical professionals from many companies, including IBM. As the standards appear, they are built into customer procurement standards, such as the Federal Information Processing Standards (FIPS) used in the public sector in the US. IBM has announced support

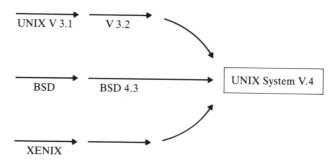

Figure 4.3.   Convergence of UNIX versions.

for the first of the POSIX standards, 1003.1, in the AIX products, and its intention to support them on the MVS/ESA mainframe and AS/400 mid-range systems.

4.5   Standard UNIX

As we saw in the last chapter, by the mid-1980s there were more than a hundred different versions of the UNIX operating system being sold in significant numbers on a wide variety of machines. More detail on the background to this situation is given by Gray (1991).

Three different versions of UNIX gradually began to dominate: UNIX System V as supplied by AT&T; Microsoft's Xenix, popularized by the Santa Cruz Operation (SCO) in a packaged form for Intel-based systems; and Berkeley Software Distribution (BSD), originating from the University of Berkeley. IBM's AIX is a development of UNIX System V with some BSD features and many that are IBM-specific.

During 1988 AT&T worked together with Microsoft, SCO and Interactive Systems (now part of the Sun Microsystems subsidiary SunSoft) to merge Xenix with UNIX System V in such a way as to retain compatibility for all the applications that had been developed to run on either version. This resulted in a standard version of the UNIX operating system for the PC, Intel-based market.

At the same time, AT&T worked closely with Sun Microsystems, the most advanced user of BSD UNIX, to merge UNIX System V with BSD, incorporating the best features of each in the final product. Known as UNIX System V.4, this was released by AT&T in 1989, by which time all three popular versions became merged into one. This UNIX System V.4 is now regarded as the standard version of UNIX as supplied under licence with that name (Fig. 4.3).

4.6   Competitive pressures

As the demand for UNIX systems built up in the marketplace, the major computer manufacturers started to supply them, licensing UNIX from AT&T in order to do so.

During the 1980s Sun Microsystems emerged as a serious competitor in the technical computing market previously dominated by Digital Equipment Corporation and Hewlett-Packard. Sun's product line is entirely based on UNIX. Unlike the established computer manufacturers, its phenomenal growth has not been held back by the need to balance new UNIX systems with the requirements of an installed base of proprietary technology.

The close relationship that developed between Sun Microsystems, the most successful vendor of UNIX workstations, and AT & T, owners of UNIX technology and itself a vendor of UNIX-based computers, made other companies uneasy. How could they license a strategically important operating system product from a company with which they expected to compete? And would Sun itself obtain a competitive advantage through being part of the UNIX development team?

4.7   The Open Software Foundation

The situation was exacerbated in 1988 when AT & T made an equity investment in Sun Microsystems. A group of major manufacturers, including IBM, Hewlett-Packard, Digital Equipment, Siemens, Philips and Hitachi took steps to protect themselves from the perceived competitive threat. In 1988 they founded an international software development organization which they named the 'Open Software Foundation' (OSF). Its brief was 'to define specifications, develop leadership software and make available an open, portable application environment'.

The current computer vendor membership of OSF is shown in Fig. 4.4, and the planned deliverables as of July 1992 in Fig. 4.5. More detail on the OSF and its deliverables is contained in Appendix 1.

An early objective of the Open Software Foundation was to provide a new operating system, OSF/1, as an alternative to UNIX. Initially this was to be produced from base technology supplied to the OSF by IBM out of its own AIX work, supplemented with software from other sources.

At the time, the formation of the OSF and its announced intention to provide yet another 'standard' operating system environment caused consternation among those people who were working hard to merge some of the variations that already

---

Sponsors   *Members*

IBM
Groupe Bull
Hitachi
Philips   200+ worldwide
Digital Equipment Corporation
Hewlett-Packard/Apollo
Siemens/Nixdorf

Mission

Develop specifications, leadership software, and make available to industry under fair and equitable licensing terms a general-purpose, vendor-neutral, open software environment

---

Figure 4.4.   The Open Software Foundation.

Special interest groups		Product function
Base communications		
Documentation		OSF/1 base function
User environment		
DOS interface		Motif
Security		
Database	Request for	Distributed computing
Distributed application	technology	environment (DCE)
Internationalization		
System management		Architectural neutral
Case		distribution format (ANDF)
ANDF		
Commercial extensions		Distributed management
Object definitions/guidelines		environment (DME)

Figure 4.5.   Open Software Foundation deliverables.

existed. Not only would there continue to be several versions of the UNIX operating system resulting from manufacturers' proprietary enhancements, but there was now OSF/1 to contend with as well.

OSF/1 can only add to the number of operating system variants if several manufacturers supply it for their systems in addition to the UNIX versions they are already shipping. So far this does not seem to be happening. Instead, vendors such as IBM are moving their own UNIX versions into conformance with OSF/1 at the interface level, but are not removing their proprietary enhancements to UNIX underneath.

4.8   Compatible systems?

In the medium term the major manufacturers are not likely to offer source or binary-code-compatible UNIX or OSF/1 systems. Instead, there will continue to be several implementations of a 'standard' operating system conforming to the standard interface definition.

Some of the vendors may call their implementations 'OSF/1' rather than 'UNIX'. However, since OSF/1 is likely to continue to incorporate some UNIX code, the OSF/1 licensees will still pay UNIX royalties. The users will probably continue to refer to all implementations by the generic name 'UNIX'.

4.9   UNIX International and the UNIX Systems Laboratory

Following the formation of the Open Software Foundation, AT&T moved its UNIX software development activity into a separate division of the company. In cooperation with a number of other manufacturers, among whom were NCR (now a fully owned subsidiary of AT&T), Sun Microsystems, Unisys and ICL, AT&T formed an association called UNIX International (UI) to specify and manage the further development of UNIX on behalf of the industry as a whole.

In 1991 the UNIX division of AT&T became a separate corporation called the

UNIX Systems Laboratory (USL). Shares were offered to a number of partners, and taken up by Sun, ICL, Novell, Fujitsu and others, with AT & T continuing to hold a majority stake. When the PC network specialist Novell became the largest of the new shareholders, the importance of UNIX to its own development strategy was clearly acknowledged. From the start, AT & T stated its intention for USL to become a publicly owned company.

Through these actions, AT & T made it possible for other interested parties to input to UNIX development plans. By separating UNIX development from its other activities, it sought to minimize any conflict of interest issues. Unfortunately, it was not able to do this fast enough to prevent the formation of the OSF, and OSF and USL are now software development companies in direct competition. However, in the time that has elapsed since their formation, the two organizations have learned to coexist. They are working together in a number of ways, particularly in the area of distributed computing, hopefully to the eventual benefit of the customers of either organization.

4.10   X/Open Limited

In the early 1980s each major European country had at least one strong indigenous computer manufacturer—ICL in the UK, Siemens in Germany, Olivetti in Italy and Bull in France. But although each was strong in its home market, none was able to maintain that strength outside its own borders.

In each country IBM was a significant supplier, with shipments close to those of the indigenous manufacturer. This meant that IBM was by far the dominant supplier across Europe as a whole. Consequently, it was the only manufacturer able to offer pan-European supply and support of compatible machines— something which not one of the indigenous suppliers was close to being able to do alone.

In 1984 a group of these European manufacturers—specifically Bull, ICL, Siemens, Olivetti and Nixdorf (now part of Siemens)—formed a jointly owned company in order to deal with this issue. Originally called BISON from the initials of the founding members, its brief was to define a system specification which could be used by all of the shareholders, thus allowing them to produce compatible systems which could be made available across Europe.

When other manufacturers such as Digital Equipment, IBM and Hewlett-Packard applied to join, the decision was taken to widen the brief. The name was changed to X/Open Company Limited, and the not-for-profit company given the task 'to facilitate, guide and manage the process that will allow commercial and government users, software vendors, standards organizations and systems makers to solve the information technology dilemmas caused by incompatibilities in their systems and software components'.

Current corporate members and shareholders of X/Open are shown in Fig. 4.6. As can be seen, the major computer vendors are not only represented directly—

X/Open corporate members and shareholders:
Amdahl Corporation
Compagnie des Machines Bull
Digital Equipment Corporation
Fujitsu Limited
Hewlett-Packard Company
Hitachi Limited
IBM Corporation
International Computers Limited
NCR Corporation
NEC Corporation
Ing C Olivetti & Co, SpA
OKI Electric Industry Company Limited
Siemens Nixdorf Informationssysteme AG
Sun Microsystems Limited
Unisys Corporation
Unix International

Non-shareholder members are grouped within the following:
X/Open User Council
X/Open Independent Software Council
X/Open System Vendor Council

X/Open's Mission:
To develop the common application environment (CAE) specification and promote its
implementation.

Figure 4.6.   X/Open Company Limited.

some also appear indirectly, through their membership in UNIX International.
Over time, membership has been extended to users, independent software
companies, systems integrators and smaller system suppliers.

Today X/Open is an international organization. It has the principal responsibility of defining and coordinating the development of a 'Common Applications
Environment (CAE)' sufficient to achieve the practical realization of open systems
as embodied in its mission statement (Fig. 4.7). This means determining and
specifying the best available standards, *de facto* or official, for each of the

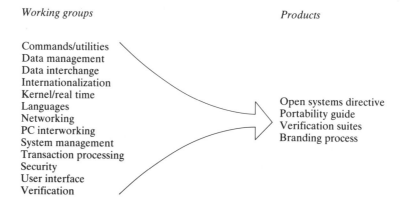

Working groups

Commands/utilities
Data management
Data interchange
Internationalization
Kernel/real time
Languages
Networking
PC interworking
System management
Transaction processing
Security
User interface
Verification

Products

Open systems directive
Portability guide
Verification suites
Branding process

Figure 4.7.   X/Open deliverables.

POSIX	International Portable Operating System Interface Standard; developed within IEEE, based on SVID and Uniforum work
XPG	X/Open's Portability Guide; mixture of public and *de facto* standards, covering all aspects of open system requirements; conforms with POSIX
FIPS	US Federal Informational Processing Standard, conformant to POSIX and XPG

Figure 4.8.   Current public standards.

components that make up complete information systems implementations. Detail on the CAE is contained within a set of books known as the *X/Open Portability Guide* (*XPG*) and available from X/Open (see Appendix 1).

Developing the CAE is a huge and constantly evolving task. To accomplish it, progress is made in a series of well-defined steps. The first of these provided definitions of the interface to the operating system in line with the POSIX work. Following this the international standards for programming languages—C, COBOL, Fortran, ADA—were adopted, together with the SQL standard for data access. SQL technology was first supplied to the international standards process by its developer, IBM. More recently IBM has also supplied X/Open with technology for mainframe data access.

X/Open's networking and communications standards are based on the ISO Open Systems Interconnect (OSI) work. The *de facto* X Window standard from MIT has been adopted for window management but no decision has yet been taken on standards for the user interface itself. Within X/Open, on-going work mirrors that of POSIX and other international standards efforts. Committees are active in the areas of security, network and systems management, transaction processing and many others.

The relationship between POSIX, XPG and the US Federal Information Processing Standards (FIPS) is shown in Fig. 4.8. While POSIX defines the Open Systems Environment (OSE) through the formal process, XPG is a mixture of public and *de facto* standards, which combine to cover all aspects of open systems requirements, including those that have not yet been formalized. The XPG gives a 'snapshot' of the best set of standard technologies that are available at a particular time, and includes the POSIX standards. The FIPS standard is that particular set of choices that need to be made within the standards if a product is to meet the procurement requirements of the US Federal Government, and FIPS is conformant to POSIX and to the XPG.

X/Open is at the center of open systems activity, with responsibility for coordinating the work of many different groups. The XPG is the most widely used open systems procurement specification worldwide.

4.11   Broader membership

X/Open, UI and OSF have all extended their memberships to include other constituents of the market, specifically user organizations, software vendors and

systems houses. A full list of members of these and other standards-related organizations can be obtained directly from each of them (see *The World of Standards*
—details in the Bibliography).

4.12   User Alliances

Stating that 'the user community lacks both a process and a vehicle to exert
collective pressure on vendors to meet open systems needs', the User Alliance for
Open Systems (UAOS) was formed in the USA in 1989. Founding members
include Boeing, Eastman Kodak, Du Pont, Exxon, Ford, General Electric, General
Motors and Hughes Aircraft. UAOS is affiliated to the US Corporation for Open
Systems, COS. Groups similar to UAOS have since been formed in other countries.

Companies with common interests are also beginning to form groups to deal
with open systems issues. The Petrochemical Open Systems Corporation (POSC)
is one such.

While potentially powerful, it is not clear that these organizations will ever be
organized in such a way as to be able to influence developments in the computer
industry to any great extent. Although users are clearly frustrated by the time it
takes for standards to be agreed, their main interest is in using the results of
technological developments for the better running of their businesses. It does not
make sense for them to devote significant, scarce and expensive resources to
defining what the computer industry should be doing in order to meet their needs.

4.13   IBM and UNIX

Although IBM is a UNIX licensee, it is not a member of UNIX International, nor
does it participate directly in its activities. Instead, IBM directs its activities
through the OSF, of which it was a founder member, and through X/Open, of
which it is a member. Nevertheless, AIX is based on UNIX System V, is IBM's
strategic product for the UNIX market, is POSIX-compatible, and will evolve to
remain in conformance with the standards that the market demands.

Most software developers regard IBM's AIX as a complete and professional
UNIX implementation. For large corporations, IBM's enhancements provide
many of the professional systems support and network management utilities that
they have come to expect in the mainframe environment and that are not always
supplied directly with UNIX.

4.14   Open systems definitions

Having followed the development of open systems in earlier chapters from both the
user and vendor viewpoints, it should come as no surprise to find that there is no
universally accepted definition of open systems. The only definition that there is
agreement on is so general that it incorporates almost all possibilities. There are
many reasons for this.

As a concept:	Freedom of choice
	Portability of software
	Minimum training/retraining
	Ease of communications
	Ability to use any peripherals
	Access to all data sources
For implementation:*	DOS, UNIX, OSF/1, POSIX. . .
	Netware, TCP/IP, OSI. . .
	C, COBOL, FORTRAN, ADA. . .
	SQL, RDA. . .
	. . .
	. . .
	. . .

*What technologies are to be used? And who controls them?

Figure 4.9. Open systems: theory and practice.

'Open systems' can refer to the concept of some sort of compatibility or freedom of choice, and also to the technology used to implement the concept (Fig. 4.9). Users are applying the concept of open systems to solve many different problems. As a result, the technologies they use for implementation vary considerably.

For suppliers, an acceptable definition of open systems is affected by economic and political factors associated with their uptake. Their various vested interests have produced a definition of open systems that suits as many of them as possible. This necessarily means that it can be only of a very general nature.

4.15   Open systems and software portability

In today's computer market, it is highly desirable that large populations of systems be compatible. This is driven by economic considerations:

- For the hardware manufacturers, sharing development costs in organizations such as X/Open, USL or OSF reduces their individual costs, and having compatible systems increases the population of software available for each of them.
- For the software vendors, software which is portable across several vendors systems increases the potential market without increasing development and support costs. As Bill Gates, Chairman of Microsoft, once graphically illustrated to a predominantly UNIX user audience, without a population of at least 500 000 completely compatible machines, it is difficult for a software company to build to critical mass (Fig. 4.10).
- For the users, hardware and software should be cheaper, owing to the economies of scale experienced by the vendors in a commodity market. When the same software is able to run on many different machines, the user has freedom to change hardware vendor without changing the software. This enables it to take advantage of competitive pricing without paying a penalty in terms of loss of investments made in software or training. If the same software

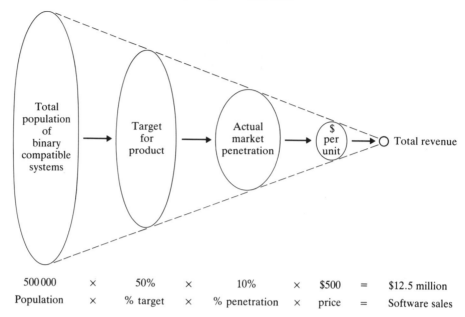

Figure 4.10.   Binary compatibility and software sales.

can be run on different machines in different departments, people can be moved from one department to another without the need for retraining.

In order to satisfy the business requirements for IT discussed in Chapter 2 (Fig. 2.9), the definition of open systems must include the capability for the same software to run on a population of machines, of varying size and performance. These characteristics are known as 'portability' and 'scalability'.

PCs running DOS offer software portability across machines but only for those using the Intel processors. They do not provide scalability to any great degree. UNIX runs well on systems ranging from portables to mainframes, and using many different processor designs. UNIX therefore provides a very high degree of both portability and scalability. In this sense, UNIX can be regarded as more 'open' than DOS.

4.16   Open systems and interconnection

Large organizations have information systems that have evolved using various computers from many manufacturers. As the need to communicate between these has grown, so also has the requirement for standard methods for interconnection and communication.

In Europe, where communications standards have always had a high priority, work to define international standards for computer connection and communication began in earnest in the late 1970s. This culminated in the international collection of standards known as Open Systems Interconnection (OSI), described in some detail by Gray (1991). These have now been accepted as part of the general open systems requirements.

4.17   Open systems and interoperability

As the realization of the importance of open systems standards grows in both user and supplier companies, it is clear that the computer industry needs to define standard interfaces for any and all of the components that make up information technology implementations. These must incorporate both present and future technologies. When this has been accomplished, hardware and software components purchased from conformant vendors will work efficiently together —a property referred to as the ability to 'plug and play'.

'Plug and play' is at the heart of open systems requirements. It defines the characteristic of 'interoperability' in its broadest sense. When interoperability is achieved in full, portability, scalability and interconnection follow automatically.

4.18   Interoperability extended to proprietary systems

In the late 1980s the focus of the open systems movement was on the standardization of the operating system interface in order to achieve portability and scalability, and on defining standards for interconnection (Fig. 4.11). Once this was done, emphasis moved to incorporating OSI into UNIX, and adding to that environment the features that commercial users required. These included improving security, adding transaction-processing capabilities, developing graphical user interfaces, integrating system and network management technologies, and investigating new technologies.

In the user base, UNIX systems provided portability and scalability, while market standards such as TCP/IP and Sun's NFS provided interconnection. Systems incorporating these technologies were regarded as 'open' and were purchased in ever-increasing numbers. Some of these were replacement systems, while others were additions to those already on site.

UNIX systems could be connected easily and were able to communicate efficiently with systems using other technologies. The same was true of proprietary systems when these were from a single vendor, or incorporated standard communications products such as IBM's SNA or Digital's DECNet.

P, portability:	The ability to move applications, people and data from one computer to another easily
S, scalability:	The ability to run the same software systems efficiently on machines of very different size and performance
I, interconnection:	The ability for machines to communicate efficiently, independent of the internal environment
P+S+I = interoperability:	The ability of hardware and software components to 'plug and play' together

Figure 4.11.   Three basic requirements.

Slowly but surely, the requirement grew for interoperability between the two sets of systems—those based on UNIX and regarded as 'open' and those using proprietary operating systems and regarded as 'closed'. This need was felt particularly strongly by IBM, which had by far the largest installed base of proprietary systems, which were rapidly being thought of as closed.

4.19   Software portability across open and closed systems

The requirement for portability of software across open (UNIX) and closed (proprietary) systems was solved in part by the software vendors. They moved their products to any machines for which the sales volumes were sufficiently high. Moving from one proprietary system to another, for example from a DEC to an IBM system, involved a great deal of work. This was greatly reduced when each system ran a variant of UNIX.

Much of the early success of the relational database company, Oracle, can be attributed to its software porting policy. By supplying and supporting its products on proprietary systems, the UNIX environment, and to some extent DOS, Oracle enabled a corporation with a multivendor hardware purchasing policy to standardize on a single database vendor across the entire enterprise. It has only recently been recognized that this has dangers of its own in that users may become locked in to the software supplier. To protect against this, there are now requirements for standards for database access.

Since software porting and subsequent support costs for each proprietary system are high, software vendors can afford to support their software only on machines sold in sufficient volume. As a result, small manufacturers of proprietary systems which were slow to move to UNIX have been driven out of the market. Only the largest manufacturers have been able to maintain sales of two product lines: one proprietary and resulting from the past, and the other open and designed for the future.

4.20   The POSIX open systems definition

The original POSIX definition of the open systems environment (OSE) was: 'a comprehensive and consistent set of international information technology standards and functional standards profiles that specify interfaces, services, and supporting formats to accomplish interoperability and portability of applications, data and people' This was modified in 1991 to that shown in Fig. 4.12.

Every word in this definition is important. The standards must be comprehensive

---

Open systems environment (OSE)
'The comprehensive set of interfaces, services and supporting formats, plus user aspects, for portability of applications, data or people as specified by technology standards and profiles.'

Figure 4.12.   Open systems: POSIX definition.

- Applications environment
- Communications
- Media
- Peripheral support
- Software
- Multimedia, imaging and other emerging technologies
- Parallel and distributed computing
- . . . and many others

Figure 4.13.   Standards required.

and consistent, covering all the components that are required (Fig. 4.13) in IT systems, both now and in the future. They must be internationally supported through the formal process; globalization requires this.

The standards must specify interfaces definitions, so that different products from a variety of suppliers may conform to them, if that is desired. They must not refer to specific products or technologies. Since the standards must cover all possible needs, sets of standards will need to be more tightly defined for specific requirements—these are the 'functional profiles'.

Portability and interoperability are required for software, data and people. It is not sufficient to be able to move software from machine to machine easily. People should also be able to move from one system to another while carrying their accumulated know-how and experience with them. They should not have to be retrained in the process, and the user interface to the system should remain consistent.

In today's integrated information systems, data on one system must be easily accessible from any other, and its interpretation and meaning must be consistent. As we shall see later, obtaining agreement on standards for data and data access within organizations is generally difficult to achieve in practice.

The POSIX open systems definition has been criticized in some quarters for its all-encompassing nature. But it is a fact of life that discussions on strategically important matters that take place between a large number of companies having highly competitive objectives will result at best in only very general agreement. Nevertheless, the POSIX definition is a starting point on which all the important players, including IBM, have now agreed.

The market may well tighten up the open systems definition over time through the technologies that it chooses to use for practical implementation. Indeed, with the rapid growth of UNIX systems, for example, this is already happening.

4.21   Variations in standards

The availability of the POSIX definitions and their acceptance by the international community enables any company to design new products, or modify existing ones, to meet the standards if it wishes to do so. Since the standards are definitions of interfaces, and not of products, it is the interfaces that must be modified, and not the products themselves.

Standards are seldom defined rigidly; usually there are choices available to the implementor at a number of places within the specification. This means that many products can be produced that theoretically meet the standard without these being compatible in a practical sense.

There are two reasons for the existence of choice. The first is that, in defining a standard to be used for many purposes, it is impossible to produce a rigid specification that meets all the requirements. The second is that, in a process where there are many conflicts of interest, agreement will only be reached on a compromise. The POSIX standards are compromise standards in this sense.

4.22   Two interpretations of POSIX

There are two main interpretations of POSIX common in the market today. Each is used as a definition of open systems, and together they are responsible for much of the confusion that exists (Fig. 4.14).

Interpretation 1: POSIX is UNIX

POSIX (and the open systems concept) is most commonly implemented today through use of a variant of the UNIX operating system. This is not surprising, since it was on AT&T's UNIX System V operating system interface that the POSIX standard was built. UNIX systems are supplied in volume by many manufacturers, including IBM, and these dominate open systems shipments at present.

UNIX systems offer a high degree of compatibility across vendors, but are not usually binary compatible. Most manufacturers have added their own specific features, either because they felt these were needed for customer applications or

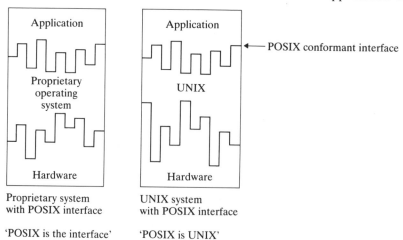

Figure 4.14.   Two interpretations of the POSIX interface standard.

because they were unable to resist the temptation to do so, in order to achieve competitive differentiation. As pointed out by Gray (1991), unnecessary variations can be damaging to the software market, and thus to the UNIX market as a whole.

Interpretation 2: POSIX can be applied to proprietary systems

POSIX defines standard interfaces. Proprietary operating systems can be adjusted to conform to these, should the manufacturer deem it to be of advantage. When this is done, software becomes more easily portable across different vendors' systems, albeit at the source code level and with some effort.

Conformance to international standards, including POSIX, is increasingly required in procurements, particularly those from government agencies. Consequently, most manufacturers have announced their intention to move their proprietary operating systems to POSIX conformance. To some extent the fact that they are able to do this indicates that POSIX is a weak standard. However, since conformance to POSIX eases the problems of software portability, the moves should be welcomed.

4.23   The IBM view

Based on extensive market research, IBM believes that its customers want the flexibility to enhance existing applications or install new ones without being forced to move to a new environment or necessarily being constrained to a single-system environment. Research also shows that its customers want to do this without unnecessary replication of data and software. At the same time, these users want the comfort of knowing that they are protected by conformance to publicly agreed standards.

Many customers have made heavy investments in IBM proprietary products. They have spent many years developing software applications for them and in building the technical resources to understand and run them. It is more attractive to such users to move to open systems in an evolutionary way, through the POSIX interface approach for proprietary systems, than it is to make any sudden and dramatic changes to their systems.

4.24   The effects of two interpretations of open systems

Ideally, previous investments made in hardware, operating systems, software applications and skills should be protected as much and for as long as possible. Applications, old and new, should be able to draw upon databases, files or other applications wherever these reside. But new and emerging technologies must also be used as appropriate, particularly when these have cost or performance advantages for the users.

Two approaches to the implementation of the POSIX standards are therefore needed in the short term. One is based on the protection of current investments and provides an evolutionary approach to an open architecture by opening up proprietary systems. The other gives the immediate benefits of open systems through a revolutionary approach based on new technologies. Which is 'best' depends on the situation that applies in the customer site.

4.25   Implications for vendors of IT products

For vendors, the need to support two methods of implementation of open systems concepts—through UNIX or through POSIX—has a number of important technical and economic implications (Fig. 4.15). These depend on the particular vendor's current position in the marketplace, and the characteristics of its installed base:

- Those having a strong proprietary installed base must offer a controlled migration path as they move their proprietary systems to POSIX conformance. At the same time, they must offer new, UNIX-based technologies in order to stay competitive in that part of the market showing most rapid growth. This means that for the immediate future they must continue to develop and enhance two overlapping and sometimes competitive product lines.

  This strategy will be expensive and difficult to implement, and only the very largest companies will be able to maintain it. Even they can be expected to merge the two product lines eventually, since it is likely to be too expensive for them to maintain both families in the long term.

  IBM is by far the largest company in this category, and therefore has the most difficult balancing act. It has the largest installed base of proprietary systems. IBM's customers have traditionally been very loyal to IBM. They can be expected to remain so, provided that IBM supplies appropriate services and products as and when they are needed, and at prices that are competitive.

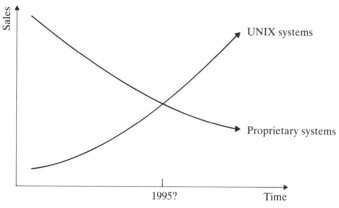

Manufacturers supporting two product lines
have a very difficult balancing act

Figure 4.15.   Effects of two families.

- Smaller manufacturers of proprietary systems will not be able to manage their way through the problems that the emergence of open systems causes them. They will either disappear or move to open systems based on UNIX, probably saving development costs and time to market by licensing technology from others. Bull is in this second category, having opted to take UNIX systems from IBM rather than develop its own. Wang, which ran into severe financial difficulty when it moved late to open systems, may yet survive as a reseller of IBM systems.
- Newer manufacturers such as Sun, whose business is based entirely on UNIX systems, can afford to compete very aggressively on price and performance. They are able to spend all their R & D money on further developing a single product line. However, they will have difficulty penetrating large commercial accounts at a strategic level. Organizations with a large investment in proprietary systems must adopt an evolutionary approach to 'going open' and financial factors will dictate when they will be ready to embark on a replacement strategy.

Moving to an open systems architecture raises many issues of integration and migration in the customer base. The company that can supply the appropriate products and services now should have an advantage in the future. As we will see in Chapter 11, IBM is directing significant resources at the supply of such services.

4.26   Open systems market trends

Despite the confusion that exists in the marketplace over the variations in UNIX, the two interpretations of open systems, and the competition between proprietary and open product lines, the penetration of the market by systems that customers deem to be 'open' is increasingly very rapidly.

Proprietary operating systems such as VM, MVS, OS/2 from IBM and VMS from Digital are moving to POSIX conformance. By the end of the 1990s, today's proprietary operating systems will have disappeared, except perhaps in some niche application areas. This will happen in controlled stages—first through the conformance of proprietary systems to POSIX and related standards, and more slowly through the convergence of each of the two operating system environments maintained by the dominant suppliers.

4.27   Market standards

In spite of the massive effort expended on open systems standards activity over the last few years, few formally approved standards exist today (Fig. 4.16). Those that do exist are not implemented in the same way by different vendors. Standards do not yet exist in many important areas, for example, at the user interface level or for transaction-processing.

It is likely that many of the gaps will be filled by market-generated standards. For example, IBM's CICS, the most widely used transaction processing software in the mainframe environment, should quickly become a *de facto* standard now

---

Standards *do not* yet exist for:
- Systems management
- Network management
- User interface
- CASE tools
- Transaction processing
- Distributed applications
- Distributed data

Figure 4.16.   Today's standards.

that it is available in the UNIX environment for IBM, HP and others. The graphical user interface Motif, supplied by the Open Software Foundation is a *de facto* standard already.

Although public standards are desirable in theory, in practice the real needs of users and the delays in the standards process mean that standards will often be set by the market (Fig. 4.17). This is not a problem, provided that the technologies are made available to other vendors on acceptable commercial terms.

4.28   The future

Although suppliers are moving to standards conformance, a single-standard operating system or application environment is not expected to emerge for the computer industry as a whole.

Technology is continually evolving while new products are being developed. There will always be a need to evolve new standards to incorporate these. The alliance between Apple and IBM, for example (discussed in Chapter 7) is expected to produce a new operating system environment for desktop machines that will incorporate object-oriented software as well as support for emerging multimedia technologies.

There are no signs that the biggest vendors in the IT market will ever fully cooperate to produce totally compatible machines. Nor is it clear that the market would be best served if they did so. Instead, we can expect that three or four groupings of vendors will appear, each centred on a major hardware manufacturer controlling a particular microprocessor technology.

Within each of these groups, a high degree of compatibility can be expected. But across them there will be only as much compatibility as can be built into the specifications for international standards.

The practical problem is to provide interoperability between the major groups. Since all can be expected to conform to the OSF's Distributed Computing Environ-

---

- Microsoft   DOS, Windows
- Unix Systems Laboratories   UNIX
- Open Software Foundation   Motif, DCE
- IBM   SNA, SQL, CICS

Figure 4.17.   Market standards.

ment specifications (see Appendix 1), this should be a manageable problem for most organizations.

Whatever the major groups turn out to be, it is clear that IBM intends to be at the heart of one of them. It already has agreements with other vendors under which they can resell its UNIX products. These will be extended into licensing arrangements for the AIX operating system software, as well as for other software products. In addition, the results of the Apple/IBM/Motorola development will lead to a microprocessor that will be licensed widely to other system manufacturers.

4.29   Summary

In previous chapters we saw that open systems is both a concept—users want freedom of choice to build systems from components from any vendor—and a set of technologies to implement the concept. Recognizing that the concept requires interoperability of hardware and software—the ability of components to 'plug and play'—the issue is to define the required technologies, and specify how they are to be controlled.

In this chapter we have followed the development of open system standards and technologies. We have seen that standards emerge both from the formal process and from the marketplace, but in spite of an enormous commitment of resources the process is often considered too slow for practical needs. Various groups have emerged to deal with the definition of user requirements for open system standards, the most important of which is X/Open.

Suppliers such as IBM, having a large installed base of proprietary systems, have no other choice but to continue to develop and sell these systems, while bringing them into conformance with international standards. At the same time, they must produce and fully support a complete line of UNIX systems in order to retain their positions in the market.

This situation has led to two common interpretations of open systems. One requires POSIX conformance and allows hitherto proprietary systems to be described as 'open'. The other relies on using a standard operating system, currently UNIX. Both interpretations will survive in the short-term since users need a migration path from the systems of the past to those of the future. Ultimately, competing product lines from a single supplier can be expected to converge.

The applications environment must constantly evolve to incorporate new technologies. As a result, standards converge as technology matures, and diverge again as new technologies appear. This is a logical, healthy and acceptable situation.

In the next chapters we will consider open systems issues as they apply specifically to IBM and its strategy. We will start by looking at the problems that are created by IBM's simultaneous support of its proprietary (but open) SAA line and its open (but proprietary) UNIX AIX family, and the ways in which it is dealing with them.

5
Supporting two families

5.1 Introduction

The evolution of enterprise computing and the rise of open systems has left traditional manufacturers with the problem of supporting and further developing two product lines—a proprietary family which dominates the installed base and a UNIX-based family, considered by the market to be today's fullest implementation of open systems concepts (Fig. 5.1).

While sales of proprietary systems are in general decreasing (IBM's AS/400 line being the notable exception), sales of UNIX systems are increasing rapidly in all parts of the world and all segments of the market. Margins on proprietary systems have always been high and therefore able to support a corresponding high level of support structure costs. Competition forces much lower margins on the UNIX systems, and services can no longer be included; they must be priced and sold separately. Sales methods must change to accommodate the reduced margins, and revenue per employee for most hardware manufacturers must increase considerably.

As the uptake of UNIX systems continues to accelerate, manufacturers that are forced through their history to support two competing product families must manage their companies through a very difficult transitional period (Fig. 5.2).

IBM has the largest installed base of proprietary systems of any vendor. These are based mainly on its Systems Applications Architecture (SAA) technology, command high margins and have traditionally been supplied 'bundled' with sophisticated support services. While IBM must continue to develop the SAA family and protect the investments of its current customers, it must also grow in the UNIX market with high-performance, innovative and price-competitive products.

As open systems become ever more important in the marketplace, IBM must develop its products accordingly. It must change its corporate structure so as to be able to respond to customers' needs while still providing a good performance for its shareholders. The changes required are vast and extremely complex.

In this chapter we look in some detail at IBM's two families of products—the proprietary SAA and the UNIX-based AIX product lines—and examine the relationships between them. We look at the tools that IBM is providing in order

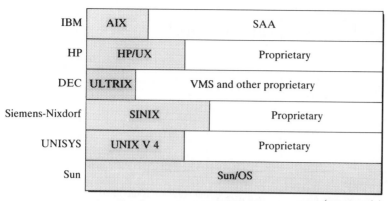

Figure 5.1.   Installed base of proprietary and UNIX systems.   (not to scale)

to facilitate interoperability between them, and the plans that it has announced to increase this further.

We will find that, while the systems in these two product lines are increasingly competitive, they are also slowly converging. Both are doing well in the market-place. By the end of the chapter we will see that the needs of many users can be satisfied through IBM's two-family strategy, and we will have laid the foundation for understanding the reasons behind IBM's open systems strategy.

5.2   Two-dimensional portability

In the early stages of IT use, IBM, together with other manufacturers, offered systems based on several different hardware architectures and system control programs (now known as 'operating systems'). By pursuing a multiple-architecture

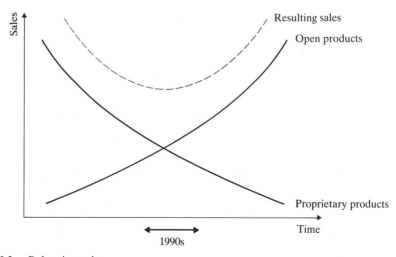

Figure 5.2.   Balancing sales.

One-dimensional, proprietary view

	IBM	DEC	HP
System 1	√	×	*
System 2	√	×	*
System 3	√	×	*
System 4	√	×	*
System 5	√	×	*
"			
"			

√ = Software runs on IBM ⎫ but software is modified
× = Software runs on DEC ⎬ for each manufacturer
* = Software runs on HP ⎭

Figure 5.3.   Software portability and scalability: proprietary view.

strategy, IBM was able to provide products with a wide range of price/performance, supporting many different information-processing needs.

This was an appropriate strategy at the time, and it still is today for certain specialized applications. But as the need for integrated information systems grows, there is an increasing need for compatibility and connectivity across systems. This applies both to those systems supplied from a single manufacturer, and across systems from several manufacturers.

When application software is portable across a complete line of a manufacturer's own systems products, development and support costs are lowered for the computer manufacturer and customers are provided with a level of scalability and upgradability. IBM, in common with other computer vendors, recognized the advantages of this many years ago, and started to develop compatibility across its own systems (Fig. 5.3).

Until the advancement of open systems concepts, it was not generally understood that the demand for portability and scalability was two-dimensional, running across many manufacturers' products, and not one-dimensional, across those of a single manufacturer (Fig. 5.4). Once software vendors and users realized the advantages of portability and compatibility, they wanted it both down a particular vendor's product line and across the product lines of different vendors (see Gray, 1991).

5.3   IBM's proprietary Systems Application Architecture (SAA)

By 1987, IBM had evolved a strategy for delivering portability and scalability across its own product line through the development of a new family of systems based on its proprietary Systems Application Architecture (SAA).

SAA was designed to make it easier for customers to build integrated enterprise information systems by improving the consistency and connectivity across four

Two-dimensional, open view

	IBM	DEC	HP
System 1	●	●	●
System 2	●	●	●
System 3	●	●	●
System 4	●	●	●
System 5	●	●	●
"			
"			

● = Same software runs on all
    systems from many manufacturers

Figure 5.4.   Software portability and scalability: open view.

major IBM proprietary environments—the mainframe MVS/ESA and VM/ESA; the mid-range OS/400; and the desktop OS/2. SAA was to do this through the use of three IBM-defined standard interfaces (Fig. 5.5):

- Common user access (CUA)
- Common communications support (CCS)
- Common programming interface (CPI).

Taken together, these three interfaces were designed to enable SAA-compliant applications to be built by software vendors and customers, as well as by IBM itself. Applications built to the standards would run on any of IBM's SAA hardware platforms.

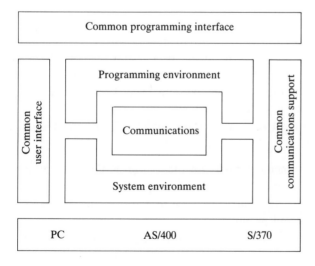

Figure 5.5.   IBM's Systems Application Architecture.

Common User Access (CUA)

The Common User Access (CUA) architecture defines those user interface components that should be common across applications. It is based on a set of generally accepted user interface design principles, optimized for ease of use.

The fundamental objectives of CUA are to provide usability and consistency within an application and consistency across applications. When the guidelines are followed, all conformant products will appear to work in much the same way. When this is achieved, user productivity and satisfaction with the product should be increased, and error rates reduced.

When software products have the same 'look and feel', a user is able to transfer knowledge obtained from one product across to other products. That this is true has already been proved by Apple users. The user interface for applications has always been tightly controlled by Apple, and as a result software products have a high degree of consistency. If a user learns to use one product with the Apple interface, he or she can quickly learn to use any other product built with the same interface. The CUA seeks to obtain the same degree of compatibility and skills portability across applications running in the SAA environment. Software portability across hardware systems and skills transfer across software products is a fundamental part of the POSIX open systems definition discussed in Chapter 4, which requires the equivalent of CUA to be available on all systems, not just those from IBM.

Serving two worlds

Most of the international standards activity concerning the user interface is concentrated on graphical user interfaces (see Gray, 1991). However, IBM's customers include many organizations with substantial investments in 'dumb' terminals, the population of which is still increasing. There are many applications for which such devices are still suitable from both a technical and a cost-effective point of view.

Until its customers are ready to move from character-based terminals, it is IBM's responsibility to provide products which are suitable for them now, and to define a controlled migration path for the time when the economics are right for them to make a change to other technologies.

CUA therefore defines two user interface models—Entry and Graphical (Fig. 5.6):

- 'Entry' is the recommended model for the non-programmable terminal environment that exists in many hundreds of thousands of real-world applications. It is best suited for data-entry-intensive applications using character-based panels with menus and prompts.
- The graphical model is recommended for programmable workstation applications. It makes extensive use of windows, action bars with pull-down menus,

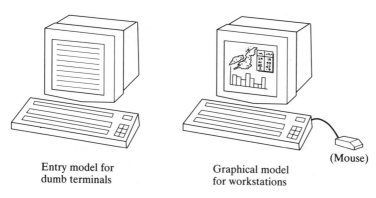

Entry model for
dumb terminals

Graphical model
for workstations

(Mouse)

Figure 5.6. Common User Access.

and standard graphical cues such as check boxes. The workplace environment is an extension of the graphical model that is suitable for the integration of applications as objects that appear as icons on an electronic representation of a real workplace, and can be controlled by a mouse.

The fact that IBM emphasizes both CUA models shows its continuing responsibility to the installed base of users.

IBM has introduced object-based enhancements to the original CUA workplace environment for programmable workstations. Known as CUA 91, it is supported in OS/2, the IBM operating system for PS/2 desktop systems, and by development tools in AD/Cycle, IBM's application development methodology.

Common Programming Interface (CPI)

The Common Programming Interface (CPI) consists of a broad and consistent set of languages and services that programmers can employ directly or through higher-level application development tools. By using this interface, developers can create cooperative applications or write major application modules without concern for the environments in which they will eventually run.

When programs are written in conformance to the CPI, programming skills become portable across all those machine environments that support it. This can help both individuals and organizations to protect investments made in training. Again, this is the one-dimensional parallel to the two-dimensional objective expressed in general open systems concepts. Protection is provided by IBM's CPI only if the individual or user organization confines itself to the use of IBM products, whereas open systems definitions seek to provide portability of skills across systems from many vendors.

The elements of the CPI include the support of standard languages as shown in Fig. 5.7, and the programming services indicated in Fig. 5.8.

C:	Based on ANSI standard X3J11 with some IBM extensions
Cobol:	Based on ANSI standard COBOL X3.23-1985
Fortran:	Based on ANSI standard FORTRAN X3.9-1978
PL/1:	Based on the OS PL/1 V2 for Systems 370

Procedures
Language: Based on the REXX language
RGP: Based on the RPG/400 product on AS:400

Application
Generator: Based on elements of the interfaces found in the IBM cross-system product

Figure 5.7.   Common Programming Interface: languages.

Application Development: AD/Cycle and AIX/CASE

Computer-aided software engineering (CASE) is the discipline which has evolved to help organizations manage the development of sophisticated software systems. Many CASE tools exist to handle aspects of the software development and maintenance cycle, but the lack of an integrated tool set capable of handling the entire process has hindered their uptake and use.

Many industry groups, standards bodies and consortia are working together to define API specifications that will enable the integration and interoperability of software tools. These specifications need to embrace existing legacy data, applications and platforms, as well as provide leadership into the next generation of systems.

AD/Cycle is a set of offerings from IBM that are designed to address the need for significant improvement in the productivity, quality and manageability of the software development process. Based on SAA, initially it is supported by staged implementation of integrated tools, data storage facilities and an open architecture

Communications interface
  Provides high level interface to SNA LU6.2 advanced program-to-program communications
Database interface
  Based on ANSI standard SQL X3.135 and IBM's own SQL
Dialog interface
  CUA structure implemented by the OS/2 Dialog Manager
Query interface
  Based on interfaces in the Query Management Facility (QMF) and the OS/2 EE Query Manager
Presentation interface
  CUA structure implemented by the OS/2 Presentation Manager
Print/manager interface
  Defines a consistent means to request print services throughout an enterprise
Resume recovery interface
  Defines a consistent interface to ensure that commit or backout updates are made completely or not at all
Repository interface
  Based on interfaces in the Repository Manager/MVS

Figure 5.8.   Common Programming Interface: services.

for interfaces. The functions are provided by IBM together with a set of AD/Cycle partners.

IBM also provides a set of integration services for CASE environments for AIX developers. These allow tools from IBM, other vendors or customers to be integrated using consistent interfaces and data formats, to support the entire software development life cycle.

AIX CASE uses the European Computer Manufacturers' Association (ECMA) Reference Model in the specification of its services and components. This includes the ECMA Portable Common Tools Environment (PCTE) and will incorporate other object oriented standards, as these emerge.

From IBM's point of view, AD/Cycle is the appropriate environment for those customers who require support for the development of applications in the SAA environment with OS/2 as the primary development platform. AIX CASE is appropriate for developing UNIX applications with the RISC System/6000 as the primary development platform.

IBM will continue to develop both the AD/Cycle and AIX CASE environments, while still themselves increasing interoperability between the two. This will be provided by the consistency of tools in the two environments, standard languages such as COBOL and Fortran, and products such as The Integrated Reasoning Shell (TIRS), a knowledge-based tool that can be used for development in both environments or to target execution in either system.

There is clearly a requirement in the user base for a consistent CASE solution across IBM's SAA and AIX platforms that provides common tools, interchange of tool data and a consistent set of platform services. The IBM CASE solution should evolve so that the developer may choose either OS/2 or AIX as the development environment and build applications to be run on SAA, AIX and, potentially, other non-IBM platforms.

As standards emerge, such as PCTE for ECMA, IBM can be expected to implement them in both environments. It is working with worldwide standards committees such as those within the European Strategic Programme for Research in Information Technology (ESPRIT), the European Computer Manufacturers' Association (ECMA), the Japanese MITI sponsored consortium SIGMA, as well as cooperating with a number of US CASE efforts, including the Software Technology for Adaptable and Reliable Systems (STARS) and the COMMON APSE Interface Set (CAIS) initiatives.

Common Communications Support (CCS)

The SAA Common Communications Support (CCS) defines architectures and protocols that allow standardized communication to take place among devices, application programs, systems and networks. It consists of IBM protocols and Open Systems Interconnection (OSI) standards chosen to allow both IBM and

Object Content Architectures
- Presentation text
- Image
- Graphics
- Font
- Formatted data

Data Streams
- 3270 Data Stream
- Document Content Architecture
- Intelligent Printer Data Stream
- Mixed Object: Document Content Architecture
- Character Data Representation Architecture

Application Services
- SNA Management Services
- SNA Distribution Services
- Document Interchange Architecture
- Distributed Data Management Architecture
- Distributed Relational Database Architecture
- File Transfer, Access and Management
- X.400 Message Handling System
- OSI Association Control Service Element

Session Services
- LU 6.2
- OSI Presentation Layer
- OSI Session Layer
- OSI Transport Layer

Network
- LU Type 2.1 Low Entry Networking
- Connectionless-Mode Network Services using Internet
- Connection-oriented Network services using Subnetwork Interface to X.25

Data Link Control
- Synchronous Data Link Control
- IBM Token Ring LAN
- X.25

Figure 5.9.   Common Communications Support.

non-IBM systems to be interconnected efficiently. The elements of SAA CCS are given in Fig. 5.9.

When CCS architectures are implemented consistently, networks can be built up from systems of vastly differing architectures and capabilities. It is a general objective of the open systems movement that such facilities are available for all systems, based on architectures that are freely available in the marketplace, and based on internationally agreed, not vendor-controlled, standards. The concept of CCS therefore has much wider implications than those of SAA alone.

IBM announced in 1991 that it had extended the SAA CCS to include Integrated Services Digital Network (ISDN) support for standard signalling protocols based on International Telephone and Telegraph Consultative Committee (CCITT) recommendations. It is making enhancements in support of image and bar code object content architectures and multiple object Document Content Architecture (DCA) standards.

SAA in other environments

Although SAA was designed to support the IBM architectures of MVS/ESA, VM/ESA, OS/400 and OS/2, certain elements are also available in its mainframe VSE and PC DOS environments. For example, COBOL and C are available in VSE and DOS, while the SQL requester function is in DOS. However, VSE and PC DOS are not defined as part of SAA, and so all elements of SAA are not guaranteed to be available in them.

Applications Software

Many independent software vendors have developed and now supply products for the SAA environment. IBM itself has added to these. The SAA Catalog, available from IBM, describes more than 500 products from over 240 vendors. Since many of these are software languages and tools used to build other applications, this catalog gives only an indication of the vast range of software available for SAA systems.

Summary of SAA

SAA provides a consistent framework upon which customers can build productive and effective enterprise-wide information systems, provided they are willing to base these primarily on IBM proprietary technology. In support of the installed base, IBM must continue to develop and expand SAA in response to customer requirements, competitive pressures and technological innovation.

In the past, a single-vendor strategy would have been acceptable to many major organizations. This is no longer the case. Many companies now realize that IBM alone, even with massive resources, cannot meet all their needs. Even if it could do so internally, information systems are starting to link across to other enterprises which may use systems from another vendor. It is therefore no longer sufficient to have compatibility within a single manufacturer's systems. Instead, adherence by all vendors to a set of global standards is required in order to provide compatibility across several manufacturers' systems.

In the definition of each of the individual elements of SAA—CUA, CPI, CCS —IBM showed that it understood the forces driving many of the user requirements for open systems. It must now extend the functionality of its solutions to non-SAA products, both its own UNIX systems and products from other vendors.

5.4   IBM's UNIX—Advanced Interactive Executive (AIX)

In 1988 IBM announced the Advanced Interactive Executive (AIX) family of operating systems, designed to address the needs of the fast-growing UNIX market. Within the AIX family, IBM provides a collection of interfaces, conventions and protocols parallel to those offered within SAA. These are designed to give consistency across the ESA/370 and ESA/390 mainframe processor families, the RISC/6000 architecture and the IBM Personal System/2 computing environments.

The multiple-architecture UNIX strategy gives customers a wide choice of function and hardware. By making the AIX operating system environment available on multiple-processor architectures, portability of people, data and programs is provided across a broad range of price/performance solutions. As a result, the IBM UNIX offerings are as strong or stronger than those of any other UNIX system vendor.

In common with the SAA product line, the AIX family incorporates many formal and informal industry standards and specifications. It is steadily evolving and will be extended over time to incorporate new technologies.

There are six related elements of the AIX family definition

- AIX Base System
- AIX Programming Interface
- AIX User Interface
- AIX Communications Support
- AIX Distributed Processing
- AIX Applications

AIX Base System

The AIX Base System defines operating system calls, libraries, commands and utilities. Specifications and functions include the UNIX System V Release 2 and Release 3 operating systems, and the Berkeley Software Distribution Release 4.3 (4.3 BSD). The definition includes most commands and routines from these environments, together with IBM specific enhancements. It conforms to the IEEE POSIX Standards, the X/Open Portability Guide Issue 3 (XPG 3) specification, and the OSF Application Environment Specification (AES).

National Language Support (NLS) is included in the AIX family definition, and the AIX Base System conforms to X/Open's Specification for Internationalization.

AIX Programming Interfaces

The AIX Programming Interface defines those services and interfaces, such as languages, that are available to applications developers. The AIX family definition includes the ANSI standards for the C, Fortran and Cobol languages, together with the extensions to the languages, as defined by the SAA CPIs described earlier (Fig. 5.7).

AIX User Interface

The AIX family definition for the user interface is based on the Open Software Foundation's OSF/Motif (see Appendix 1), together with the presentation services

---

User interfaces and presentation services:
- AIX Windows, based on OSF/Motif and X Windows
- X Window system
- C Shell
- Bourne Shell
- GKS and graPHIGS graphic routine libraries
- XGSL (GSL graphics routines integrated with X Windows)

Note: Some of these are supported on workstations only.

Figure 5.10.   AIX user interfaces.

shown in Fig. 5.10. Certain of the presentation services, for example the X Window server and the graphics routine libraries, are supported on workstations only.

AIX Communications Support

The AIX family supports a full range of communications facilities (Fig. 5.11). Some of these, such as Ethernet, X.25 and OSI, are public industry standards; others, such as SNA LU 6.2, are IBM proprietary technologies in common use. The communications support offered in AIX is as complete as that of any other UNIX vendor, and has the additional advantage of providing efficient and well-supported methods of linking IBM SAA, IBM AIX and non-IBM systems.

AIX distributed processing

The AIX family definition includes distributed processing facilities that provide users and applications access to programs and files on other systems that implement compatible functionality. For example, Sun's Network File System (NFS) is supported in the AIX family definition, as are commonly used UNIX remote functions.

AIX applications

Almost all the products that exist in the UNIX world have been ported to the IBM AIX environment, and several thousand applications products are now available. These range from simple utilities to complex multi-function vertical applications.

- X.25, including new applications and an application programming interface
- Ethernet and IEEE 802.3 support
- Token Ring and IEEE 802.3 support
- ANSI 3.64 protocol for connection of asynchronous ASCII terminals
- TCP/IP facilities, including end-user commands and an application programming interface
- UUCP, allowing users to copy files from one UNIX operating system to another
- OSI
- SNA LU 6.2

Figure 5.11.   AIX communications support.

The catalog of applications software for the AIX family is constantly updated by IBM.

AIX and OSF/1

In 1991 IBM announced its intention to migrate the AIX family to the Open Software Foundation's OSF/1 (see Appendix 1).

AIX/ESA, the System 390 member of the AIX family provided on the ESA architecture, extends IBM's mainframe UNIX offering beyond AIX/370 for those customers who require the high performance and large capacity provided by the ESA processor. The migration path is relatively easy, since a high degree of binary and data compatibility exists between the two environments. AIX/ESA is built upon the Open Software Foundation's OSF/1, with additional IBM enhancements designed to exploit the capability of large processors.

AIX for the RISC System/6000 family already has many interfaces and standards in common with the OSF/1 product. Modifications for full OSF AES operating system conformance should be included in time. IBM has stated that it intends to migrate AIX/6000 to an OSF/1 operating system base.

For the PS/2 platforms, IBM will maintain and advance the current AIX PS/2 offerings. IBM has said that it intends eventually to incorporate OSF technology into the IBM PS/2 computing environments.

IBM intends to offer the OSF Distributed Computing Environment (DCE—see Appendix 1) on the AIX/ESA platform and to provide a suite of DCE products for a future release of AIX for the RISC/System 6000. It will support the OSF Distributed Management Environment (DME), when this becomes available.

5.5   Foundations for an open systems architecture

Organizations today are not building integrated information systems from scratch, on green field sites. Instead, they are building systems for the future while making best use of prior IT investments. Recognizing this fact is fundamental to understanding IBM's open systems strategy.

IBM is building its open system solutions on the architectures provided by both the SAA and AIX families (Fig. 5.12). Each of these environments incorporates many established and emerging industry standards. Both can be expected to evolve to incorporate others as they emerge from the standards process. In the sense of 'conformance to international standards', IBM is positioning both the SAA and AIX families as 'open'.

The SAA family has the larger installed base, but the number of AIX users is growing fast. IBM's obligation to its customers is to provide migration and integration paths between the two families.

While SAA may provide the capability to optimize a particular solution, AIX provides a full and standard UNIX implementation across a wide range of

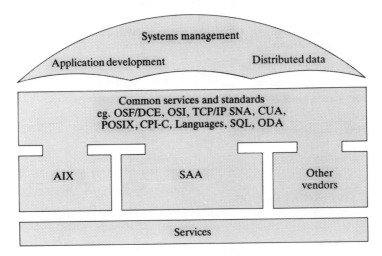

Figure 5.12. IBM's open enterprise.

platforms. IBM standards for reliability, availability, serviceability (RAS) and extensive use have made the SAA functions of truly 'industrial strength'. With AIX, IBM is now bringing the same standards of quality and reliability to the UNIX market.

In 1990 IBM announced that SAA and AIX are both key software strategies, and its intention is to make each of them 'best in class'. Although the two families are independent, technologies and capabilities will be shared between them (Fig. 5.13). The resultant interoperability of SAA and AIX should allow customers to build enterprise solutions that incorporate both SAA and AIX, if they so desire. Interoperability features will be extended to facilitate the integration of other vendors' systems.

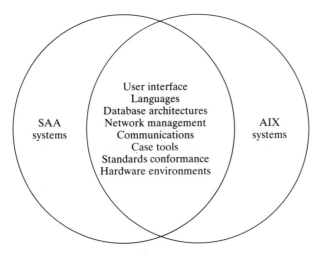

Figure 5.13. Commonality across SAA and AIX systems.

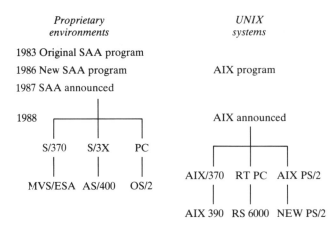

Figure 5.14.   IBM's two architectures. (*Source*: ITG)

5.6   Interoperability of SAA and AIX

Developed in parallel through the 1980s (Fig. 5.14), SAA and AIX are now complementary and strategic IBM architectures, each capable of delivering a wide range of customer solutions.

IBM has announced products and statements of direction that demonstrate its intent to provide a significant and increasing level of interoperability between the SAA and AIX families. This should facilitate comprehensive enterprise solutions when both operating environments are required. The interoperability functions that exist between SAA and AIX systems can be grouped into the following three types:

- Common functions available on both SAA and AIX systems, for example, database technology, OSI communications, OSF DCE
- Bridges between SAA and AIX, performing data translation and conversion, for example, mail interchange facilities, NetView network management software
- UNIX function options in AIX made available on SAA systems, for example TCP/IP, NFS, X Windows.

The specific areas of interoperability between SAA and AIX as announced by IBM are: sharing of data, file transfer, presentation services, communications protocols, mail exchange, network management and a common set of standards-compliant languages.

Sharing of data

Relational database support is available as standard on all SAA systems. Extensions to the SAA Relational Database Management System were added in 1988 to support access to data distributed in remotely interconnected IBM systems —an increasingly common customer requirement.

To support the sharing of relational data between SAA and AIX systems, IBM will provide AIX distributed relational databases that harmonize with SAA distributed database implementations (DB2, SQL/DS, OS/400 DBM, OS/2 DBM...). The SAA and AIX relational database managers will work together to support a distributed database capability, which will allow both SAA and AIX users access to data in all environments. In this way, SAA and AIX users will be able to share common relational data.

The AIX-distributed relational databases will conform to the ANSI SQL and FIPS standards and the X/Open SQL specifications as defined in the XPG.

Shared files

The ability to share files between applications executing on SAA systems and those on AIX systems is a common requirement. Today this is accomplished using Sun's Network File System, NFS.

The OSF's DCE will improve distributed file sharing among heterogeneous systems. It will be supported in both SAA and AIX, and will significantly enhance their file-sharing capability.

Presentation services

For AIX systems, presentation services and user interface management for advanced applications are provided by the X Windows and AIXwindows. The X Windows system supports both local and distributed application access through its client/server support. AIXwindows is based on the OSF/Motif graphical user interface and utilizes the X Windows System Client Support.

For SAA systems, presentation services for applications are provided by Presentation Manager (PM) and Common User Access (CUA).

Although AIXwindows and PM are different implementations of presentation services, they produce similar user interface styles—known as 'look and feel'. This means that, although the developer must customize software for each environment, to the user the application will appear to behave in the same way on AIX or SAA systems.

For customers requiring a consistent set of presentation services across SAA and AIX systems, it is IBM's goal to provide X Windows and AIXwindows support as standard on all AIX systems, and as options on all SAA systems. With this available, AIX workstations will be able to display local X Windows and AIXwindows applications which execute on remote AIX and SAA systems.

OS/2 workstations will also be able to access X Windows and AIXwindows applications which execute on remote AIX and SAA systems. Using PM support on OS/2, SAA applications will also be able to be displayed.

Communications and connectivity

Connectivity was the early interpretation of interoperability and remains central to it. IBM has products such as TCP/IP, LU 6.2 and OSI, for both the SAA and AIX environments and intends to expand the protocol and connectivity support between them. The goal is to support SNA LU6.2, OSI and TCP/IP communications protocols on all SAA and AIX systems, operating on standard physical connections such as Token Ring, Ethernet and X.25.

Mail exchange

AIX, in common with other systems derived from the UNIX operating system, support the *de facto* standard for electronic mail systems, Simple Mail Transfer Protocol (SMTP).

IBM supports mail exchange between SMTP and its proprietary office products through bridging functions which run on MVS, VM or OS/400. The bridges for MVS and VM are supplied through IBM Business Partner, SoftSwitch. AIX and SAA systems will support the OSI mail protocol X.400 and it is IBM's intention also to support X.400 mail exchange between its office products.

Network management

Network management is one of the biggest problems that users face when they implement multivendor networks.

IBM provides products that give customers the ability to manage their networks by collecting information about the status of network components, using the network to transport this information to a centralized location selected by the customer, analysing the information, and using it to control the network.

SNA, OSI and TCP/IP network architectures each define different methods of collecting and transporting information. In OSI, it is the Common Management Information Service/Protocol (CMIS/CMIP) while in TCP/IP, it is the Simple Network Management Protocol (SNMP). These architectures define both 'agent' and 'manager' functions. Managers collect and analyse data sent by agent functions residing on nodes on the network.

IBM provides network management for mixed SNA, TCP/IP and OSI networks incorporating SAA and AIX systems. It is expanding support for SNMP agent functions and CMIS/CMIP agent functions to both SAA and AIX environments and enhancing its NetView network management products to provide manager functions for both TCP/IP and OSI networks. Mixed SNA, TCP/IP and OSI networks can then be managed from a single NetView focal point.

Although IBM originally defined the focal point for network management to be on the IBM mainframe, it is clear that many users would like to manage their networks from other servers. As a result, IBM now offers network manager functions on other SAA and AIX platforms.

Subject	AIX/6000	AIX PS/2	AIX/ESA	MVS/ESA	VM/ESA	OS/2	OS/400
Languages: C	AV	AV	AV	AV	AV	AV	AV
COBOL	AV	AV	SOD	AV	AV	AV	AV
FORTRAN	AV	AV	AV	AV	AV	AV	AV
Relational Database (SQL/DRDA):	SOD	SOD	SOD	AV	AV	AV	AV
Data files: NFS Client	AV	AV	AV	–	–	AV	–
NFS Server	AV	AV	AV	AV	AV	AV	SOD
Transaction Monitor: CICS	An	–	–	AV	AV	AV	An
Distributed Computing Environment (OSF DCE): RPC, Security, Directory, Time	An	–	SOD	SOD	–	SOD	SOD
User Interface: OSF Motif	AV	AV	AV	AV	AV	SOD	SOD
Mail: X.40	AV	SOD	SOD	AV	AV	–	AV
Connectivity (X.25): SNA	AV	SOD	–	AV	AV	AV	AV
OSI	AV	SOD	SOD	AV	AV	–	AV
TCP/IP	AV	AV	AV	AV	AV	AV	AV

AV	IBM product available
An	IBM product announced
SOD	Statement of Direction for IBM product
–	no IBM announcement

Figure 5.15. Summary of SAA and AIX interoperability.

Common languages

IBM provides standard implementations of commonly used languages C, Fortran and Cobol on both the SAA and AIX platforms. These support the ANSI standards and implement the SAA CPI. The availability of these increases the potential for portability of software between SAA and AIX environments.

Summary of interoperability capabilities

Figure 5.15 summarizes the interoperability capabilities for the SAA and AIX environments as of November 1992. This chart changes continually as IBM improves the level of interoperability.

To ensure interoperability between dissimilar systems, test and verification procedures are required. IBM is working with verification organizations such as the Corporation for Open Systems (COS) and X/Open to certify that its systems conform to their defined interoperability standards.

5.7   New technologies

There are many exciting and innovative technologies emerging in the computer industry today. Technical professionals from IBM development laboratories contribute to various cooperative industry-wide activities set up to define standards for these. Examples are:

- Services to support the transparent execution of an application across a distributed set of processors
- Data definition technologies which help an application understand not only the existence of information but its context
- Object-based application systems which permit the simultaneous use, and reuse, of discrete pieces of data by multiple applications
- Information security which controls access to information resources regardless of their physical location
- New ways of presenting information, including full motion video, enhanced video, holograms and music.

Whatever new technologies emerge and whatever standards are set, for the immediate future IBM can be expected to deliver them on both the SAA and the AIX platforms.

5.8   Summary

In this chapter we have described IBM's SAA and AIX product families. Although SAA was developed internally within IBM, the concepts of portability and scalability on which it was based are closely connected to those driving the open systems movement. The principal difference is that whereas SAA focuses on IBM proprietary products, open systems runs across all manufacturers' products.

IBM has worked hard to maximize the level of interoperability between its two product families, and this is increasing continually. Portability between SAA and AIX is facilitated by the existence of common languages, and communications by the implementation of many of the same technologies in both environments.

IBM must continue to develop and maintain both the SAA and the AIX product lines, at least for the immediate future. Some of its customers have made, and continue to make, heavy investments in SAA, while others want to standardize on open systems implemented through the use of UNIX. As a result, IBM is committed to offering parallel products for SAA and AIX, and to continuing to improve their interoperability.

In the long term the costs of developing and maintaining two overlapping and sometimes competitive product lines will eventually strain even the huge resources of IBM. Thus we can expect that the two product lines will continue to converge wherever possible.

The fact that IBM is actively supporting and developing two product families, one based on its own proprietary technology and the other based on *de facto* standard UNIX software, both of which it describes as 'open', has made it difficult for people to understand IBM's position in the open systems market.

In the next chapter we will describe IBM's concept of the open enterprise, in which integrated information systems are built of products which conform to standard interface definitions. We will see that this reflects a much broader definition of 'open systems' than many advocates of the concepts originally proposed. Nevertheless, the IBM interpretation is based on the requirements it has identified in its customer base, an important component of which relates to preservation of previously made investments in hardware, software, data and skillsets.

6
Opening IBM

6.1 Introduction

> Open systems will enable a more effective and timely implementation of a global market system .... IBM fully intends to be the open systems Vendor of Choice.
> (Michael Armstrong, *Uniforum Keynote Speech*, 1991)

Open systems are now recognized by all vendors of IT products to be the key to information systems architectures now and into the next decade. Open systems offer new opportunities to both users and vendors to produce innovative IT solutions in support of changing business requirements.

For IBM to gain a position of leadership in the open systems market, it must visibly demonstrate its commitment to open standards. It must continue to develop and enhance its SAA and AIX product lines while moving both into conformance with the standards that the market demands. It must provide for interoperability between the SAA and AIX families, as well as between its own and other vendors' products, both proprietary and UNIX-based. And it must further develop its range of support services, extending them to support its competitors' products along with its own.

We have pointed out earlier that there are many interpretations of the meaning of 'open systems'. In this chapter we review the definition of open systems that IBM uses, and analyse its implications. We investigate IBM's level of commitment to the international standards-setting process, and relate this to its product development strategy. Finally we review the services that IBM is providing specifically for the open systems market.

In doing so we are building up the background to IBM's overall open systems strategy and beginning to identify the key factors that logically must be embedded in it if it is to be successful in the long term.

6.2 Open systems—reconciling views

As we have seen in earlier chapters, and as Gray (1991) details, the definition of open systems varies according to the needs of the users. Basically, this is because

Method	*General*	*IBM*
Use a standard operating system	UNIX MS-DOS	AIX PC-DOS
Use a standard interface to the operating system	POSIX	AIX and SAA both conformant
Implement the same functionality for the user	Port applications across many environments, including SAA and AIX	

Figure 6.1.   Open systems: levels of implementation.

'open systems' is both a concept—usually based on the purchaser's desire for freedom in some sense—and a set of technologies for implementation of the concept in a particular set of circumstances. IBM's position is that, ultimately, the only valid definition of open systems comes from user requirements, and it is on this that its own definition and subsequent strategy are based.

Open systems implies the use of technology that is generally available, either through the public domain or through open licensing arrangements. But as we have seen in Chapter 3, definitions exist on many levels (Fig. 6.1).

One view, taken early in the development of the concept, suggests that a common standard operating system can provide for most open system requirements. Such an operating system could be implemented on a variety of hardware platforms, and applications would then be portable across those systems. Once standard communications were built into the operating system, applications could be distributed, and system components designed for interoperability.

This view is most popular in the market today, with implementation accomplished through use of the UNIX operating system. To a lesser extent, MS-DOS is also viewed as 'open' according to this definition. IBM provides open systems products to this definition in its AIX and PC-DOS families.

An opposing view contends that using a standard operating environment might limit the ability of the user to utilize the functionality of the hardware architecture to its fullest extent. In this case, the argument is for agreement on a standard interface to the operating environment, rather than agreement on the operating system itself. This view is most often taken by manufacturers that have made heavy investments in non-UNIX operating environments, but it is also supported by big users of proprietary technologies that wish to preserve their investments until the time is right for a major change.

IBM also supports this second definition of openness. Consequently, it is implementing many internationally agreed interface standards in its proprietary SAA product family as well as in its AIX systems. In the process, it has encouraged the movement of vast amounts of application software into both the SAA and AIX environments.

The availability of the same software in different environments can lead to yet another definition of openness—one in which standard facilities are available to users and developers in support of the tasks which they need to perform. In this case, the user's view of the system remains the same, regardless of the operating system or hardware involved. For example, now that Lotus Development Corporation has made its spreadsheet product, Lotus 1-2-3, available on environments ranging from the Apple Mac, through PCs, to UNIX machines and even the IBM mainframe, users of the product see the same basic functionality regardless of the system they a:e actually using.

IBM believes that its customers want the flexibility to enhance existing applications or install new ones without necessarily being constrained to a single-system environment, and without unnecessary replication of data and software. Applications should be able to draw upon databases, files or other applications, wherever these reside. Investments in hardware, operating systems, applications and skills must be protected. But it must also be possible to use new and emerging technologies as appropriate.

6.3   IBM's potential open systems customers

From the IBM point of view, customers with an interest in open systems come from a variety of enterprises but show some common characteristics: their information systems have been developed over a considerable time, and they have been designed using many different systems, architectures and products. Within this general characterization, they can be classified (Fig. 6.2) into one of four groups:

1 Long-term IBM customers that are predominantly users of IBM proprietary technology. These enterprises are currently committed to the IBM mainframe proprietary MVS environment, and have usually accumulated huge investments in hardware, software and training related to it.

   Such organizations are likely to design IT systems for the immediate future around IBM's proprietary SAA. They are probably already users of relational database technology and will recognize the advantages of adopting a standard user interface—CUA in the SAA implementation.

   Their requirements are for timely and relevant development of the SAA family, and for interoperability between it and other systems that they may also have on site, or that their customers and suppliers use.

2 Companies that have standardized on UNIX systems for the bulk of their requirements, with a significant part based on IBM's AIX. UNIX will have been chosen as the implementation method for an open systems strategy, and AIX picked either because of the technical or price/performance advantages to the IBM AIX systems, particularly the RISC System/6000 architecture, or because the support services offered by IBM are attractive.

   For these enterprises, the immediate requirement is for interoperability between the UNIX systems and the variety of systems that they will already

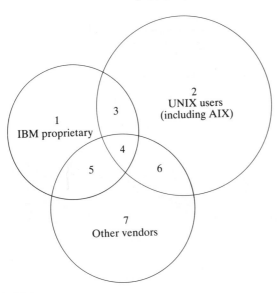

1: SAA
2: UNIX
3: SAA and UNIX
4: SAA, UNIX and other proprietary
5: SAA and other proprietary
6: UNIX and other proprietary
7: Other proprietary

The basis of IBM's open enterprise is SAA, AIX,
SAA–AIX interoperability and multivendor interoperability

Figure 6.2.   Customers for open systems.

have on site, and for the professional management and support services that
they are accustomed to having available in the proprietary environments.
3   IBM sites that are significant users of both SAA and AIX, who recognize that
    there are potential advantages in using each of them. Their pressing need is for
    interoperability between the two environments, which includes a requirement
    for migration and integration tools and services.
4   Users of multivendor systems of all sorts, both proprietary and UNIX, IBM
    and non-IBM. These organizations have the most complicated requirements
    for interoperability. If the needs of this group are met in full, the needs of all
    others follow, at least in principle.

6.4   IBM's formal open systems definition

What makes a system open? Interoperability and data/user portability in a
heterogeneous environment.

(Mike Saranga, *AIX Expo Keynote Speech*, 1991)

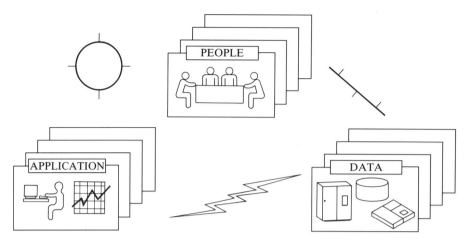

Open systems environment (OSE)
'The comprehensive set of interfaces, services and supporting formats, plus user aspects, for portability of applications, data or people as specified by technology standards and profiles.'

Figure 6.3.   IEEE POSIX open systems definition.

IBM's public position on the definition of open systems is to support that developed within the US IEEE Technical Committee on Open Systems (TCOS) (Fig. 6.3). This is believed to provide an appropriate representation of the objectives and requirements of IBM customers.

In the IEEE statement, 'The comprehensive set of interfaces, services, and supporting formats, plus user aspects, for portability of applications, data or people as specified by technology standards and profiles.' This set of standards is being defined within a large number of committees which go under the general heading of 'POSIX'.

AIX is compliant with the first of the POSIX standards, 1003.1, and will evolve to remain compliant with all other POSIX standards as they emerge from the formal process. Since such standards will be adopted by major purchasers worldwide, it must do so. At the same time, IBM must incorporate its own proprietary technologies into the evolutionary standards process (Fig. 6.4).

IBM will provide POSIX 1003.1 compliance for its proprietary mainframe systems using MVS/ESA and for the mid-range systems running OS/400. This is expected to be extended to other POSIX standards as they became accepted by the international community.

6.5   Open systems standards development

No single vendor, not even one of the size and resources of IBM, can supply all of today's IT user needs. Nor can a single vendor define or control the definition of open systems standards. Recognizing this, IBM is working actively with customers, other vendors, industry consortia and standards organizations in many countries

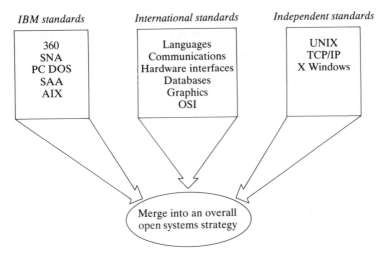

Figure 6.4.   IBM's open systems evolution.

to help evolve the required standards (Fig. 6.5). At the same time, it is developing conformant products of its own that can be used to provide effective business solutions for its customers.

As a major vendor, IBM has been active in the international standards committees for many years, and has supplied much of its own technology to the process. For example, the SQL standard for data access is based on technology which IBM supplied to the appropriate standards bodies. SQL is now an internationally accepted public standard.

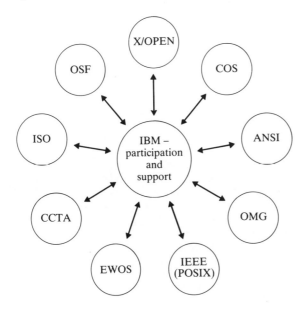

Figure 6.5.   IBM and open systems standards groups.

Standards have always been important in the computer industry, and the organizational structure for setting standards has been in existence for a long time. The development of open systems has only served to emphasize their importance.

IBM is an active participant in open systems standards work, and cooperates with many of the formal and informal bodies that exist. Along with other contributors, it recognizes that an open systems infrastructure cannot exist without internationally agreed standards, and that these must be defined for all the hardware and software components that make up IT systems. It also recognizes that independent tests of conformance are necessary to ensure that the standards are actually met, and has funded the development of some of these.

6.6   IBM's Standards Management Programme

IBM's annual commitment of resources to standards-setting activities is vast. Currently, it has more than 1200 people actively engaged in standards work taking place in more than 1100 standards committees (Fig. 6.6). At an estimated cost of $100 000 per person per year, this represents an annual investment of more than $120 million.

IBM has set up an internal organization specifically to manage its standards work. At the center of its Standards Management Programme is the IBM Standards Programme Authority (SPA). This is a single person, usually a senior architect or designer, who is responsible for the technical direction of all standards-

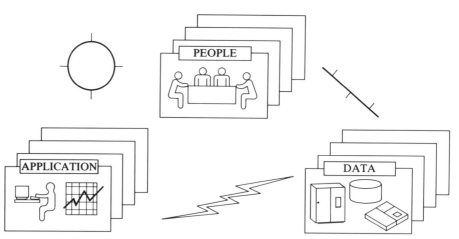

Over 1200 IBM employees participate
in more than 1100 standards committees

• IBM supports industry accepted
  and widely available standards
• IBM works with appropriate
  standards groups to develop
  emerging standards

Figure 6.6.   IBM's standards commitment.

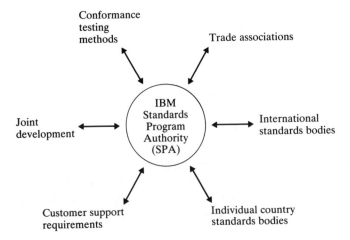

Figure 6.7.   IBM's standards management.

defining activities in a given subject area. The SPA is usually resident in the product laboratory responsible for producing products in the particular area, but works closely with a network of IBM people around the world who are involved in related industry activities (Fig. 6.7).

Through this process, IBM tries to minimize the technical differences that might arise because several organizations are working on the same standard without realizing it. Because of its size and the number of industries in which it is involved, IBM is one of the few companies able to play this coordinating role—known as 'harmonization' in the standards world.

Today IBM has several hundred SPAs covering virtually every area of information technology—those for which it already has products and some which are still regarded as emerging technologies, and for which it can be expected to have products in the future.

IBM's commitment to standards

For many years IBM has publicly maintained an unswerving commitment to standards activities. It actively offers IBM technology to the standards process, and works with customers, research institutions, other vendors, and industry consortia to promote the definitions and availability of open technology standards.

Although IBM maintains an active role in standards support, this does not mean that it will implement every standard in every possible product. Support will be provided only if the standard meets the needs of IBM's own customers and can be demonstrated to be a prudent business investment.

Setting market standards

The complex system by which international public standards are set is described by Gray (1991). Although the system results in a democratic process, it is often criticized for being too slow for practical requirements. When this is in fact the case, the market usually votes with its dollars, and a *de facto*, or market, standard gets set. This may be formalized after the event if the technology in question is submitted to the standards process.

IBM is conceivably the only company large and powerful enough to be able to set market standards on its own. Other companies such as Microsoft or Novell can do so only by licensing their technology to many others. Nevertheless IBM is increasingly offering its own technology to the standards process, and licensing technology or products to other vendors. For example, IBM's technology for accessing mainframe data was supplied to X/Open for inclusion in the CAE while its CICS for UNIX has been licensed to Hewlett-Packard, among others. By making its technologies available in this way, IBM may have an even greater impact on emerging standards than it will achieve through participation in the formal bodies.

Divisive standards

IBM has offered its distributed SQL protocols, Distributed Relational Database Architecture (DRDA), to the standards groups. This technology has been developed by IBM in cooperation with some of its largest customers and contains many features that these customers have stated that they require. However, it is not clear that DRDA will be accepted by the standards bodies, since competitive technology is also on offer from the SQL Access Group (SAG).

Should DRDA not be acceptable as an international standard, IBM will be forced to support both it and the finally agreed standard. It must support DRDA because it meets its own customers' specific requirements in the area, and it is publicly committed to supporting internationally agreed standards, when that makes good business sense.

This is an example of a situation where IBM must dedicate resources to try to converge what might otherwise end up as two different standards. Having two to support is certainly not in IBM's interests. More importantly, it is not in the interests of the users, big or small. From their point of view, any two competitive but standard technologies should be converged to one over time.

6.7   Development choices for vendors

A computer vendor developing a systems software strategy for today's marketplace is faced with a variety of design and business alternatives (Fig. 6.8):

• An established vendor with a large installed base can continue to focus only on

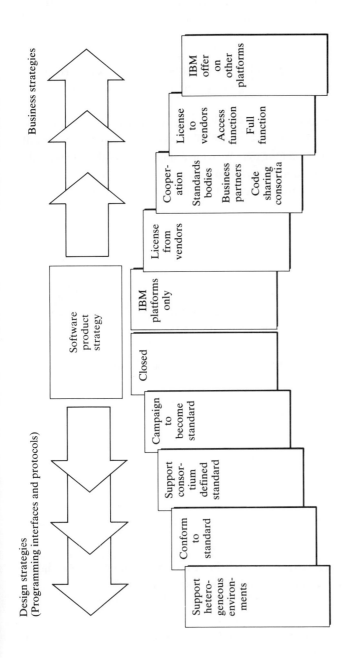

Figure 6.8.   Product development choices.

its unique, closed and proprietary architectures. Vendors that do this in spite of the momentum building up behind the open systems movement are likely to suffer severe consequences. Only niche players can stay concentrated solely on proprietary systems, and then only in highly specialized market segments and in the short term.

- A strong vendor can focus on its own technology and launch a campaign to gain acceptance of it from users and other vendors. To some extent, IBM did this with its communications protocols, SNA, and produced a *de facto* standard in the process.

- A vendor may choose to provide a standard set of interface protocols and define these externally. These may eventually become *de facto* or formal standards. Alternatively, a vendor may provide a migration path to externally defined standards from within its own products.

- While focusing on its own design strategy for the long term, a vendor can gain time and additional functionality in its products in the short term by licensing technology from other vendors or associations, who may have already implemented a public standard or may own an emerging *de facto* standard. IBM's licensing of Novell's PC networking technology, NetWare, falls into this category.

- As part of a program to promote its own technology, a vendor may license the capability to others. This might extend its use further than the originator could do alone, even if the vendor is as large as IBM. IBM has licensed technologies such as SNA, SQL and NetView to other vendors, and has also provided many component technologies to standards organizations such as the Open Software Foundation (OSF).

- The vendor can choose to develop and market implementations of its own solutions on other vendor platforms. There are problems associated with this, some concerning competitive differentiation and others involving conflicts in the distribution channels.

6.8   IBM's path

IBM could provide a complete open systems portfolio of products in many different ways:

- IBM could build products from scratch in strict conformance to standards
- Current IBM products could be migrated to standards over time
- Functionality not available from IBM directly could be licensed from other sources and incorporated into IBM products
- IBM's own technology could be offered to the standards community for eventual formal standardization
- Technology could be licensed to other vendors and perhaps become a *de facto* standard in the process.

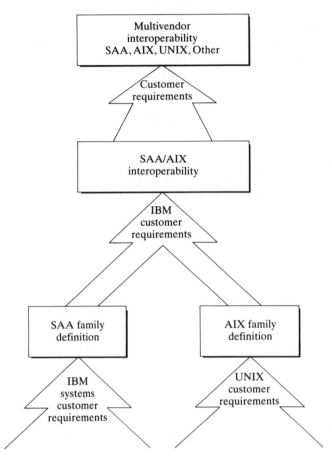

Figure 6.9. Evolution of the interoperability strategy.

IBM can be expected to use any or all of these in order to provide its customers with the most effective solution to their requirements, and to achieve a leadership position in the open systems market as quickly and efficiently as possible. For example, IBM will license technologies such as AIX to other vendors and offers CICS for other vendors' UNIX platforms.

6.9   Vendor positions

IBM must develop its SAA product family to provide interoperability with AIX and with UNIX systems from other vendors (Fig. 6.9). At the same time, other vendors of proprietary and UNIX products must provide interoperability with IBM's proprietary technology, because IBM products dominate in the installed base. In this respect IBM is in a better position than many other manufacturers; while they must learn to interoperate with IBM proprietary products, IBM does not necessarily have to do the same with theirs.

IBM has to provide interoperability basically between two product lines—SAA and UNIX (which includes its own AIX) systems—but other manufacturers must provide it for three—SAA, UNIX and their own proprietary products. In the long term few will be able to support the extra investment that this requires, and will be forced to drop their own proprietary products.

6.10   Problems of supporting two families

If IBM is to maintain its dominant position in the computer market, it must supply products and services that meet the needs of each group of its potential customers. This is going to be difficult. The two currently distinct IBM product lines, AIX and SAA, each have a significant and growing installed base. Users of each expect continual delivery of innovative new products designed to give them a smooth upgrade path, and they expect to be provided with the related software and services. Furthermore, many of them demand maximum interoperability between the two product families as well as between other systems they may have on site.

IBM customers are used to receiving a very high level of professional services, bundled in with the hardware and software systems. In the highly competitive UNIX market, hardware is becoming a commodity and hardware margins are dropping fast. As a result, services can no longer be bundled into the price; they must be charged for separately. Furthermore, since the open systems market encourages multivendor purchases, these services, if offered, must be extended to support other vendors' products, both UNIX and proprietary.

As a result of economic pressures almost all proprietary environments other than those supplied by IBM are static or in decline. While IBM has the resources to continue development of two strategic product families at present, even it may not be able to justify doing so for ever.

6.11   Opening and closing systems

IBM has two strategic product families, the proprietary SAA line and the AIX UNIX line. These two families taken together are the foundation for IBM's open systems strategy (Fig. 6.10).

Both the SAA and AIX families support a significant number of open standards and interfaces, and more are continually added. Both lines also support a multivendor networked environment which will be enhanced over time. The functionality of both families in the multivendor environment will be extended, increasing their overall interoperability. In this sense both families are 'open' in IBM's definition.

Specific features can be expected to be added to both families in order to provide competitive differentiation without jeopardizing the conformance to standards. However, these will reduce the ability to port software across from other systems, and so reduce the level of interoperability. In this sense the AIX family could be considered 'proprietary' open, in that features have been added to a standard product that make the UNIX version specific to IBM, while the SAA family is

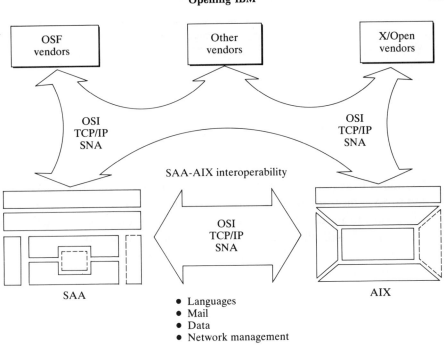

Figure 6.10.   Foundation for an open systems infrastructure.

'open' proprietary, being a closed proprietary system that has been opened up by modifications leading to standards conformance.

Because IBM is moving forward with two interpretations of open systems implemented through the SAA and AIX architectures, its open systems strategy is sometimes viewed with suspicion. However, its stated reasons for doing so—to protect and enhance the investments made in either or both architectures by many of its major customers—would appear logical and justifiable. In any case, most other major vendors are moving in similar directions, 'closing' their 'open' systems in order to differentiate themselves from their competitors, and 'opening' their 'closed' ones in order to conform to required standards.

6.12   IBM's open systems strategy

IBM's open systems strategy is based on results of its research into the needs of its customer base, coupled with certain business decisions that have to be addressed as both customers and IBM migrate to the open environment.

The results of many studies of the IT user base, conducted by X/Open, IBM and various market research companies, consistently show that the principal requirements of many enterprises can be described as:

- The ability to implement an information structure architecture that allows for non-disruptive growth

To provide customers with the ability to implement enterprise-wide open systems infrastructures
through:

- Commitment to standards
- Superior technology and innovation
  - architectures
  - system frameworks and structures
  - infrastructure products
- Extensive service and support

Figure 6.11.   Components of IMB's open systems strategy.

- The ability to acquire new products, hardware and software, from any vendor, and to have these interoperate with the systems already installed
- The ability to protect existing investments in hardware, software and skills development, while allowing the exploitation of new technology
- The ability to access and manage information resources, and the business information they support, in a multivendor environment, both across and beyond the enterprise.

IBM's open systems strategy is designed to address each of these issues. There are four main components to it—a commitment to standards, development of innovative products, provision of an integrated infrastructure for customers, and extensive services and support (Fig. 6.11).

We have seen the huge commitment that IBM has made to standards, and identified the two strategic platforms, SAA and AIX, on which new technologies will be supported. With these families as building blocks, IBM will deliver a broad set of products and services designed to allow its customers to implement complete open systems information infrastructures.

While these will be based as much as possible on IBM products, there are no longer any hard and fast rules. IBM software products may be supplied on other vendors' systems; products licensed from third parties may be supplied by IBM in conjunction with its own systems; services will be offered across multiple vendors' platforms; IBM products and technologies will be licensed to others for sale. In this sense, IBM is opening up its entire product strategy.

6.13   Infrastructure products

The open systems infrastructure product strategy broadly addresses the following (Fig. 6.12):

Networking

The networking strategy addresses the requirements for multivendor and multi-architecture networking, and must therefore handle the most common environments. For IBM, it will be implemented through the major protocols of OSI (the international standards), TCP/IP (the *de facto* standard for the UNIX world) and

- Networking
- Data management
- Security
- Client–server architectures
- Systems management
- End-user interface
- Transaction processing
- Application development
- Desktop environment
- Enterprise applications

Figure 6.12.   Infrastructure products.

SNA (the standard for communications to IBM proprietary systems). It must also address the issue of bridges and routing capabilities to other popular vendors' networks, and specifically must integrate PC networks into the systems as a whole.

Enterprise data management

The strategy for data management must provide 'transparent access to data' in any of three formats—relational, record format and byte-stream. In addition, systems management and remote printing facilities relating to the access to data across the enterprise must be included.

Enterprise security

Many organizations are concerned about the management and control of access to confidential information, particularly when this resides on multivendor networks. While many suppliers, including IBM, implement various levels of security on their own systems, an open systems strategy must address the requirements for security on multivendor networks running both within and between enterprises.

Client/server architectures

Many users require access to remote resources from the desktop, together with at least an element of local processing and presentation of the information. Applications in the user base range from executing software on a remote platform from the desktop, through downloading information into an executive information system for local action, to managing or trouble-shooting systems from afar. The IBM open systems strategy must incorporate client/server architectures that meet these requirements.

Systems management

Most manufacturers of computers provide proprietary system management tools, but as yet these conform to no generally accepted standards. Customers must have a cohesive and consistent way to manage a multivendor, mixed architecture environment. The IBM open systems strategy involves supplying to this requirement by working with a number of industry partners to an overall architectural design for systems management that it has defined in cooperation with them.

End-user interface

Many organizations wish to provide a common user interface across all the systems in the enterprise, possibly customizing this for their own internal use. IBM recognized this in its SAA product line when it introduced CUA. In the wider, open systems environment, IBM must address this need, staying in synchronization with international standardization efforts while at the same time offering a level of consistency with CUA.

Enterprise transaction processing and management

High-volume transaction-processing (TP) applications are fundamental to the business requirements of many organizations. Open systems based on the UNIX operating system have until recently been perceived as inappropriate for high-volume TP requirements.

IBM has always been strong in the TP market. It developed and 'owns' CICS, the *de facto* standard language used for implementation of TP applications on systems in thousands of commercial sites. Porting of CICS to AIX and other versions of UNIX, licensing CICS to other vendors and supplying migration support services is an important part of IBM's open systems strategy.

Application development

Integration of data sources and subsequent use of information in new applications is recognized by many organizations as the key to their profitable future. New software development tools, computer-aided or object-oriented, must be provided within the overall product plan.

The desktop

The importance of information, coupled with the explosion in the amount available, is driving the development of new technologies for accessing, presenting and assimilating information. Under the general heading of 'multimedia', these can be expected to be incorporated into desktop technologies in the next few years. The IBM strategy for the desktop component of open systems architectures must recognize this.

Enterprise-wide application

IBM's open systems activity can be expected to expand to the delivery of complete application solutions. Examples are: electronic data interchange (EDI), which is fundamental for inter-departmental or inter-enterprise communications and trading; computer integrated manufacturing (CIM), which defines a structure for integrating solutions in the manufacturing and instrument control areas, and requires defining standards for interfaces between computers and control devices; and transaction processing, as already mentioned.

All of these require the integration of many different technologies, and will have to be based on an open systems architecture in order to maximize interoperability and minimize support issues.

6.14   Frameworks

No single vendor today is able to provide all the hardware and software products and services that individual clients may need. IBM is no exception to this. As a result, it is evolving partnerships with many other companies in order to deal with those requirements that it cannot itself directly provide. In particular, it has defined the concept of 'frameworks' for key technologies and application areas, under which companies may work together to solve particular problems in the user base.

In these frameworks, the overall definition of a systems or application area—for example, multivendor systems management—is defined and broken into multiple manageable segments. Interface definitions between the segments or tasks are then defined to allow the segments to work together, so that the software components become interoperable. These definitions are made generally available to the marketplace as a whole, but particularly to software developers.

Under the framework concept, technology from multiple sources can be brought together, and then used to address a major business or system objective. Key IBM frameworks designed to support the open systems environment are:

- SystemView, incorporating NetView, for systems and network management
- AD/Cycle and AIX CASE for computer-aided software development
- Information Warehouse, for management of the enterprise data.

Each of these is discussed further in later chapters. As the frameworks evolve, IBM plans to work closely with national and international standards bodies to define the protocols and interfaces incorporated within them.

6.15   Information systems architectures

The SAA and AIX families, the interoperability functions that exist between them and the systems frameworks, will allow IBM to bring specific product solutions to the marketplace, based on customer requirements for a complete information infrastructure. Parts of these solutions will involve IBM products; others will be supplied by partners. Products from various sources will be blended together with the aid of the system frameworks. The infrastructure as a whole includes networking, data, transaction management, systems management, client/server architectures, security, application development tools, end-user interface, distributed applications, and emerging technologies.

6.16   Services and support

A major change in IBM's strategy for service and support has taken place over the last few years. Where IBM engineers once looked after IBM equipment only, the attitude now is: 'We will support whatever our customers have and want us to look after.'

In the open systems environment this comes as a great relief to many organizations. Those that know and trust the quality of IBM's support services have been reluctant to move into the open environment without it, even though they recognize the benefits that the use of standards-based products could bring. On IBM's part this new policy is a recognition of the strength of the open systems movement within its customer base, an acknowledgement of the need for a high level of support of the multivendor networks that result, and a desire to increase both its product and its service businesses.

The scope of services offered range from defining and detailing a suitable multivendor architecture for the enterprise to installing a local area network with mixed vendor clients and servers. In this sense, IBM is building a new and extensive systems integration and consultancy business, covering the technical and business needs of its customers.

IBM's strategy is not based on offering a fixed 'turnkey' open systems solution to its clients. Rather, it relies on being able to meet a wide spectrum of customer requirements by having a variety of hardware and software products, services and support available from which to build customized solutions. This is a recognition of the fact that, although many organizations wish to have an open systems architecture in the long term, implementation is highly dependent on the starting position.

6.17   Business issues

A manufacturer's product design strategy must always be balanced with an appropriate business strategy for itself, its shareholders and its customers. Sometimes, conflicting demands put the vendor into a difficult situation.

Commitment towards an open environment by any vendor with an installed base of proprietary products forces that vendor to offer several alternatives for one or more functions. These arise both from its own proprietary products, perhaps even as these evolve towards compatibility with standards, and from its own standards-based products. For example, IBM must offer CUA and SNA for SAA; OSF/ MOTIF and TCP/IP for AIX; and OSI for both.

In this sense the more recently established computer vendors which supply only UNIX products have an advantage. Without an installed base of proprietary systems that must be protected and enhanced, such companies do not have to deal with the complicated integration and migration issues facing IBM and its customers.

High margins have been the norm in the proprietary systems market, where hardware and software were often bundled with services. In the highly competitive UNIX market, hardware margins are under severe pressure. The technical and financial demands made by the need to develop and support two competing product lines with very different margin structures are high. Every established manufacturer is opening up its proprietary product line, while building a parallel UNIX family and providing interoperability between the two. IBM is not unique, but as the manufacturer with the largest installed base of proprietary systems it faces the greatest challenge.

6.18   The new IBM

In November 1991 IBM announced a plan to create autonomous businesses from its previously monolithic structure. As reported in *Business Week* (December 1991), these businesses may eventually be new companies with their own stock and board of directors. Those likely to gain autonomy are shown in Fig. 6.13.

These companies—Facilities Management, Maintenance, Software, Systems Integration, Personal Computers and Workstations, Printers, Storage Products and Semiconductors—cover many of the components of the integrated information system. By separating them out IBM allows them more easily to supply and support non-IBM products, and to compete with one another, as the market allows.

For example, the Systems Integration Division must supply and support non-IBM products, and technologies that bridge between IBM and non-IBM products, if it is to be successful in the marketplace. Separating it from those primarily concerned with IBM's own products makes it easier to do this.

If IBM is to sell its own software products on other vendors' platforms, then it needs an organization set up to do so, separated from its own computer business. An independent software business could provide this.

Although not described by the analysts or by IBM as part of the open systems strategy, this reorganization is clearly very closely associated with it. It would be almost impossible for IBM to compete in the open systems market without a radically different structure from the monolithic one that was appropriate for the mainframe era.

6.19   Summary

In this chapter we have taken an overall look at IBM's open systems strategy. It has proven to be very comprehensive. Although using a broader definition of open

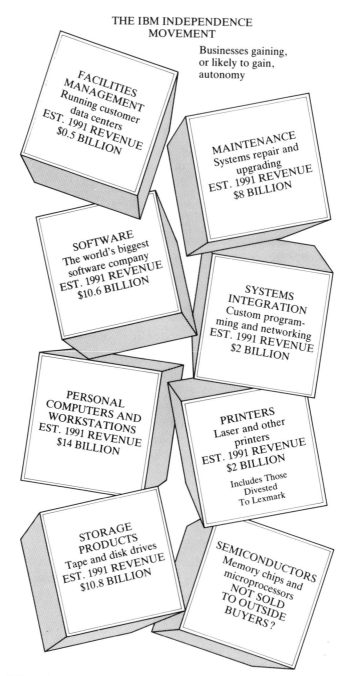

THE IBM INDEPENDENCE
MOVEMENT

Businesses gaining,
or likely to gain,
autonomy

FACILITIES
MANAGEMENT
Running customer
data centers
EST. 1991 REVENUE
$0.5 BILLION

MAINTENANCE
Systems repair and
upgrading
EST. 1991 REVENUE
$8 BILLION

SOFTWARE
The world's biggest
software company
EST. 1991 REVENUE
$10.6 BILLION

SYSTEMS
INTEGRATION
Custom program-
ming and networking
EST. 1991 REVENUE
$2 BILLION

PERSONAL
COMPUTERS AND
WORKSTATIONS
EST. 1991 REVENUE
$14 BILLION

PRINTERS
Laser and other
printers
EST. 1991 REVENUE
$2 BILLION

Includes Those
Divested
To Lexmark

STORAGE
PRODUCTS
Tape and disk drives
EST. 1991 REVENUE
$10.8 BILLION

SEMICONDUCTORS
Memory chips and
microprocessors
NOT SOLD
TO OUTSIDE
BUYERS?

Figure 6.13. The new IBM. (*Source: Business Week*)

systems than that of the UNIX-only vendors, the strategy appears to be logically justified and based on user needs.

The two technologies in common use for open systems implementation—that of the standard operating system, usually UNIX, and that of the standard interface, defined through POSIX—justifies IBM supporting two product lines, AIX and SAA, for now and the immediate future. While one may be more appropriate for new systems, the second allows an evolutionary approach for systems which are already installed, and in which huge investments have so far been made.

The need to develop, continually enhance and support two strategic product lines, and the falling margins on UNIX systems, result in difficult business conditions for IBM. In the next few years it must balance the sometimes competitive SAA and AIX product lines, deal with the conflicting economic factors driving its own and its customers' decisions, and continue to perform well for its shareholders.

IBM is working in many different ways to strengthen its open systems strategy, often in close cooperation with other companies and licensing technology as necessary. In this sense it is facing a major open systems issue head-on—that of cooperating while competing with other companies, to the benefit of both vendors and users of the technology.

The moves which IBM is making to change its organizational structure are in response to customer requirements for integrated information systems requiring an open and multivendor approach. Only the results will prove that these moves are the right ones, and that they are sufficient to protect IBM's leadership position in the long term. At present, the pointers in the marketplace all support the position IBM is taking.

In the next chapter we will look more closely at the partnerships that IBM is building in order to address those issues which it cannot tackle alone. We will see that they are very wide-ranging and provide some interesting pointers to the future.

7
Strategic alliances

7.1 Introduction

In the global information systems market, organizations are fighting for competitive advantage using technologies that are advancing at ever-greater speed. Customers for IT products are demanding 'open' interoperable components that allow them to build integrated information systems that will meet their requirements in the long term, independent of the technologies of any particular supplier.

No single company, even one with the resources of IBM, can supply all of the products and services that the market needs in the time-scale that it demands. Consequently, many companies that are natural competitors are trying to find ways to work together. This forces them to learn a new skill—how to cooperate at one level while continuing to compete on another.

In this chapter we examine this trend as it applies to the open systems movement and analyse the relationships and alliances in which IBM is involved. We will discover that some of the strategic partnerships that IBM is now developing could have a dramatic and long-term effect on the future of open technologies.

7.2 Business alliances

An alliance is a formalized way for companies to work together in some respect. Alliances between companies that are otherwise competitive have been common in Japan for many years, but have not often been developed in other countries. This is changing fast as business alliances evolve in many industries, particularly those that deal internationally.

Companies in the computer industry are no exception to the trend. For example, many consortia (see Fig. 7.1 and Gray, 1991) have been formed to handle particular standardization issues relevant to the open systems movement. These demonstrate how companies with competitive interests can work together on matters of common interest. While participating in many of these group efforts, IBM has been steadily forging a number of strategic relationships on its own behalf over the last 10 years or more, with competitors, suppliers and customers.

To be successful, business relationships must serve the interests of all parties

IBM is a member of many computer industry consortia and organizations. Among these are:

- CBEMA—Computer and Business Equipment Manufacturers
- COS—Corporation for Open Systems
- ECMA—European Computer Manufacturers' Association
- EIA—Electronic Industry Association
- ODA—Open Document Architecture Consortium
- OMG—Object Management Group
- OSF—Open Software Foundation
- OSINET—Open Systems Interconnection International Network
- PDES—Product Data Exchange Specification Consortium
- UNICODE—Unicode Consortium
- X/Open—Worldwide open systems organization

Figure 7.1.   Examples of computer industry consortia.

involved, providing something definite to each partner. This might be capital, skills and expertise, access to new markets, or access to new hardware or software products. A major objective of most relationships is for the partners to avoid spending time and resources duplicating each others' efforts.

7.3   IBM's international alliances

In the last 15 years or more IBM has formed hundreds of alliances around the world, consisting of an assortment of joint ventures, equity investments, business partnerships, joint research and development projects and product licences (see Fig. 7.2). The IBM World Trade Units in Europe and Japan have been particularly active in recognizing the potential of, and developing, such partnerships. Today IBM has one of the most extensive sets of alliances in the computer industry.

Although some of the IBM alliances, particularly that with Apple, have been given worldwide headlines, the company has in fact been growing this part of its business in various ways and for many years, particularly in countries other than the USA.

Japan

In Japan the IBM salesforce is outnumbered five to one by its three biggest competitors, Fujitsu, NEC and Hitachi. In order to narrow the gap in as fast and as economic a way as possible, IBM Japan has formed more than 70 alliances since the early 1980s. These consist mainly of joint ventures designed to broaden its market coverage and improve its overall solution offerings.

For example, IBM Japan and Toshiba created a new company, Display Technologies, in order to manufacturer color flat-panel displays required for laptop computers. Each partner contributed capital and skills to the new venture. By working together, both companies expect to be able to bring new technology to the market faster than would be possible by acting alone.

Mitsubishi was the first company to be licensed to market certain of the IBM ES/9000 mainframe technology under its own name. As a result of the agreement,

Joint ventures

New companies created by IBM and its partners to pursue emerging growth markets. In consulting, IBM formed Meritus with Coopers & Lybrand: in color flat-panel displays, Display Technologies with Toshiba; a key to the Apple alliance is a joint venture company to develop powerful software based on object-oriented technology.

Equity investments

By buying a stake in a partner, IBM infuses capital needed to grow the business and can also reap financial returns. Investments in software companies encourage them to write applications that support IBM platforms and architectures.

Joint development/manufacturing

Allows IBM and its partners to share costs, skills, risks. 64-megabit memory chip development and 16-megabit chip production with Siemens are examples.

Original Equipment Manufacturer (OEM)

A new business thrust for IBM. When IBM serves as an OEM supplier, as in the Wang accord, it sells components, software or complete systems to companies that build them into their products or sell them under their own logos. Besides fresh revenue, OEM provides another outlet for IBM products and helps fully utilize IBM's vast manufacturing capability.

Product licensing

Access to innovative products allows IBM to offer complete solutions, and it can give its partners a marketing boost. IBM's agreement with Lotus, for example, enhances IBM OfficeVision software. Its pact with GO Corp. gives IBM access to GO's pen-based operating system.

Business partners

Thousands of IBM-authorized agents, dealers, and remarketers who reach customers, worldwide.

Figure 7.2. IBM alliances.

Mitsubishi can sell IBM technology into customer sites, particularly in the public sector, that might otherwise be closed to IBM.

Europe

In Europe, IBM has invested in more than 215 alliances since the mid-1980s, and the number is growing steadily. Many of these are equity investments into small, specialized companies that offer software applications or services that IBM does not offer directly. IBM does not usually try to control the companies. Instead it prefers a minority investment sufficient to ensure that the company supplies and supports its products on the IBM platforms, and retains a basic loyalty to IBM.

Other countries

IBM Canada formed an alliance with Westridge Corporation in order to expand its services offerings by indirect means. Westbridge specializes in 'outsourcing' —managing a company's IT systems from outside the company, under contract. IBM is building a substantial outsourcing business, particularly in the USA and Europe, and the relationship with Westbridge complements this.

Until recently some Latin America countries—Mexico, Argentina and, particularly, Brazil—have had 'market reservation' policies that have essentially prohibited certain computer imports. In Brazil, for example, the mid-range, workstation and PC markets were reserved for domestic producers. Although this policy may give short-term advantages to the indigenous manufacturers, it is now recognized as holding back the development of IT in those countries. As a result IBM Latin America has consolidated at least 10 strategic alliances in the area that are primarily aimed at gaining market access by linking up with the local suppliers.

For example, in the mid-range systems area, IBM provides Brazil's Itautec with AS/400 processor kits and disk drives, which Itautec then assembles, tests and markets as its own 'S/400' product line. A similar joint venture with SID Informatica for personal computers was approved by the Brazilian government in 1991 and is now operational.

In 1992 Brazil lifted many of its market reservation policies. But, as is the case in many other countries, the government is still expected to provide incentives to ensure that locally made products will be favored over those that are imported. The IBM alliances made in Brazil are therefore expected to remain valuable even now that restrictions on trading directly have been lifted.

7.4 The scope of the alliances

The IBM alliances attract a great deal of attention from the world's press, in part because of the sheer number and scope of them. Figure 7.3 shows the announcements for the three months from May to July 1991 as an example.

May 1991	• Borland announced agreement to develop software for OS/2
June 1991	• IBM announced plans to tailor Novell's NetWare for the RISC/6000 family
	• IBM and Wang announced agreement under which Wang will sell IBM's PS/2, RS6000 and AS/400 systems
	• Lotus Development Corporation announced licensing of Lotus Notes and cc:mail to IBM to enhance IBM's OfficeVision products and for inclusion in OS/2
July 1991	• Apple, IBM and Motorola announced long-term strategic relationship to work together on technology for personal computing
	• Siemens and IBM announced partnership to produce 16-bit memory chips at the IBM facility in France

Figure 7.3.   IBM alliances: May–July 1991.

The pace shows no sign of slowing down. IBM is clearly determined to work with any company that it believes will help it to maintain and grow its business in the highly competitive global market.

7.5   Grand strategy or clutching at straws?

Analysts sometimes question whether the scope of the IBM alliances indicates the building of a grand strategy or whether it simply indicates that IBM is doing everything possible to retain its leadership position, hedging its bets and spreading the risks.

In fact, many of the alliances appear to result from decentralized decision-taking and a more open attitude within IBM as a whole. Separate business units have been given the freedom to negotiate cooperative agreements as they see fit for local requirements. This has resulted in many partnerships which are particularly suited to a local territory and has also led to an ability to move fast—for example, the Wang agreement is reputed to have taken no more than 60 days from inception to signing of the contracts.

'Open systems' affects more than the technological components of the solutions that organizations implement. As a result of access to information, organizations themselves are becoming more 'open'. Attitudes are changing, and barriers to trading are disappearing. With the changes that are taking place in the way in which it does business, IBM is in fact responding to the open market in its broadest sense.

7.6   Partnerships with software companies

The many partnerships that IBM has with software companies range from joint marketing and sales programmes through equity investments and shared development to full ownership of the companies. While many of them have been formed for the specific requirements of customers in a particular territory, some, in particular the AD/Cycle, Information Warehouse and SystemView partnerships, are fundamental to IBM's own long-term software strategy.

Members of the IBM International Alliance for AD/Cycle:
- Bachman Information Systems Inc
- Digitalk Inc
- Easel Corporation
- KnowledgeWare Inc
- Micro Focus Ltd
- Sapiens International Corporation
- Synon Corporation
- VIASOFT Inc

Note: On a country-to-country basis, consultancy and services for AD/Cycle are offered both by IBM itself and by third parties related to IBM.

Figure 7.4. International Alliance for AD/Cycle.

AD/Cycle

AD/Cycle is one of the most important of IBM's software partnerships and is the basis of IBM's application software development strategy. Although originally announced for SAA, a parallel development now exists for AIX, and IBM is responding to the pressures of the open market by bringing the two environments together.

AD/Cycle is a framework designed to help improve the productivity, quality and manageability of software development and maintenance work. Its main purpose is to define methodology to enable software development tools from different vendors to work together. The object is to be able to cover the spectrum of user requirements with an integratable product set, even if separate tools are purchased from a number of different vendors.

For open systems users, interoperability of software components is at least as important as that of hardware components. In that respect, AD/Cycle is yet another response to the market's demand for openness.

In support of its AD/Cycle strategy, IBM has established long-term business relationships with leading vendors of AD/Cycle tools and services, including taking an equity position in some of them. Members of the International Alliance for AD/Cycle have signed worldwide marketing agreements with IBM. They have extensive relationships with IBM AD/Cycle development sites and participate in strategy, requirements, system testing and some joint development activities; members are listed in Fig. 7.4.

IBM's Application Development Consulting Practice offers education, consulting, project management and implementation services designed to assist corporations to use AD/Cycle. As general contractors, they utilize a number of firms for specific services. Firms that have service contracts with IBM in this area are different from country to country.

Members of the IBM International Alliance for Information Warehouse:
- Bachman Information Systems Inc.
- Information Builders Inc.

Development partner:
- Comshare Inc.

Note: International Alliance membership involves partnership in marketing as well as in development.

Figure 7.5.   International alliances for Information Warehouse Framework.

AIX CASE

IBM's AIX CASE framework is designed to bring its AD/Cycle and AIX UNIX software engineering worlds closer together. AIX CASE is modelled on the ECMA reference model for open-distributed software development.

The basis of the principal components of IBM's AIX CASE is Hewlett-Packard's Softbench, which has been licensed to IBM and other companies, and is fast becoming a *de facto* standard technology. More than 30 CASE suppliers have indicated their intention to support AIX CASE.

Information Warehouse Framework

The Information Warehouse defines a set of database management systems, interfaces, tools and facilities designed to manage and deliver reliable, timely, accurate and understandable business information to authorized individuals for business decision-making. It therefore provides comprehensive data management and access capability across the enterprise.

In order to implement the Information Warehouse, IBM is forming a set of business relationships with software and service providers that have products and services which are complementary to its own. Some of these belong to the International Alliance for the Information Warehouse Framework (Fig. 7.5).

In cooperation with its Information Warehouse business partners and with other vendors, IBM has stated its intention of guiding the evolution of the framework in such a way as to satisfy the needs of the data-processing and end-user communities, protecting customers' investments as much as possible in the process.

SystemView

SystemView is IBM's strategy for planning, coordinating, operating and managing heterogeneous, enterprise-wide information systems. It establishes the structure for management of all multivendor information resources including host, network, database, storage and business administration.

SystemView supports all relevant industry standards, and IBM publishes the application programming interfaces and guidelines so that other vendors may participate in SystemView if they wish. In this sense, SystemView is an open

---

Members of the IBM International Alliance for SystemView:
● Bachman Information Systems Inc.
● Candle Corporation
● Information Retrieval Companies Inc
● Platinum Technology Inc

Development partner:
● Legent Corporation

Note: International Alliance membership involves partnership in marketing as well as in development.

Figure 7.6.   Business partners in SystemView.

structure. Current business partners cooperating in SystemView development are
listed in Fig. 7.6.

7.7   OEM contracts

Original equipment manufacturer (OEM) contracts allow a company to buy
hardware components, software or completely finished systems from another
company, and build them into its own products or sell them under its own name.
Such deals have always been common in the computer industry. For example, IBM
has had a highly successful OEM business for many years supplying large disk
drives to other computer manufacturers.

Worldwide, the OEM business is worth more than $100 billion, and is growing
fast. In future, more companies are expected to move away from manufacturing
and into systems integration, using products obtained under OEM arrangements,
and so the growth is expected to continue.

At present, international OEM business is dominated by Asian suppliers. IBM
has aggressive plans to grow its OEM business very rapidly through various
alliances, intending to reach revenues of $3 billion by 1993. In order to get to this
level, it is willing to make virtually its entire product line and base technologies
available on an OEM basis.

Benefits of OEM deals

IBM has huge development and manufacturing resources. With improvements in
automation and quality control, these can produce substantially more products
than IBM can sell on its own. The Wang agreement, under which Wang became
an OEM for IBM, added an additional 15 000 Wang customers for IBM PC and
mid-range products. The Mitsubishi OEM agreement for ES/9000 technologies
widens the mainframe customer base. These and other OEM deals help to take up
any slack in manufacturing, increase the overall volumes, and should help IBM
and its OEMs to maintain highly competitive pricing.

OEM deals provide good tests for products. Since an OEM can buy products
from wherever it wishes, it is free to take those showing the best quality, innovation

and price/performance ratios. If a manufacturer cannot match up to the competition, it will not get the deals. This puts increased pressure on the design and production areas of the manufacturer's business. The result is that the original manufacturer's own products, incorporating the same cost-competitive components, cannot fail to benefit.

If IBM does not take the OEM deals, someone else—a direct competitor—will. The direct and indirect benefits will then accrue to it, while IBM itself will have a new and direct competitor in the OEM.

Once the OEM arrangements are in place, IBM licensees will compete directly with IBM, using compatible, or even identical, products. OEM relationships therefore provide yet another example of the problem of 'competing while cooperating', which is characteristic of the open systems market.

Case study of an OEM deal—IBM and Groupe Bull

In the late 1980s Groupe Bull in France ran into financial difficulties. Losing large amounts of money, it needed a fresh injection of capital to finance a restructuring program and for development of new products. Many of its problems were attributed to its late entry into the UNIX market, and to its inability to handle the conflicting demands of a proprietary and an open product line.

When the problems became critical, Bull sought a partner who could not only supply cash but could also help to revamp its product line fast. In particular, it wanted a high-performance UNIX product line with which it could compete in the open systems market. This product line had to be one that was well supported by the French software industry, so that a catalog of applications software was available for it.

IBM is very strong in France. Nevertheless, it could not afford to allow a competitor to achieve a strategic alliance with Bull and so increase its position in France. It was therefore very important that IBM reach an agreement with Bull, and the French government, on the terms of the contract.

Early in 1992 IBM and Groupe Bull announced a partnership involving a wide range of technologies and products, and under which IBM would take an equity stake in Bull. The main points of the agreement are shown in Fig. 7.7

In spite of the closeness of the agreement, Bull and IBM will remain competitors in France. But the result of the contractual arrangement with Bull is that IBM's products will continue to dominate in France, regardless of which of the two companies sells them. This will be helped by the fact that software suppliers will be able to provide their products for either

- Bull will adopt the RS/6000 processor in its UNIX systems.
- Bull will adopt the Power PC chip, to be developed through the IBM/Apple/Motorola partnership, when it is available.
- Bull will lead in the development of the multi-processor versions of IBM's RISC systems.
- IBM will resell portable PCs from Bull's Zenith Data Systems subsidiary under its own name.
- Bull will manufacture circuit boards and subassemblies for IBM in France.
- IBM will manufacture RS/6000 systems for Bull at its plants in France.
- Bull will have access to the Power PC development center in Austin, Texas, run jointly by IBM, Apple and Motorola.
- Other manufacturing and technology cross-licensing arrangements will follow.

Figure 7.7. The IBM/Bull alliance.

IBM or Bull customers without having to make any changes in their code —the systems will not just be binary-compatible, but will often be identical.

Bull has many commercial customers but is particularly strong in government sites. In the UK, for example, it is the principal supplier to the Inland Revenue for the implementation of a large UNIX-based network for the control of income-tax information. The position of the IBM RISC System/6000 UNIX systems in France and in other Bull strongholds has obviously been greatly strengthened by this agreement.

There are other possible indirect benefits for IBM from this partnership. Until recently, Bull was an active member and supporter of the ACE Consortium, which standardized on the MIPS RISC processors. Bull's relationship with IBM has given additional and public support for the IBM Power processor as a potential standard for the future.

7.8 Research and development partnerships

Competitive pressures, soaring research and development costs and the risks involved with innovation make technical development partnerships highly desirable in many fields. Partners can share the required investment costs, expertise and resources, as well as the risks of failure. For each partner, the result can be shorter development times and a better return on investment.

Some examples of IBM's technology partnerships are:

- IBM and Siemens in Germany have formed a partnership to develop 64-megabit memory chips jointly, as well as to manufacture 16-megabit chips at the IBM facility in France.
- IBM and Go Corporation, originators of an innovative pen-based operating system, have a development and marketing agreement under which IBM will use its marketing and financial resources to promote the GO technology, and its technical capability to help develop and support it. Go's operating system has the potential to be incorporated into many future IBM products.

- IBM and Auspex Systems have announced a joint development agreement relating to high-end file servers.
- IBM and Hewlett-Packard have a strategic alliance to develop and manufacture a family of fiber-optic components that will be marketed to computer manufacturers for designing low-cost, high-speed communications into computers and peripherals.

As demonstrated by these examples, IBM has many technologically based alliances. Nevertheless, the one signed in 1991 between IBM, Apple and Motorola has received the most publicity. This is because it is thought to have great potential for influencing the long-term development of the computer industry. We therefore examine it in some detail.

7.9   The IBM/Apple/Motorola alliance

There are three significant opportunities for IBM to gain broad market acceptance (*de facto* standard status) for its technologies. Although these are in their infancy at present, each will be a vital component of the computer industry in the long term. They are—RISC chip technology, multimedia and object-oriented software.

RISC technology is important because it allows very high performance computing in a cost-effective way. Multimedia—the combination of sound, vision, video and touch on the desktop—is important because its use will revolutionize the user interface to computers, bringing the technology to more people than ever before. Object-oriented software is a vital element of open systems, since it allows the development of modular, reusable and interoperable software components

The alliance between IBM, Apple and Motorola addresses all three of these components—hence its fundamental importance. We will examine in turn the contributions that each of the partners is expected to make to the alliance as a whole, and the particular open systems issues that it allows each of them to address.

Apple's role

> Apple brings breakthrough object-oriented technology, individual computing design focus, leading-edge multimedia technology, and an additional channel for IBM's RISC technology.
>
> (Apple/IBM/Motorola, 1991)

Long regarded as the most 'closed' of the system environments, Apple's operating system has nevertheless achieved a high degree of respect for its quality and ease of use. Considered by commentators to be years ahead of the standard PC-DOS environment, it has made sophisticated software usable by many, pioneering the 'friendly' graphical user interface approach.

Apple's software has been built on a deep understanding of user requirements on the desktop. It is continuing to improve the user interface, in the process researching the use of object-oriented technologies for the development and integration of operating system software. It has developed innovative multimedia support technologies and embedded them into its desktop machines. More than any other computer company, it has shown that it understands the implications of the convergence of computer and consumer electronics.

In spite of its technological breakthroughs, Apple is not of sufficient size and strength to be able to market its technologies at the level that is required if they are to become standard. It has not been able to become a viable supplier of enterprise systems, having only achieved significant penetration on the desktop. It needs a high-performance RISC processor for its next generation of systems. Up to now its supplier has been Motorola.

Motorola

Motorola brings world class design and manufacturing talents and worldwide chip marketing and distribution capability.

(Apple/IBM/Motorola, 1991)

Motorola has long been one of the world's leading microprocessor design and manufacturing companies, highly respected for the outstanding quality of its products. In spite of this, it has not been able to win the big computer manufacturers over to its own RISC designs, mainly because they (IBM, HP, Digital and Sun) all have RISC chip designs of their own. Nevertheless, its 88K chip, well respected for its performance, is embedded in systems from several smaller manufacturers and is widely used in industrial design.

Motorola understands that the support of independent software companies is vital for the success of any microprocessor design. It has consistently funded and supported 88open, the organization with responsibility for porting software to 88K-based systems and testing systems for conformance to the 88K ABI. By so doing, it has ensured that systems using the 88K are able to access a vast catalog of well-supported and tested applications software.

Motorola needs a strategy that will enable it to compete fully with its competitors, and allow it to utilize its high-quality manufacturing facilities to maximum capacity.

IBM

IBM contributes technology leadership with the RISC POWER processor architecture used in the RS/6000 range, a functionally rich open standards-based operating system in AIX, key object-oriented technologies, and a deep understanding of enterprise computing.

(Apple/IBM/Motorola, 1991)

IBM knows that the future machine for the desktop has not yet been defined. Nevertheless, it is clear that customer needs demand full support of object-oriented software and multimedia technologies, which themselves require high-performance RISC-based systems with new operating system technology.

Multimedia has the potential to address a whole new set of applications needs, but the lack of standards and development tools make development risky, expensive and slow. Object-oriented software promises to improve the economics and development cycle time of software. This should facilitate more rapid delivery of customizable applications solutions to customers, and allow the re-use of software components. Although IBM has much of this technology under development itself, Apple is currently the acknowledged leader in the field. For IBM, the fastest and safest route to market is through an alliance with Apple.

There are as yet no generally accepted standards for multimedia or for object-oriented programming techniques. By working with Apple, IBM should reduce the risks in development and improve the chances of the resultant technology becoming a standard acceptable to a wide community.

Purchasers of chip technology always like to have a second source of supply. This ensures that pricing stays competitive, and that supply lines stay open. If IBM is to make the POWER architecture a standard in the marketplace, it must have an alliance with at least one other chip manufacturer. Motorola, with its outstanding reputation for quality and its minimal competitive position today, is the clearly preferred microprocessor partner for IBM.

The alliance objective

The objective of the IBM/Apple/Motorola alliance is to build and proliferate technology in the three areas—RISC technology, multimedia and object-oriented software—in such a way as to gain broad market acceptance.

Customers will require software portability and vendor choice across these new technologies, and so the technologies that emerge from the alliance must be made openly available on good commercial terms. Provided that this happens, the market should expand fast, producing new revenue growth opportunities for all three partners as well as for their licensees.

While all three companies will work together within the alliance, they will still be in competition, both between themselves and with others to whom they may license the technology. This is the ever-present dilemma in the open systems market —how to compete when products are technologically compatible and developed in cooperation.

Alliance components

There are five major components to the IBM/Apple/Motorola alliance (Fig. 7.8):

1 Object-oriented software development

IBM and Apple have formed a new independent company, Taligent, that will develop and market a new software platform using object-oriented technology.

Apple, IBM and Motorola will cooperate (and compete) in five areas:
- Object-oriented operating environment (TALIGENT)
- Networking
- RISC chips (Power PC)
- Power Open Computing Environment
- Multimedia technologies (KALEIDA)

Apple and IBM also announced a cross-licence of patents and displays, including a 'limited licence to the Macintosh visual displays.'

Figure 7.8.   The IBM/Apple/Motorola alliance.

This company will license its products to IBM, Apple and other systems vendors. The software is planned to run on Intel, Motorola and IBM processor architectures. Initial products are targeted for the mid-1990s.

The open systems concepts supported are: portable software, interoperability of software and freedom of choice of vendor.

2 Enterprise networking

The enterprise networking alliance is an agreement to enable better integration of Apple's systems into IBM networks. The agreement does not include any provisions for joint marketing or joint development of products. IBM and Apple will continue their separate developments, cooperating only to the extent of ensuring that products work together.

The open systems concept supported is: interoperability, between Apple and IBM systems.

3 PowerPC—RISC chip development and distribution

IBM, Apple and Motorola are combining resources to develop a new PowerPC family of single-chip RISC microprocessors. IBM and Motorola are forming a design center which will be staffed by engineers from all three companies. Motorola will manufacture and market the PowerPC technology worldwide, while IBM will continue to manufacture RISC chips for its own products. PowerPC will become the basis for new products from IBM and Apple, and potentially for other vendors.

Applications based on the IBM RISC System/6000 will be binary compatible with the PowerPC. Products are expected to be available in the mid-1990s.

The open systems concepts supported are: software portability, upward compatibility and scalability.

4 PowerOpen computing environment

This alliance encompasses two major cross-licensing agreements and is the basis for a new computing environment called PowerOpen. The PowerOpen computing environment will be based on the PowerPC RISC hardware platform, a new release of AIX and two user interface options—the OSF's Motif and Apple's Macintosh desktop.

IBM will build the new release of AIX based on OSF's OSF/1 operating system, and will provide an application binary interface (ABI) to enable the portability of software. Apple will port its Macintosh Desktop (the Apple proprietary user interface) to the new version of AIX and will provide the ability to run Macintosh System 7, A/UX (Apple's UNIX version) and Motif/AIX applications.

Both IBM and Apple will develop and sell PowerOpen-based products to their respective customers. Products are expected to be available in two to three years.

The open system concepts supported are: portability of software across all PowerOpen systems, portability of Macintosh applications to AIX platforms, compatibility across operating systems, and standard interfaces.

5 Multimedia joint venture

IBM and Apple have formed a new independent company, Kaleida, which will develop and promote multimedia technologies, products and specifications to be made available to the industry on attractive commercial terms. The focus of the work will be on reducing the complexity and costs associated with the implementation of multimedia applications.

The joint venture will specify, develop and license multimedia enabling software and designs to manufacturers, software houses, creators, content owners, packagers and distributors of information products. It will develop software products, such as a device-independent multimedia application scripting language, and portable run-time environments, as well as data formats and specifications for multimedia platforms.

Initial products are targeted for the market in two to three years.

The open systems concepts supported are: standards for new technologies (prior to the formal process), and portability of software.

Conclusions on the IBM/Apple/Motorola alliance

Both IBM and Apple recognize the importance of emerging multimedia technologies for the desktop machines of the future. While each could have been a strong contestant for dominance in this area, together they form an impressive alliance. Apple's desire to provide products for 'the rest of us' complements IBM's knowledge of corporate needs. Combining the innovative minds and technical resources contained within both companies should produce exciting technology appropriate for the 'window onto the information network'.

Over the next few years, many other manufacturers can be expected to align themselves with the IBM/Apple/Motorola alliance, and to commit to the resulting technologies. If the research and development work is successful, it is likely that *de facto* standards will emerge from the joint work.

7.10   Managing alliances

Alliances can be versatile and powerful tools if the relationships are handled well. If not, as IBM's experiences with SBS, Discovision and Rolm showed, it is best to end them. To be successful, the interests of both partners must be well served—the 'win-win' deal—and one partner must not expect to impose its culture, style or methods of management on the other.

While working to make the alliance succeed, each partner will also be working hard to compete with the other in certain markets and opportunities. This often makes the management of the relationship difficult and its interpretation by the outside world confused.

While the benefits for IBM, its partners and its customers can be profound, the reasons for forming alliances are usually straightforward. IBM is using alliances to become more responsive to customers' needs, more efficient in its structure and faster in its response times, to enter new markets, to optimize its R & D investments, and to help focus its people and resources where they will be most effective. Knowing this, it is trying hard to manage them well, having learnt much from its previous experiences.

7.11   Summary

In this chapter we have examined the scope and the nature of the strategic alliances which IBM is developing. Some of these are with software companies with which it has traditionally cooperated, and others with hardware companies more often considered its competitors. The problem of learning to cooperate while competing is fundamental to the open systems movement.

The alliances allow IBM to move much faster, into restricted markets and with a broader product line than it could possibly manage alone. The products which it is developing with its partners may significantly affect the development of the computer industry. In particular, the results from the Apple/IBM/Motorola relationship may change the nature of the desktop system in a way that can be only guessed at today.

The concept of cooperating while competing is in tune with sociological and political trends. The 1990s have already shown that the global market of the future is going to be very different from that of the past. Cooperation and freedom of choice are its principal characteristics. Any company that does not recognize this and change accordingly can expect to suffer the consequences.

The evidence shows that IBM knows this and is moving accordingly. Whether it can move sufficiently fast, and carry enough of its people and customers with it as it does so, remains to be seen. But as John Akers, Chairman of IBM, has said: 'Alliances are important. They give us a chance to better control our future—and to lead from strength in the key areas that drive the industry.'

8
Integrated information systems

8.1   Introduction

In earlier chapters, we discussed the need for integrated information systems (IIS), and presented this as a major driving force behind the open systems movement.

Much of today's enterprise data is held on the corporate mainframe, and is most often found in the IBM proprietary environment. The issue of how to build integrated information systems within and across enterprises generally includes finding ways to integrate with, or migrate from, this environment to one with a more open design.

In this chapter we investigate IIS concepts in detail and analyse IBM's approach to them. We look at some of the products which it is developing and supporting, and the relationships it is building with other companies working in the field. We will see that IBM has clearly recognized and is responding to customer needs for the integration of data from many different sources, and is gradually opening up its own technologies to accommodate these.

8.2   The business perspective

To be successful in business today requires having quality information about the business and the market at the fingertips of the people who need to react quickly to it. This information comes from a multitude of sources both inside and outside the enterprise (Fig. 8.1). The challenge is to find efficient ways to deliver it in a timely, accurate and understandable way so as to enable effective decision-making by the authorized individuals.

Businesses today are run with little margin for error. Success depends on knowing when changes take place in the internal or external environment, knowing what response to make and when, responding very rapidly if required, and being able to assess the response to actions taken. The margin between success and failure can hinge on the ability to analyse which parts of the business are profitable and which are not, on knowing who is or is not buying a particular product and why, or even on being able to analyse in detail the profitability of one major contract. If there is a problem it is not enough to know where it is; the individual,

140

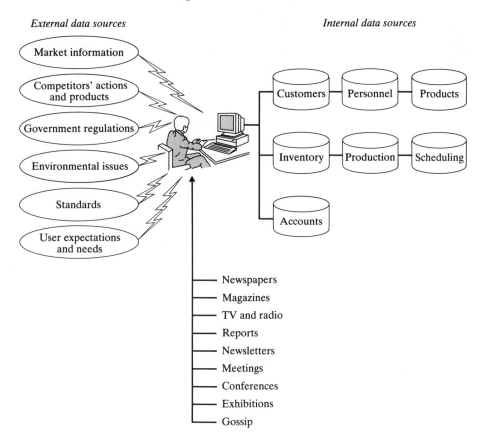

External data sources

Market information

Competitors' actions and products

Government regulations

Environmental issues

Standards

User expectations and needs

Internal data sources

Customers — Personnel — Products

Inventory — Production — Scheduling

Accounts

— Newspapers
— Magazines
— TV and radio
— Reports
— Newsletters
— Meetings
— Conferences
— Exhibitions
— Gossip

Problem: To manage the delivery of timely, accurate and understandable business information to authorized individuals to enable effective decision-making.

Figure 8.1.   The information user.

group or company must also know what actions to take, and be able to measure the response to these. Knowing where the business stands in relation to the overall market and the positions of specific competitors can help to decide the choice of actions to be taken.

In the 1990s and beyond, businesses will continue to reduce inventory and production times, while speeding up workflows and cutting costs. But the emphasis for competitive advantage will move to service, quality and dependability, all of which require shortened response times. Ingenuity and effective decision-making will be required at all levels; both require rapid access to relevant information.

For most businesses the information that could be used to answer many vital questions usually exists somewhere in the enterprise. The problem for most people is in finding out where it is and how to use it effectively. Too often the relevant facts are scattered throughout the company, exist in different forms in different places

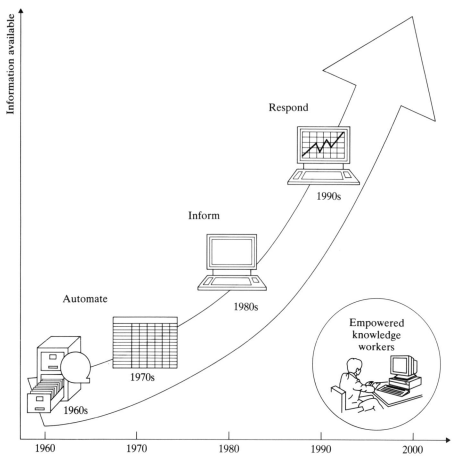

Figure 8.2.   The information explosion.

(sometimes in the heads of key people who may not be easily accessible), are often duplicated and can even be contradictory. Although they know it might ultimately help them to do the job better, people sometimes find it too time-consuming and difficult to obtain the information they want within the time frame they have available.

8.3   The information explosion

The problems of finding and using information are compounded by the fact that the amount available is growing at an accelerating rate (Fig. 8.2). A study from AT & T's Bell Laboratories estimates that the amount of available data is doubling every five years, yet because of the difficulties in accessing it effectively and practically people are able to use only about 5 per cent of it.

Over the years, as the capacity of systems increased and costs declined, enterprises continually automated more and more of their operational processes. This made much of the internal operational data available for analysis and use. With data collection devices such as bar coders, scanners, automated tellers and computerized documents now linked to the internal systems, data in the sense of raw facts is pouring into businesses. The desire now is to turn this data into information by applying intelligence to it and using it in new applications for maximum advantage to the business.

For example, the key to profitability in a distribution business lies in keeping inventory to a minimum while still being able to supply to customers' requirements quickly. Bar coding of products is essential for commercial just-in-time delivery systems, where people in the business need to know exactly where things are and when they will arrive at their destination. As the use of these systems grows so does the amount of data available from them, and so does the requirement for easy access to it and applications that allow new uses of it.

8.4   The fragmentation of data

As automation progressed and the demands for information increased, users often became frustrated with the central systems in place in their organizations. They grew tired of waiting for the central DP department to build the applications that they needed—the application backlog in many large organizations is several years long. As PCs and departmental systems increased in number, users started to buy their own query and graphics tools, spreadsheets and database systems. As a result, individual users and their departments accumulated data and information independent of the central DP organization. This situation continues today.

Until recently few corporations imposed rules or guidelines for the software tools purchased and used on PCs and departmental systems. As a result, the data which has accumulated now exists in many forms and on diverse systems, managed by a number of different data management systems, and used in a wide variety of custom-built local applications. Enterprises are only just beginning to realize that the totality of this data is a very valuable corporate asset and that, as such, it should be carefully managed and intelligently used. This cannot happen unless and until the data is standardized in some sense, and made more generally accessible.

8.5   Consequences of data integration

Technicians in the computer industry are working to help users reintegrate their data into information systems that can be accessed efficiently and easily by all those who need to do so. They are also developing methods by which the vast amount of information available can be sorted according to its relevance for particular people and tasks. Technologies such as touch screens and embedded video are evolving in applications that make information more easily accessed and assimilated by people who may never before have used a computer in its conventional sense.

Integrated information systems, which by their nature must be built on open systems technologies, generally lead to fundamental changes in the organization as a whole, and in the attitudes of some of the people within it. In particular, when more information is more easily accessed by more people, the organization becomes more open in every respect. And when middle managers are no longer needed as conduits and controllers of information, the organization becomes generally flatter.

8.6   Departmental systems

As separate business processes were automated over the years, major application systems were built to serve the needs of particular operational aspects of the business. Examples are accounts, personnel, manufacturing and marketing. Operational data, resulting from the processing of a particular application, grew with that application and was tightly coupled to it (Fig. 8.3).

Many of these early applications were transaction-oriented, with each transaction creating a valuable piece of data—placing an order, changing an order, recording a customer enquiry, recording a payment or manufacturing a part. Users who needed to review, analyse and understand the business processes relevant to their own department selected or developed software tools to help them to do so, dictated by the job at hand. The tools then also became tightly coupled to the

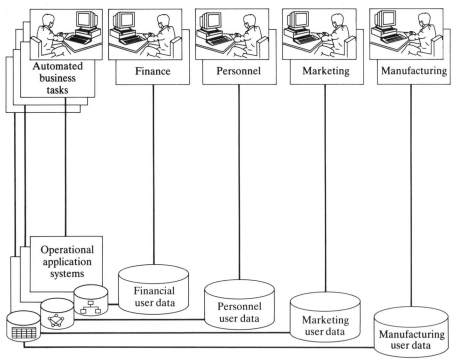

Figure 8.3.   Departmental systems.

individuals and departments that selected and used them, since they were chosen for their particular needs.

As more business processes became automated, each application area fostered its own user community with its own set of tools and data. Users began to copy, collect and build stores of data suitable for their own needs. As new applications were added, so the data grew. Users familiar with the data relevant to their own area had little or no knowledge of complementary—or contradictory—data resident elsewhere.

Many organizations contain these almost self-sufficient and independent departments that use their own particular aspect of the corporate data. These departments may access the data directly from the source, extract and download it from somewhere else, or even collect it themselves, as their needs dictate. The departments have become accustomed to selecting and using a particular set of tools in order to manipulate the data. Over time their application systems have gradually evolved to take on the technology, style and characteristics of the management philosophy in place in the department at their outset.

As long as departments operated fairly independently, this situation was accepted. But problems appeared once users began to reach across departmental boundaries for other relevant information—marketing looking for financial information, for example, or sales investigating inventory. Once users tried to access information 'owned' by others, the problems caused by lack of standards became apparent.

8.7 The problems of diversity

The problems created by the lack of standards are many and various (Fig. 8.4). Locating and accessing data from within another department can be difficult and time-consuming. Data definitions may be inconsistent and unfamiliar—for example, the finance and sales departments may have different meanings of 'account', and while some places in the organization call a contract a contract, others may call it a job. Getting everyone in an organization to agree on the meaning of such basic terms is one of the most difficult of the tasks involved in building integrated information systems.

Special programs have sometimes been written to provide data to a particular set of users. Another set of users with similar, but not quite identical, needs might have their own set of programs. A third group may go to another department to get what they want rather than do it themselves. Different personalities, locations, platforms and cross-functional needs can produce a range of unmanaged and often costly data acquisition techniques.

Each data source tends to spawn its own set of preparation programs—applications programs or procedures to periodically select, copy, transform, subset, or combine data in order to produce the information the users want. If the data-

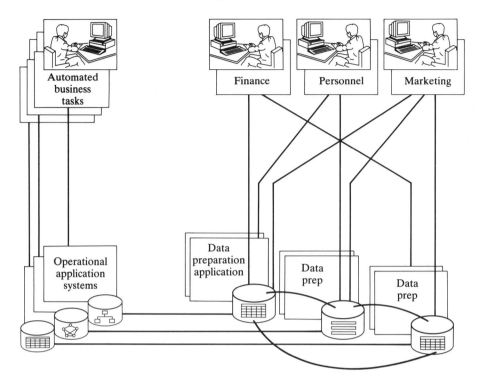

- Locating and accessing data across departmental boundaries is difficult.
- The data descriptions, formats and access methods may be unfamiliar.
- Different platforms and cross-functional needs spawn costly data acquisition techniques.

Figure 8.4.   Information systems impact.

processing department is required to produce these, it probably adds to the already substantial backlog of work, and is unlikely to command a high priority.

The programs by their nature are usually very sensitive to the data within them and consequently highly susceptible to change when the data changes. Out of necessity they are often built by the users themselves—people who were not hired or trained as programmers. They are unlikely to use the best techniques for the job, and writing the programs takes time and talent away from the work for which they were hired.

If data is extracted at different times, by different methods or from different sources, it may yield inconsistent and even contradictory results. This can be at best embarrassing and at worst disastrous. Some organizations have installed a level of internal administrative control on the data, but this is rare. More often it is understood that the individual user or department carries responsibility for the quality and accuracy of the data it uses.

New technology used in a new application or in a major replacement for an existing old application can no longer be accepted if it increases the data diversity within a department. Today additional diversity can be supported only if there is a good business case for it. Otherwise it should be recognized as a major inhibiting factor to long-term progress.

8.8   The main problem areas

There are three main areas that must be addressed before effective information delivery can be achieved (Fig. 8.5). They are:

- Standardization of the interface to the data—there is no single view of the data, and there are many interfaces in common use.
- Uncoupling of applications from data—applications which use the data are often dependent on the data itself, and are limited in the data that they can access.
- Uncoupling of tools from data, sources and platforms—if tool providers are forced to write and maintain products for many different data sources, formats and platforms, a great deal of redundancy, unnecessary costs and possible inconsistencies is likely to follow.

These three problem areas combine to waste time and resources, and reduce the quantity and quality of the information available. Each of them must be resolved if the benefits of integrated information systems are to be realized.

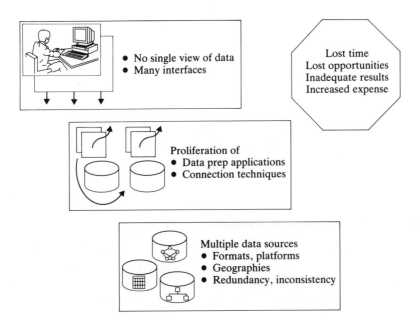

Figure 8.5. The problem areas.

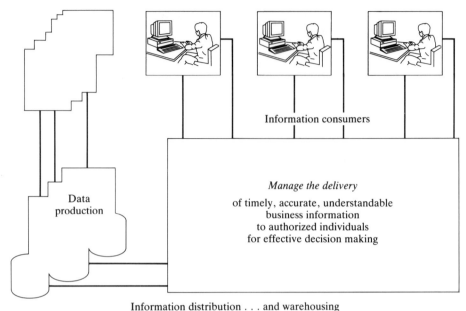

Figure 8.6.   The IBM approach.

8.9   The IBM approach

The challenge to the information systems industry as a whole is to design a
methodology that gets information from its point of origin, the production site, to
the consumer, the user who needs it, in a way that is transparent to the user. IBM
views this as a classic delivery problem (Fig. 8.6) which can be addressed by
implementing a data distribution and warehousing system. As in any such system,
the requirements are to deliver the goods in a reliable and dependable way, assuring
the quality of the goods received, and making sure the right things get to the right
customers at the right time.

Today users must search for the data they need, using tools that they select. A
key concept in the IBM approach is to provide them with 'a data delivery service'.
This is based on delivering the data to a place where it can be accessed easily
automatically.

8.10   The Information Warehouse

The overall strategy for solving the problems of information delivery and management is presented by IBM under the heading of the Information Warehouse. This
is designed to address the areas of access to information, data delivery, data
management, and integration of the data from both IBM and non-IBM data
sources (Fig. 8.7).

The Framework can be described as a customized set of tools and processes

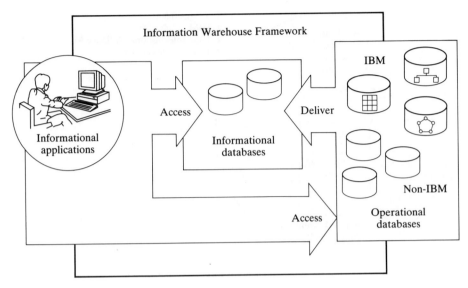

Figure 8.7.   IBM's Information Warehouse concept.

designed to gather data from any source, transform and organize it, store and manage it, maintain its currency and provide user access to it, all for the purpose of solving business problems. The specific goals are then to provide a common view of the data, to provide ways to transform data into the information needed and suitable for decision-making, and to improve the management of the data delivery process so as to provide timeliness, accuracy and consistency of the data.

The expansion, automation and integration of tools and processes to deliver the data from where it exists in operational databases to databases designed expressly for users is another important facet. These 'informational databases' could be located centrally or distributed within the enterprise. It should not matter to the users where the data is or how their access to it is achieved as long as their requests for information are easily satisfied in reasonable time frames.

The concept of an Information Warehouse Framework has been evolving in both users' and vendors' minds and products for some time. By putting a name to it, IBM formally acknowledged its importance to the long-term strategy.

8.11   The International Alliance for the Information Warehouse Framework

The products and services that are required to implement the Information Warehouse Framework will be provided by IBM and many other companies, in partnership (Fig. 8.8). Members of the IBM International Alliance for the Information Warehouse Framework are companies that work closely with IBM in the development of products, and the designation shows IBM's recognition of their role and importance in the strategy.

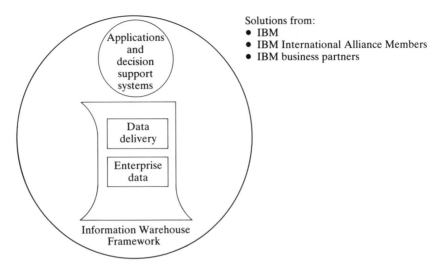

Solutions from:
- IBM
- IBM International Alliance Members
- IBM business partners

Members of the IBM International Alliance for Information Warehouse:
- Bachman Information Systems Inc
- Information Builders Inc

Development Partner:
- Comshare Inc

Business Partners:
- Work with IBM on a country-to-country basis.

Figure 8.8.   The International Alliance for the Information Warehouse.

Business partners are companies that have products that are consistent with and complement the Warehouse Framework efforts, and with whom IBM usually has marketing agreements. IBM's approach, working with these partners, is designed to make it easier for customers who have diverse data types to bring them into the Information Warehouse concept.

The Alliance sets out the rules and structure under which IBM will work with companies that are very often also its competitors. Although the Alliance is developing an open structure under which many competitive products can coexist, it is still an essential element of IBM's strategy to try to persuade customers to use the IBM relational database products wherever possible. While it will ensure that its products and strategies have open interfaces, and it will encourage other companies to conform to them, IBM will continue to compete vigorously, particularly in the data management area which is at the heart of the enterprise systems.

8.12   Approaches to data access

When diverse data exists in many different places, it can be difficult to access it in total. This situation can be improved in a number of ways—by moving to a

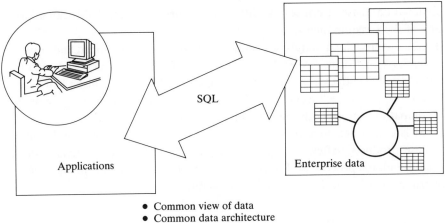

- Common view of data
- Common data architecture
- Industrial strength data management

Figure 8.9.   Common access to data sources.

common data architecture, by providing a common way to access different kinds of data, or by providing a standard delivery service for users.

A common data architecture means that standard data management structures are used. Data is more consistently organized—perhaps by putting all the data into compatible relational database management systems—and it becomes easier to access and link data in different locations (Fig. 8.9). Although many organizations are moving towards a standardized data architecture, there will still be a transition period when other kinds of data exist in the enterprise, left over from the past. There is a need for a consistent way to access the data, either through tools supplied to the user or by tools that can gather it up and deliver it to the user.

The specific approach taken to access and delivery will depend on what and where the data is today, and where it is ultimately best for the users that it resides.

8.13   The IBM view

IBM has been in the database management business for a long time. In the process, it has accumulated a great deal of information from its customers on what they require in a database in order that it manage their data effectively. The fundamental requirements are:

- Integrity—the data must be accurately stored
- Security—access to data must be controlled
- Recoverability—should the system fail, the data must be able to be recovered in its original form
- Performance—access to any particular data must be as fast as the application requires.

Relational databases from several different vendors, including IBM, can address many of these requirements.

IBM's own relational database products were originally developed and supplied for the SAA platforms—MVS/ESA, VMS/ESA, OS/400 and OS/2. Compatible products will eventually be supplied for the entire AIX family also. Third-party software suppliers, such as Oracle, already have relational database systems that are compatible across both the SAA and AIX families.

IBM is committed to support national and international standards for all its database products. After it supplied its own SQL data access language to the formal standards process, SQL was embodied in an international standard, and is now supported by all the major database vendors.

8.14   Distributed data architectures

As the world moves to distributed database structures across heterogeneous networks, it is vital that the characteristics of integrity, security, recoverability and performance of databases are maintained.

IBM has developed a distributed architecture, Distributed Relational Database Architecture (DRDA), which offers an open architecture for the access to relational data from multiple relational database systems, both IBM and non-IBM. This architecture has been published by IBM and is available to other vendors to implement if they wish.

IBM plans to implement DRDA across IBM platforms and to promote its acceptance as a standard. With DRDA on IBM platforms, interoperability with non-IBM vendors using DRDA will be provided automatically. DRDA competes with the remote data access (RDA) standard proposed and supported by the SQL Access Group (SAG), whose members include most of the major database suppliers.

At a general level, RDA is built on international OSI standards, while DRDA is built upon IBM's own SNA standards. DRDA has additional functions which have been deemed mandatory by large IBM customers—functions that enhance systems management and operational durability for large line-of-business application environments. IBM has recommended enhancements to RDA to address the requirements for additional capabilities.

IBM has offered its DRDA technology to ISO and ANSI for use in the international standards for remote data access, and is actively working within the standards committees to bring DRDA and RDA together. The DRDA Vendor Enablement Program encourages non-IBM vendors and other hardware vendors to build or update their products to conform to DRDA. This would allow IBM and other vendor systems to share the same network and interoperate so that any application could access any data.

IBM has implemented DRDA capability on all of its SAA platforms, and is extending its functionality. Customers and vendors who need distributed database functionality can implement DRDA protocols and connect their applications and databases together in an open heterogeneous system.

DRDA is based upon studies which IBM has made within its own user base, and has been designed with the upward migration of that group in mind. The places in which it differs from RDA are deemed necessary in order to provide required functionality and upward compatibility for current IBM database users. For this reason, if RDA becomes the publicly agreed standard, IBM will have to support both DRDA and RDA in the short-to-medium term, unless it can find a way to merge the two technologies prior to the formal standardization work being completed. Other vendors, many of whom have also announced their intention to follow IBM in its support of DRDA, will be forced to do likewise.

8.15   Going to the source of the data

One way of giving users access to more data is to provide decision support tools that can access a variety of data sources (Fig. 8.10). The disadvantage of this approach is that each tool must then supply access routines to retrieve data from each data source. It is up to each tool to provide a way to describe the data available to the user, and to use this information to assist them in constructing requests for information.

IBM supplies a selection of decision support tools to assist users with retrieving, analysing and presenting information for decision-making. Most of these originated in the SAA environment, and will be moved across to the AIX family. Third-party software suppliers, who have never been slow to provide products for the IBM families, will undoubtedly also provide products. There are already some excellent third party decision support tools for the UNIX environment which have been ported to the IBM RISC System/6000.

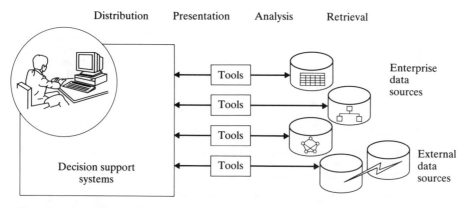

Each decision support tool
• Provides access capability to a set of data sources
• Identifies what data is available to the user
• Assists users with requesting data

Figure 8.10.   Decision support systems.

While there are advantages in accessing data from the source, there are also some drawbacks. The user is limited to the capabilities of the tool in use. If additional data sources need to be accessed, a new tool may be required. Different users develop a preference for particular tools, not all of which can access the same kinds of data. Sharing of data is more difficult. The nature of user query workloads tends to be unpredictable, and can seriously affect the efficiency of production work. If the data is remote, performance and communications must be coordinated.

If people are using data reflecting conditions at different times, changes in data that have taken place after a particular user has accessed it may not get transmitted into the work. Users themselves often change the data for use within their own applications—for example, spelling product codes in full, or using their own shorthand notation for customer names. This can lead to confusing and even contradictory results unless internal standards are agreed and adhered to.

8.16   Standard access methods

The Structured Query Language (SQL) has become the standard for data access. There are a vast number of tools available that utilize it, and many programmers and users that are familiar with it. It makes sense therefore to try to use SQL as a common way to ask for data, whatever the nature of the source.

One approach to data access is to change SQL commands automatically into the requests for all the different data types that existing systems use. Once done, this

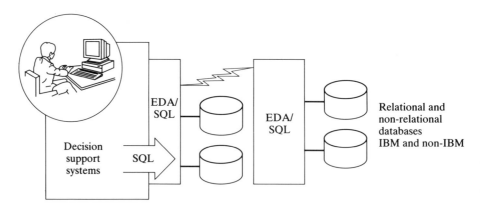

- Expands range of access to over 40 data sources
  - Local or remote
  - IBM and non-IBM platforms
- Permits data of different types to be joined together
- Provides a common access and connection technique
  across multiple tools and data sources

Figure 8.11.   Access to corporate data.

saves a great deal of work, and allows users to access more data with the tools with which they are already familiar. This is the concept behind Enterprise Data Access/SQL (EDA/SQL) (Fig. 8.11) developed by Information Builders, a member of the IBM International Alliance for the Information Warehouse Framework.

8.17   Enterprise Data Access (EDA/SQL)

EDA/SQL sits between the application and the data, and intercepts requests for data. It interprets the request, and is then able to construct a native request to the proper data source. After collecting the data, it returns it back to the application.

EDA/SQL supports access to relational and non-relational data, on IBM or non-IBM systems, locally or remote. It provides a call-level programming interface utilizing SQL as a common data access language to IBM and many other vendor relational and non-relational databases, including such well-known ones as Oracle, IDMS/R and Adabas.

Data of different types on the same platform can be joined together and returned to the user as a single result. Since the components are modular, as the need for a new platform or different data type arises, the appropriate module is added. The user tools do not have to change, and the new data is immediately accessible.

More than 40 different data sources can be accessed with EDA/SQL. The connections to all the platforms are consistent, and EDA/SQL can be used by applications running on workstations, on mid-range and on mainframe machines. In its concept, EDA/SQL is in the mainstream of open systems thinking—it provides an open interface to data. For this reason, it should make it easier to install, maintain and use data on many different and diverse platforms.

8.18   Data delivery

Although access to different data types can be accomplished using SQL retrieval techniques, the data engines that sit behind them need not have changed. Users can then access the data that they require, but not necessarily in the time frame that they want. The process of getting the data may also significantly impact the performance of the system where it resides. The data delivery aspect of the Information Warehouse is intended to address these issues.

Fundamental to data delivery is the concept of informational databases, distinct from operational needs and designed expressly for informational applications. These may be built for one of several reasons: to enhance the data, to gather data from multiple sources, to separate query work from transaction work or to put the user data where it is more convenient and easily accessible.

Since users and the tools they use should not really be aware of where the data is or how the tool reaches it, the decision to build informational databases and where to locate them is based on cost, manageability and control aspects.

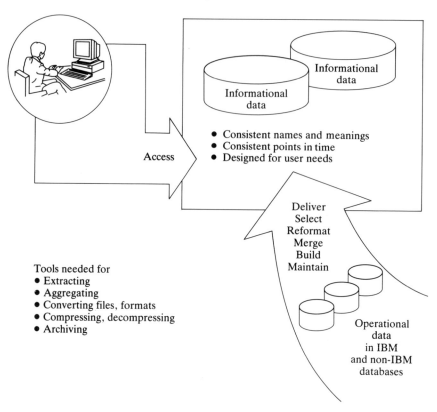

Figure 8.12.   Delivering and enhancing the data.

8.19   Enhanced data

Operational data generally needs to be 'enhanced' in order to make it more meaningful and useful for knowledge workers (Fig. 8.12). This requires various transformations to be made on the operational data. In the process, it becomes possible to improve the quality of the data, establishing consistent names and meanings, to reflect common data at consistent points in time for the shared information, and to develop a planned archiving approach. Information can be selected, merged and formatted for particular user needs.

IBM offers tools that provide a generalized way of locating, extracting, selecting and gathering information from a variety of IBM and non-IBM sources into an informational database. Once these are built, the data can be maintained by repeating the gathering and loading steps at regular intervals, applying those changes that have occurred since the last update. This means that the operational and informational databases are kept consistent. IBM provides products for this aspect of copy management when the operational data is in IBM database structures IMS/ESA and DB2, and is providing a growing level of integration among the data delivery tools for these two environments. Increasing the interoperability of its own and its partners' software tools is a primary goal of the Information Warehouse Framework.

8.20 The window onto data

Once integrated information systems have been built, the problem is how to help users more easily assimilate the information they contain. Access to vast amounts of information is of little use if people do not have the time or the ability to understand, interpret and act upon it. Graphical user interfaces, where icons are used to represent objects, and touch screens, where people no longer need to type or use a mouse, are making computers easier to use by people who may previously have been inhibited by the technology. But now the information itself must be made easier to understand, even when it is complex.

Expansion of the graphical user interface with additional object technology is a key requirement for the future. Incorporating objects for image, audio and video into the user's workplace will enhance desktop systems, as will the ability dynamically to create and manipulate objects as represented by icons as part of the application process.

IBM is working with standards development organizations to promote IBM technologies in these areas, and is joining with business partners and industry consortia such as the Object Management Group (OMG) to bring new technologies into the marketplace. Through its partnership with Apple, it is also working to develop technologies in this area and establish them as open standards, licensable to other vendors.

8.21 Summary

In this chapter we have considered the issues raised by the concept of integrated information systems. We have seen that, in order to build such systems, databases that currently exist must be 'opened up' in the sense that the data available in each of them must be made accessible with common tools. Although there are problem areas where agreement on appropriate standards has not yet been reached, most of the computer industry now recognizes the importance of data standards in the overall concept of open systems.

Queries on the database can adversely affect the production environment. To overcome this informational databases take data from the operational systems and present it in a suitable form to the people who have to use it for decision-taking. The informational databases allow a level of control to be put on user databases, ensuring that they are kept up to date with operational data, and that separate applications do not contain contradictory data.

Tools that access the various operational databases, those that format, merge and control the informational data, those that build user-specific applications from the data, and those that balance the data and provide remote access, must all be designed to work together. Interoperability of software in this area is a vital aspect of open systems development.

The main objective of IBM's Information Warehouse Framework is to provide a consistent and common view of all the data, operational and informational, that exists within an enterprise. IBM is working with a number of partners to produce this.

Although IBM is opening up its own technologies to provide compatibility with those of other vendors, in general it will always be easier to integrate from within a single vendor's product lines than across those of a number of different vendors. The 'look and feel' of the products will be comparable, levels of support will be more consistent, and the interoperability functionality will be more assured. Thus, when operational applications are based on IBM relational systems, it is likely to remain easier to build informational databases and decision applications with IBM technology than otherwise, at least for the foreseeable future.

However, until IBM provides a similar range of database access and control products and services for the AIX environment to that existing for the SAA family, enterprises committed to UNIX will be forced to go to other vendors for some of their software needs. Many of the Warehouse partners are heavily committed to the UNIX environment, and so can be expected to provide products to fill any gaps that IBM might leave.

In the next chapter we will consider the issues raised by distributed computing in general. We will discuss the problems that arise when systems from several vendors, incorporating a variety of environments, are integrated into a distributed network. As with data integration, we will find that enterprises require inter-operability of software components as supplied by many different vendors, and that the computer industry as a whole is working to provide this.

9
Networking and distributed computing

9.1 Introduction

The explosion in use of personal computers was followed by the desire to link these into information systems both inside and outside the enterprise. At present data is most often contained on proprietary systems in applications which have been developed over a long time and at great accumulated cost. If it is to be accessed from the desktop, many hitherto incompatible systems must be linked together and ways found to access the information stored on them.

The first step in the achievement of this objective is to define standard methods of communication between machines and standard methods for access to information sources on them. Dedicated single user systems will then no longer be the norm. Instead, users will be able to reach beyond the limits of their desktop computers to the features, functionality, data and performance contained on the network as a whole.

In this chapter we consider first the issue of providing standard communications between machines—the early definition of interoperability—and describe how IBM is providing for simple networking between its own and other vendors' systems. We move from this to a fuller definition of interoperability, that of designing products with standard interfaces so that they may work together. This leads into a discussion of distributed computing, where tasks may be divided up and distributed across a network.

There are many difficulties inherent in managing resources in the distributed environment. We will see that IBM is focusing much of its development efforts on solving the problems by providing practical products and services to manage the distributed environment, based on many years of experience in managing sophisticated mainframe systems.

The whole of the computer industry is moving to provide interoperability of software and hardware products. Most vendors are supporting this through the OSF's Distributed Computing and Distributed Management Environments. When these are implemented, they will enable integrated information systems to be developed, managed and used through compatible, if competitive, technologies.

A great deal of IBM and other vendors' product development work in the distributed environment is heavily tied to that taking place within the Open Software Foundation (OSF), of which IBM was a founding member. The current state of work within the OSF is reviewed in Appendix 1, where it is related to IBM's own products and strategy.

9.2   Communications and networks

In the 1970s, computer manufacturers developed and marketed proprietary networking products to allow communications between their own computers. As users

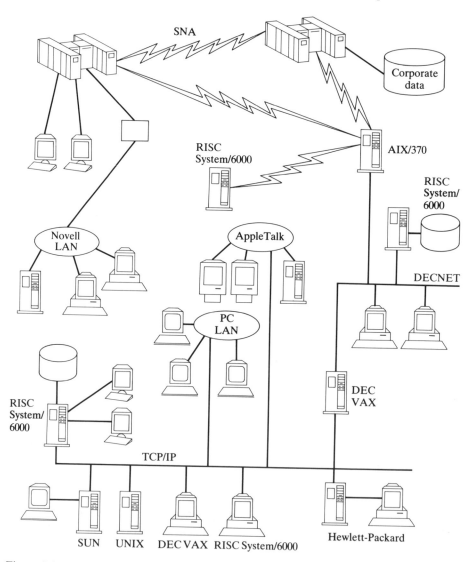

Figure 9.1. Networks in the real world.

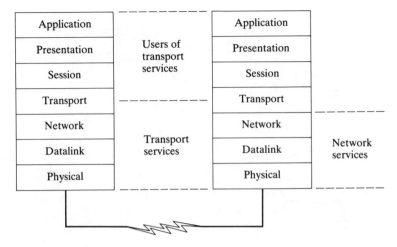

Figure 9.2. The OSI seven-layer model.

moved to multivendor purchasing, it became increasingly important that a standard communications technology was established to interconnect machines, independent of manufacturer (Fig. 9.1).

The International Standards Organization (ISO) produced a definition of such a standard in its Open Systems Interconnection (OSI) specifications (Fig. 9.2). While manufacturers and users worldwide have agreed in principle to adopt the OSI standards, in the real world there remains the problem of making connections to the networks which are already installed. Many of these are themselves *de facto* standards in very wide use (Fig. 9.3).

Among the *de facto* standards are IBM's SNA protocols, the TCP/IP protocols,

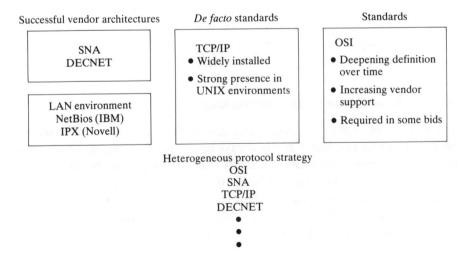

Figure 9.3. Multivendor networking.

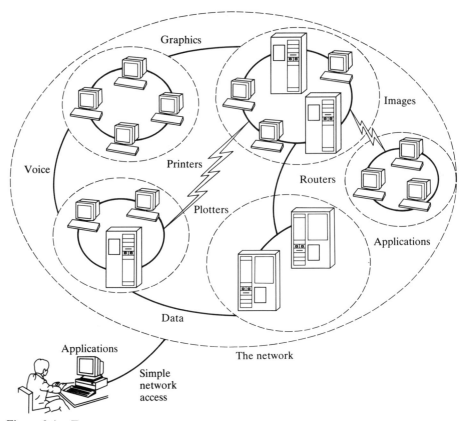

Figure 9.4.   Transparent access to resources: user view.

which are widely used in the UNIX world, and Novell's NetWare INX/IPX protocols for the linking of PCs and servers onto local area networks. There are also some widely used proprietary network technologies, such as AppleTalk from Apple and DecNet from DEC. All of these must be taken into account when integrated information systems are built. The ideal is to achieve completely transparent access to any or all of them from any point in the network (Fig. 9.4).

9.3   The evolution of open networking

The concept of 'open' networking has existed for many years, although not necessarily under that name. It has always been possible to attach other vendor devices to an exposed interface in a network if the specification of that interface was published. This was often the case with IBM products. Today the general open systems environment must support the attachment of a plethora of hardware and software devices at all layers of the network. It must also accommodate and recognize multiple network protocols and be able to manage the diversity in a comprehensive manner.

9.4   Opening up Systems Network Architecture (SNA)

Systems Network Architecture (SNA) is a set of communications products designed by IBM to allow its own disparate computer architectures to communicate with each other and with other vendors' systems.

Since the introduction of SNA in 1974, IBM has supported and encouraged an environment which would be considered 'open' according to many of today's interpretations. Source code has always been available to licensees of the SNA products, and IBM also published and made available the definitions and descriptions of the SNA Formats and Protocols (FAP).

When IBM published the SNA LU2 communications architecture and the accompanying 3270 Data Stream technology, other vendors were able to produce products compatible with the IBM 3270 family if they so wished. In the mid-1980s, IBM published LU 6.2, SNA Distribution Services (SNA/DS) and T2.1 Node architecture as strategic attachment interfaces to the SNA environment. IBM's 1986 Open Communications Architecture announcement gave examples that enabled other vendors to provide SNA-compatible hardware and software products to the marketplace, and many did so.

In 1990 IBM announced the VTAM OSI Remote Programming Interface (RPI) to support distributed applications that involve an SNA mainframe and an OSI host from any vendor. More recently, the addition of Advanced Peer-to-Peer Networking (APPN) to SAA extended the multivendor capability of the SNA End-Node architecture, further enhancing the attachment and access capability of non-IBM platforms to the SNA backbone.

SNA LU 6.2 provides a conversational communications protocol for interfacing between platforms. Since it is now available on both the SAA and AIX families, it provides an architectured structure for establishing advanced program-to-program communications (APPC). To foster its use by other vendors, IBM has published the definition of this and other SNA protocols. As a result, the OSI development effort for an OSI transaction-processing standard has accepted SNA technology, and the current OSI standard definition contains considerable similarity to SNA.

9.5   Open networking standards

IBM's 1986 announcement reaffirmed its commitment to international standards as fundamental to communications and the multivendor-distributed environment. IBM supported this commitment by announcing the availability of specifications for its implementation of the public data network standards X.21 and X.25.

As the definition of open networking evolved in the marketplace, so has IBM's support for it. Today IBM provides OSI and TCP/IP communications support across both its SAA and AIX families. It is working with many partners to provide international and *de facto* standards that will support multivendor networks,

Fiber Distributed Data Interface (FDDI) is a 100-Mbit/s optical fiber token ring system being widely adopted as a high-speed building backbone. New copper wire options make it feasible for it to be used for workstation connections to networks. High speed extension will allow the integration of voice, data and image transmission.

FDDI is defined as an international standard within ISO, and is supported across the computer industry by all major players, including IBM.

Figure 9.5.   Fiber Distributed Data Interface (FDDI).

interoperability of software and hardware on the network, and standards for the management of the multivendor-distributed environment.

The general industry support for network standards, together with IBM's own commitment to OSI, TCP/IP, SNA and the support of other vendors' networks, means that an enterprise can create the network configuration most suited for its business, secure in the knowledge that the architecture will be scalable to future needs.

IBM will continue to enhance the openness of SNA through interface extensions, provisions of new interfaces, and the submission of key interfaces and protocols to the appropriate standards bodies. It will also continue to enhance the OSI and TCP/IP products across both the SAA and AIX computing environments. It will continue to support popular LAN environments, such as Novell's NetWare and Apple's AppleTalk, and keep pace with technology evolution.

IBM, along with other vendors, will be looking to provide increasingly higher speeds to support the needs of the networks. As multimedia technologies become common, for example, they will require huge amounts of data to be transmitted quickly. Evolving standards such as FDDI (Fig. 9.5) and Frame Relay (Fig. 9.6) will need to be incorporated into network strategies.

9.6   Supporting PC networks

The *de facto* standard for local area networks of personal computers is Novell's NetWare, incorporating its proprietary IPX protocols.

In 1991, IBM and Novell announced a licensing, distribution and support agreement. This defined a relationship under which IBM would market Novell products, and the two companies would work together to enhance the

Frame Relay, also referred to as fast packet switching, is a technique which allows the fast processing of data through routers connecting networks. Emerging standards for Frame Relay are defined within the Frame Relay Forum, an organization of computer and networking equipment manufacturers and users working to speed up the acceptance and implementation of Frame Relay technology. IBM was a charter member of the Frame Relay Forum.

Specifications developed by the Forum are expected to be consistent with those being established by the Frame Relay standards committees of ANSI and the CCITT, of which IBM is a long-standing participant.

Figure 9.6.   Frame Relay.

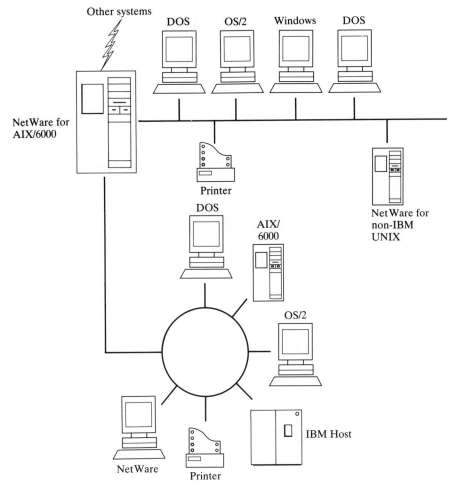

Figure 9.7.   NetWare and AIX/6000 integration.

interoperability of IBM and Novell products on networks. The object of the joint work was to improve communications in the network and to make system and network management easier. Following its agreement with Novell, IBM itself now markets and supports IPX, the LAN protocol utilized in Novell's NetWare products.

NetWare for AIX (Fig. 9.7) allows IBM's RISC System/6000 to function as a NetWare server on either Token Ring or Ethernet LANs. NetWare clients connected to the AIX system may access AIX files and printers and AIX applications. Likewise, AIX users can share files and printers with users of DOS, Windows and OS/2.

NetWare for AIX/6000 allows PC clients access to IBM hosts such as the System/390 and AS/400 through the connectivity programs available on the RISC System/6000, and across to other networks using protocols such as X.25 and OSI.

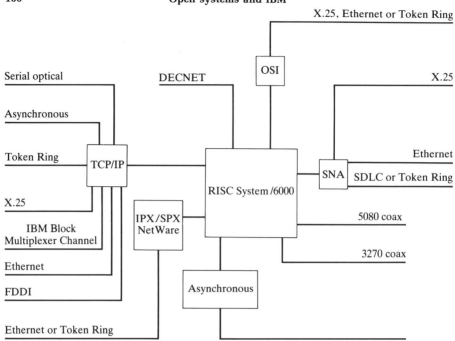

Figure 9.8.   RISC System/6000 in the network.

9.7   Cross-vendor communications

For many years IBM has been working from within the SAA product line to provide cross-vendor communication capabilities that facilitate access to enter-prise-wide information. It is now expanding these to the AIX product family (Fig. 9.8), and has implemented a consistent set of communications protocols—OSI, TCP/IP, SNA—across both the SAA and AIX platforms.

   The IBM multiprotocol network program is designed to allow the routing of SNA, TCP/IP, IPX, DECNET and AppleTalk protocols as well as the transport of SNA and NetBios traffic in a bridged or routed environment. As part of this program, IBM itself supplies routers.

9.8   IBM's base architecture for communications

IBM has defined a base architecture (Fig. 9.9) to support general communications requirements and is steadily refining it as new technologies are developed.

   There are several important aspects to note in the architecture. First, there is IBM's implicit recognition of the need to support various modes of distributed application, indicated by the presence of three types of interface: CPI-C for conversational mode, RPC for distributed function, and the emerging Message Queue Interface (MQI) for distributed messaging. CPI-C is designed to provide a consistent interface for APPC, the RPC is that of the OSF, and MQI is an evolving standard. It would be attractive to provide a single API that allows for all of these, but this has so far proved difficult to accomplish.

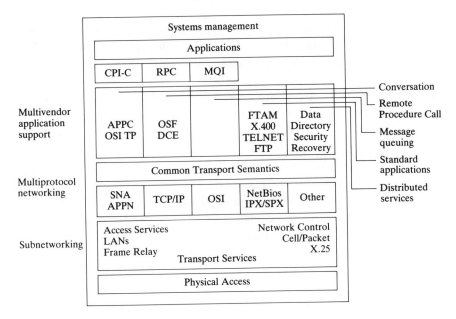

Figure 9.9.   IBM's blueprint for networking.

IBM is providing a broad set of distributed applications and services from a mix of its own, OSF and other technologies. The incorporation of IPX/SPX, for example, results from the strategic alliance with Novell, and clearly indicates IBM's intention to integrate Novell networks into the enterprise systems. It is also aiming to provide the enterprise with the management services it feels essential. The inclusion of the data recovery service is an example of this.

9.9   Advanced Peer-to-Peer Networking (APPN)

Advanced Peer-to-Peer Networking (APPN) is an IBM architecture that allows a variety of intelligent devices to simply and dynamically establish communications in a common and consistent way. It is included in both SNA and SAA Common Communications definitions, and is being extended to all major IBM platforms.

IBM has published the APPN end-node architecture, and will license the technology. This allows other vendors to design products that can participate in APPN networks if they wish. Apple, Novell, Siemens/Nixdorf and Systems Strategies are examples of vendors that intend to do so.

With the introduction of distributed multiprotocol support, IBM has continued to open up SNA. Mainframes need no longer be the core of hierarchical SNA networks; instead, mainframes, minicomputers and workstations can become network equals. In addition, with APPN users can link IBM devices with TCP/IP instead of SNA, if they so wish.

Communications flexibility has been further increased through IBM's LAN-to-

LAN Wide Area Connectivity Program, which allows communication between IBM Token Ring Networks, PC Networks and Ethernet networks which are connected by an SNA Wide Area backbone, for example, SDLC or X.25. Many IBM business partners support links to other vendor-defined networks—for example, SNA to DECNET connectivity is provided by Interlink Computer Sciences Corporation, and DECNET support for AIX by KI Research Inc.

9.10   Standard OSI profiles

Open Systems Interconnection (OSI) is a set of internationally agreed standards which define the ways in which open systems should communicate, together with the rules for implementing those standards. These standards must cover a multitude of possible applications, and there are many ways in which standards-conforming products can be implemented.

Because the OSI standards include the ability to make many choices for different application needs, it is left to groups of users to define the set of choices that fits with their own particular requirements. These functional standards, also known as standard profiles, can be specified to suppliers, who may then build products that support them.

The most important of the standard profiles are those specified by national governments as requirements for federal procurements. These Government OSI Profiles are known as 'Gosips'. There are Gosips defined by the USA, Europe and Japan, and work is in progress to reach compatibility between them—the process known as 'harmonization'.

Other important profiles are those defined by large groups of users with common needs. Prominent among these are the Manufacturing Automation Protocols (MAP) and the associated Technical and Office Protocols (TOP). Both are accepted as functional standards for the computer integrated manufacturing (CIM) industries.

Owing to strong worldwide customer support for these and other profiles, IBM must continually study, recommend and support profile definitions. It must also develop OSI products that are as much as possible consistent with the current and updated versions. It should not be expected to adopt these automatically within its product line; the particular product content and systems supported will be based upon customer requirements and on IBM's business and technical judgement.

Whereas a few years ago OSI was described as 'desirable' in major procurements, it is now more often mandatory. IBM's OSI products must therefore continue to be designed and developed so that they work with other vendors' OSI implementations, and take into account any regional differences between the USA, Europe and Asia.

SPAG/ISO:
'Interoperability is when two products collaborate to jointly offer a particular service to their respective users.'

US IEEE:
'Interoperability is the ability of two or more systems to mutually use the information that has been exchanged.'

Typical IT manager:
'Interoperability is the ability to transmit information across different proprietary systems so that it can be extracted in any part of the company.'

Typical business manager:
'Interoperability provides the tools to exploit from any point investments made in data.'

The general requirement in order to achieve interoperability by any definition:
'System components, whether hardware or software, must be designed and built to standard interface definitions so that they may "plug-and-play" together.'

Figure 9.10.   Definitions of interoperability.

9.11   Interoperability

Although the computer industry is agreed that it is moving towards the accomplishment of interoperability, there are almost as many definitions of the meaning of 'interoperability' as there are of 'open systems' (Fig. 9.10). Once again, this is because the term is used as a catch-all phrase for the solution to many different problems.

The definition of interoperability that the European Standards Promotion and Application Group (SPAG) uses in its Process to Support Interoperability (PSI) literature is based on that of ISO as used in the definitions of OSI: 'Interoperability (i.e. the capability of interworking to achieve a common task) is when two products collaborate to jointly offer a particular service to their respective users.' This matches closely with the US IEEE definition: 'the ability of two or more systems to mutually use the information that has been exchanged'.

Many different definitions of interoperability were obtained and are presented in a survey published by PA Consulting Group in 1992. Typical of these is one from an IT manager: 'The ability to transmit information across different proprietary systems so that it can be extracted in any part of the company...', while another comes from a business manager: 'Interoperability gives us the tool to exploit, at any point, our investment in data.' Both these strongly reflect the position adopted in IBM's open systems strategy and described in this book.

9.12   Distributed computing

The goal of a fully distributed computing environment is to provide users and applications with transparent access to data, resources and applications located anywhere on a heterogeneous distributed network. Users and applications should not have to worry about where a particular resource is located—linking should be

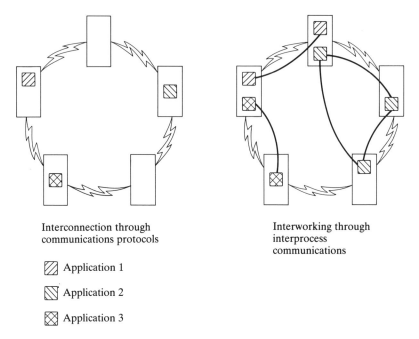

Interconnection through
communications protocols

Interworking through
interprocess
communications

[img] Application 1

[img] Application 2

[img] Application 3

Figure 9.11.   Interconnection and interworking.

done automatically. The goal can be achieved only through the use of interoperable
hardware and software products across the network.

   While networking implies interconnection, distributed computing requires interconnection and the ability to interwork (Fig. 9.11). In the first case, machines need
to be able to communicate efficiently, and send data from one to another. In the
second case, tasks are actually split up and the work shared across machines.
Distributed computing then implies that one system, the client, will request that
work be done by another, the server, with the systems jointly providing a service
to the user—the ISO definition of 'interoperability'.

   This has led to the description of distributed computing as 'client/server
computing' (Fig. 9.12). It should be noted that, while it is common to regard the
desktop machine as 'the client' since it is normally requesting the service, and the
database holder, network router, or other usually larger system as 'the server',
since it is most often providing the service, this is not required by the concept. The
requester of the service is the client, and the supplier is the server, whatever and
wherever the systems may be.

9.13   Client/server computing

The ability of users to access, share and manage distributed resources and applications is a fundamental requirement of the client/server environment. Cooperative
processing, where tasks are split up and sent to operate on one or more processors

Client/server computing: A technology which
enables transparent access to shared distributed
resources and services.

Programmable workstation clients on a LAN
transparently accessing distributed resources and
services within a workgroup and throughout the
enterprise via a server or servers.

Client/server   Client/server

Client: service requester.
Server: service provider.

Figure 9.12.   Client/server computing.

in the network, will often need to be supported across incompatible environments.
Nowhere in the enterprise is the need for open systems and interoperable technologies more urgent.

Client/server distributed computing is necessary for workgroup applications and
for efficient use of network computing resources. Implementation requires the
integration of many incompatible hardware and software technologies and will not
be easy for most enterprises to achieve. Since much of today's important corporate
data is resident on the mainframe, together with the transaction-processing
software on which many businesses rely, the client/server infrastructure must
support multiple architectures incorporating mainframes, mid-range machines and
PCs within LANs.

9.14   Problems of distributed computing

While distributed applications are hard to build, they will be even harder to
manage. Multivendor networks will require a full set of systems management tools
(Fig. 9.13). The management tools in use today for most UNIX and PC environments are a long way from the sophistication of the tools used in the mainframe
environment. These existing tools need to be extended into the distributed environment or new ones developed.

- Continuous operations
- Multi-systems support
- Systems management
- Data management
- Applications support
- Accounting
- Service agreements
- Availability
- Capability
- Integrity
- Security
- Software distribution
- Performance
- Configuration management

Figure 9.13.   System management issues.

If software is to be interoperable across many computing environments, it must clearly be defined and written in a modular way. If applications from several vendors are to work together, all must conform to agreed interface standards. To date this has been achieved only in the Apple Mac environment, where Apple rigorously controlled standards for application interoperability, and, to a lesser extent, in IBM's own SAA CUA environment.

Achieving software interoperability in general will require the adoption of internationally agreed standards for object-oriented programming. These techniques are relatively new, standards are only just emerging, and the skillsets in the programming population are scarce. The Object Management Forum (OMF—see Appendix 1) is a group of computer industry representatives working on object-oriented programming standards. IBM is a member of the OMF and participates fully in all its activities.

9.15   Middleware

Relating to the work of the OMF is the concept of 'middleware'. This term is used to describe the set of software that sits between the applications developer and the network infrastructure. It is being developed in order to deal with some of the common problems of distributed computing. Middleware provides a simple and consistent set of interfaces that can cover a range of complexity on the multiple platforms that may lie underneath.

Examples of middleware are: distributed file systems, distributed data access methods, distributed function implemented through Remote Procedure Calls (RPCs), and distributed object messaging. Over time, many standards will emerge in this area, and use of them will take away part of the onerous task of writing distributed applications.

9.16   IBM's approach to client/server networking

IBM is extending its existing hardware, software and services to incorporate client/server computing (Fig. 9.14). It regards client/server computing as a technical response to a business problem. The business problem is to provide access to resources distributed over multivendor networks in a way that is transparent to the application and easy to use. The technical response is to adopt standards and develop products and services that support the multivendor environments most commonly encountered in customer sites.

IBM has announced (November, 1992) a new business, the client/server Computing Unit, with the mission of developing products and services that will help organizations build and run distributed client/server applications.

While IBM's customers are generally very loyal and committed to IBM as a supplier, most have a mixture of IBM and non-IBM equipment and software on

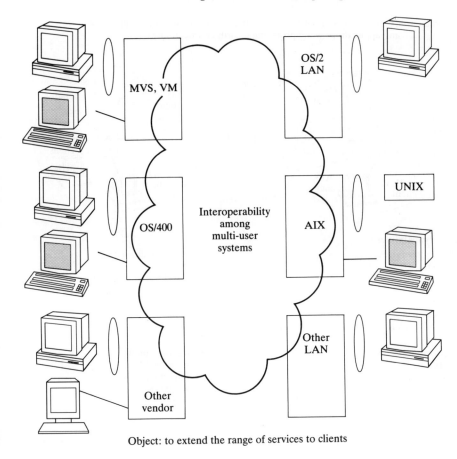

Figure 9.14. IBM's interoperability objective.

site. Responding to this, IBM is ensuring that its solutions can support both IBM and non-IBM elements by steadily incorporating the support of non-IBM technologies into its distributed client/server architecture (Fig. 9.15).

Concepts behind the strategy

IBM's stated strategy for client/server computing emphasizes the following:

- Integration of current and future technologies
- Integration of diverse and evolving standards and technologies into existing platforms
- Enhancement of base standards with additional function, ease of implementation and use, and manageability
- Facilitation of flexible placement of function throughout the network.

Requirement: To provide easy access, sharing, and management of distributed resources
and applications while providing growth and flexibility

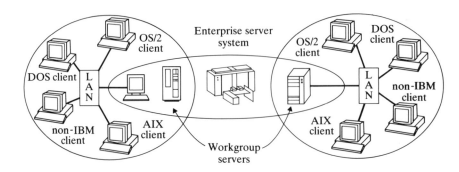

Current capabilities:

- Network services
  - FDDI
  - TCP/IP
  - SNA
  - OSI/CS
  - Token Ring
  - LANRES/VM and MVS for NetWare LANS

- Data–print services
  - DB/2
  - OS/2 DBM
  - OS/400 DBM
  - DRDA
  - TCP/IP NFS

- Systems management
  - NetView
  - LAN Network Manager
  - LAN Station Manager

- Interoperability
  - OSF/DCE
  - Directory
  - Kerberos security
  - RPC

Directions: Ensure end-to-end solutions across all configurations (SAA, AIX, other vendors)

Figure 9.15.   IBM's approach to client/server computing.

Implementation of the strategy

IBM is implementing its client/server strategy through a number of services.
Among these are:

Network services

IBM has added support for standards such as TCP/IP, OSI and FDDI to its own
SNA and Token Ring technologies. It has products and services to support these
on both SAA and AIX platforms, and will develop them further over time.

Systems management services

Networks consisting of both IBM and other vendor equipment are often best
managed from a central facility. IBM's NetView and LAN Network Manager/
Station Manager are being opened up to service both IBM and non-IBM devices
on the network from a point that may be an SAA or an AIX platform.

Data services

IBM's Distributed Relational Data Architecture (DRDA) is designed to allow dissimilar processors to share data as if it were local to the requesting processor. The ability to access from one system data which resides on another in a way which is transparent to the programmer or user is a key application requirement. Much of the DRDA architecture is based on SQL/DS, a database language pioneered by IBM and subsequently adopted by many non-IBM database vendors. As a result, IBM and non-IBM database managers can intercommunicate effectively.

Sun's Network File System (NFS) is a non-IBM flat-file implementation that is supported within TCP/IP products and therefore also supported by IBM.

Application services

Open systems implies the portability of people and skills as well as that of data and programs. Software technologies that are common across diverse systems can help to provide this. For example, making the IBM CICS interface available across MVS, VM, OS/400, OS/2, DOS, AIX and other UNIX systems allows programmers to carry their CICS knowledge and programming skills across these environments. Making CICS available on non-IBM machines, either directly or through third parties, allows a common base for client/server applications to be developed across an even wider variety of processors.

Interoperability enablers

The OSF's Distributed Computing Environment (DCE—see Appendix 1) has been accepted by the computing industry as a whole as the basis for distributed computing. The DCE includes technology for making Remote Procedure Calls (RPC), has inbuilt security features based on Massachussetts Institute of Technology's Kerberos technology, and includes directory services based on OSI's X.500. IBM will support DCE for AIX and selected elements of DCE on its SAA platforms in order to provide these common services.

Products such as IBM's CPI-CI and Cross System Product (CSP) can be used to develop client/server implementations that are common across a variety of IBM processors.

9.17   Servers

Although not a requirement of the model, in the client/server environment the desktop machine is most commonly the client requesting the service and the shared departmental or enterprise system most often the server. The functions of servers are many and varied. The most common are file servers and data managers (Fig. 9.16). Others include: systems managers, application servers, facilities servers, compute servers, electronic mail servers and communications servers.

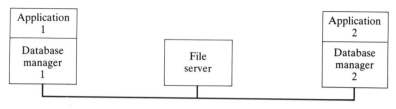

- Relevant files are shipped across network
- Network easily overloaded
- Redundant files lead to inconsistent data
- Interconnection approach

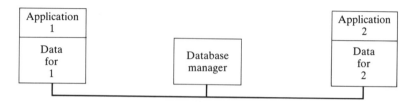

- SQL commands used by application to access data from server
- Applications all access the same database
- Data can be consistently managed and controlled
- Client/server approach

Figure 9.16.   File servers and database servers.

While the departmental server tends to provide services to a small group within a department, probably operating on a LAN, the enterprise server is likely to provide access to host data, resources, management tools and applications, as well as to provide a link between workgroups. The distinction between the departmental and the enterprise server is fading as mid-range systems such as the RISC System/6000 and AS/400 are extended to be able to support many hundreds of users.

Most of the IBM platforms commonly operate in either client or server mode (Fig. 9.17). The exceptions are the ES/9000, which is almost always a server, and the PS/2, which is most often a client.

Product	Client	Workgroup server	Enterprise server
PS/2	✓	✓	—
RS/6000	✓	✓	✓
AS/400	✓	✓	✓
ES/9000	—	✓	✓

Note: The distinction between workgroup and enterprise servers is blurring as the RS/6000 and AS/400 systems become capable of supporting hundreds of users.

Figure 9.17.   IBM clients and servers.

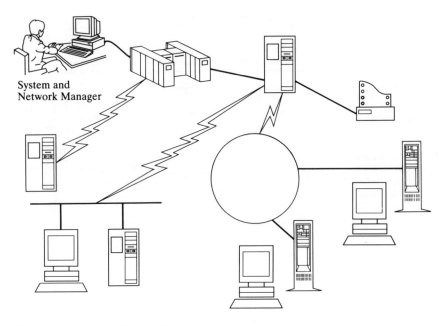

Uniform management of enterprise resources

- Networks
- Systems
- Data
- File systems
- Printers
- LANs   Directions: SystemView, OSF/DME

Figure 9.18.   Enterprise-wide system management.

9.18   Systems and network management

An integrated network of multivendor systems requires an integrated management system which covers both the network infrastructure and the hardware and software systems that are communicating on it (Fig. 9.18). There is often a requirement for management of the total resource to be done from a single point, but control may also be distributed to points on the network, and coordinated from a central point or points.

In the open systems world the management system must deal with all the normal tasks—resource management, process management, security, updates, asset management, software distribution, backups, updates and breakdowns, tuning and balancing, network management—across systems supplied by several vendors and incorporating many incompatible technologies.

9.19   IBM's open enterprise systems management

As customers incorporate standards for open systems and integrate new technologies into their networks, IBM plans to provide appropriate products and

Requirement: To provide systems management for total enterprise I/S resources

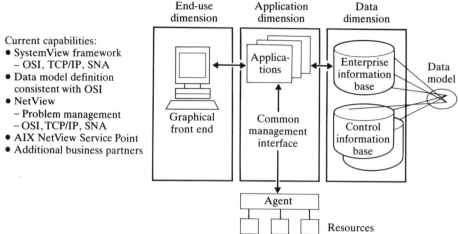

Current capabilities:
• SystemView framework
  – OSI, TCP/IP, SNA
• Data model definition
  consistent with OSI
• NetView
  – Problem management
  – OSI, TCP/IP, SNA
• AIX NetView Service Point
• Additional business partners

Directions:
• Support heterogeneous systems
• OSF/DME convergence/interoperability with SystemView
• Continue drive toward consistent user interface
• Continue SAA/AIX management convergence/interoperability

Figure 9.19.   IBM's open enterprise systems management.

services to allow customers to achieve comprehensive end-to-end management support.

The strategy is not tied exclusively to IBM products. Instead, it is based on the belief that the majority of customers' networking environments will be composed mainly of OSI, TCP/IP and SNA protocols. IBM's intention is to expand its product line continually to support these and other popular non-IBM technologies, and to provide the appropriate consultancy and support services for implementation and management. IBM states that it will support the customer's freedom to choose appropriate technologies for the circumstances. It will provide the flexibility required to create a network from diverse technologies, including those from other vendors, and the tools to manage the resulting system.

IBM's open enterprise systems management architecture (Fig. 9.19) is designed to provide its customers with the ability to collect, manage, access and integrate information among departments, locations and companies, worldwide—and to do it simply and easily. SystemView is its flagship framework for providing this, and NetView the subset of technologies for handling network management.

9.20   NetView and SystemView

IBM introduced the NetView and Open Network Management architecture for SNA in 1986. Since then it has been working with other vendors to produce comprehensive network management systems for voice and data networks. IBM's own systems management products now provide multivendor support in the areas of protocols (OSI, TCP/IP), operating systems (AIX, UNIX), and LAN management.

In 1990 IBM introduced SystemView, the framework and structure for management of all multivendor information system resources, including host, network, database, storage and business administration, as part of SAA. SystemView is based on OSI standards and developed with object-oriented techniques. It allows the management of SNA, OSI and TCP/IP networks, and incorporates NetView. Together, SystemView and open enterprise systems management architecture provide the foundation for enterprise-wide network management solutions.

NetView

NetView provides operations, problem management, change management, configuration management and performance and accounting management. Originally designed for SNA and running on the mainframe, a version of NetView has since been developed for the RISC System/6000.

The NetView approach is based on two related concepts. The first allows enterprises to manage networks from centralized points, while the second uses distributed points of control throughout the network to support both SNA and non-SNA systems and products. These points of control are used to collect network management information, forwarding it to a central site, and act as operations receiving points for commands coming from central points (Fig. 9.20).

The AIX NetView Service Point product provides for central management of AIX and UNIX devices through NetView. This product is available from IBM both for its own AIX RISC System/6000 systems, and also for other vendors' UNIX platforms. It performs the same service point function for AIX and UNIX platforms that NetView/PC provides for the DOS and OS/2 environments.

NetView incorporates a database for management which provides the basis for enhanced automation of multivendor network and system environments. Eventually, NetView will allow the management of all multivendor devices on the network from a single workstation.

Although NetView was originally conceived as a host system running on the mainframe, its subsequent implementation on AIX means that a more distributed and less host-oriented environment is now accepted by IBM. As a further indication of its more open approach, IBM uses components of Hewlett-Packard's OpenView technology, which it licensed in 1991, in AIX/NetView 6000.

The HP OpenView elements of NetView/6000 provide it with three Simple Network Management Protocol (SNMP) applications—fault, performance and configuration management. With extensions to support APPN, and the ability to manage mixed UNIX and SNA networks, management can be done from the RISC System/6000. This means that mixed SNA and UNIX networks are no longer required to be managed from the host mainframe. This is a major extension of IBM's open systems strategy.

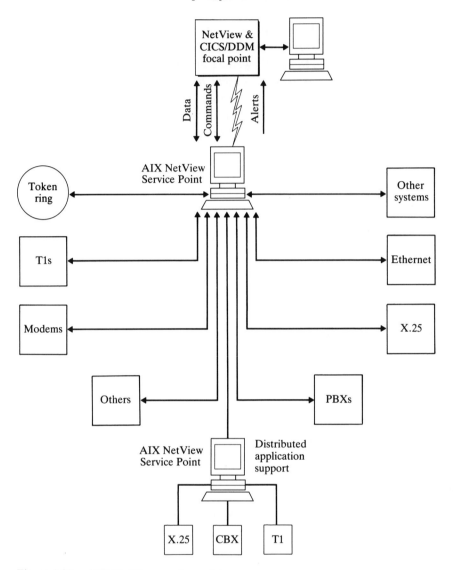

Figure 9.20.   AIX NetView service point.

Attributes of NetView

As part of the NetView product, IBM developed (Fig. 9.21):

- A specialized, user-centered, task-oriented graphical user interface (Fig. 9.22)
- Menu-driven installation and configuration tools based on the Systems Management Interface Tool (SMIT) for AIX
- On-line documentation
- Two-way comprehensive cooperative management with the mainframe NetView products.

- Graphical user interface
  - Display network nodes and devices
  - Browse through product documentation
  - Monitor critical resources
  - Display geographical, physical and logical views
- Systems Management Interface Tool (SMIT)
  - Facilities installation, configuration, device management, problem determination and storage management
  - Easy-to-use menus and help screens
  - On-line information
- Dynamic Network Discovery
  - Allows network resources to be discovered, mapped and monitored automatically
  - Flags network changes and updates maps
- Management Information Base (MIB)
  - Add standard and vendor specific MIB objects to system
  - Manage devices with vendor specific MIBs
- Cooperative management with NetView
  - Two-way interface between AIX NetView Service Point and NetView

Figure 9.21.   AIX NetView/6000.

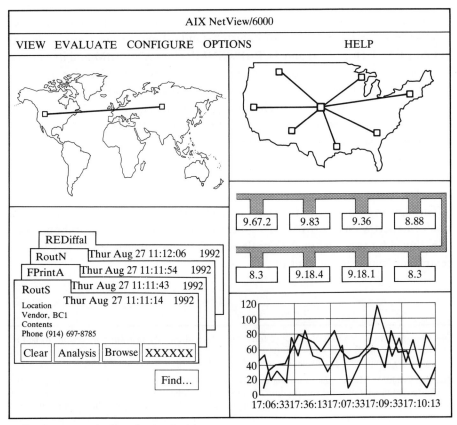

- Continuous monitoring of network status
- Alarms when pre-defined thresholds are exceeded
- Ability to set up remote diagnostics and shell

Figure 9.22.   User interface for NetView/6000. [*Source*: **IBM (USA) Ltd.**]

SystemView

SystemView is IBM's overall systems management framework for planning, coordinating and operating heterogeneous enterprise-wide information systems. It was originally part of SAA and is based on OSI and SNA standards. There are IBM proprietary additions where the standards are judged to be incomplete or do not meet IBM customers' requirements.

The SystemView framework enables the building of consistent systems management applications based on defined open architectures and standards. SystemView can manage resources across OSI, TCP/IP and SNA networks and NetView is incorporated within the SystemView framework.

According to IBM, the use of SystemView should protect customer investments in multivendor environments and provide flexibility to address new and changing business requirements. In support of this, the SystemView APIs are published, allowing other vendors to participate in its implementation, if they so wish.

9.21   Partners in network management

Using the Open Enterprise Systems Management architecture, together with open product interfaces and support of industry standard management protocols such as OSI's CMIP (Fig. 9.23) and TCP/IP's SNMP (Fig. 9.24), IBM and its partners are able to provide extensive support for management of multivendor networks.

Currently, IBM has more than 60 partners who write applications compatible with NetView and SystemView. These support the management of both voice and data networks incorporating a variety of multivendor devices.

In 1991, IBM announced an agreement with AT&T to develop a cooperative management solution for voice and data networks. The first implementation is based on the SNA Open Network Management architecture and lays the groundwork for future implementations based on OSI management standards.

Through an alliance with International Telemanagement, IBM offers the Multivendor Expert Manager (MAXM), a local management concentrator for a variety of multivendor telecommunications devices. This communicates with NetView for centralized management control.

OSI Management is a toolkit of standard functions which allow management applications to be built to observe and control other OSI-conformant systems. Some examples are: applications to manage the configuration, fault level, performance, accounting and security aspects of OSI distributed networks.

The OSI Common Management Information Protocol (CMIP) is used to transfer the information that is required for maintaining the Information Management Database. Examples of transfers include: data used to log statistics about performance, diagnose faults, reconfigure elements of the system or maintain accounts.

Figure 9.23.   Management of OSI networks.

Transmission Control Protocol/Internet Protocol (TCP/IP) was designed by the US Department of Defense around 1974, and has established itself as the *de facto* standard for UNIX networks. Although TCP/IP and OSI are incompatible, there is a clear migration path defined between them.

Simple Network Management Protocol (SNMP) is used for transferring management information around TCP/IP networks. It is the TCP/IP equivalent of OSI's CMIP.

Figure 9.24.   Management of TCP/IP networks.

9.22   SystemView and the OSF's Distributed Management Environment (DME)

IBM plans to support the OSF's Distributed Management Environment (DME —see Appendix 1) in future system management products for the AIX environment. Where appropriate, the SystemView definition will include interoperability features between AIX systems management and the SystemView standards, interfaces and protocols (Fig. 9.25). These will allow operators to extend the System-View management capabilities into AIX environments. SystemView itself will interoperate with DME systems in general.

Along with many other vendors and organizations, the OSF fully supports the object-oriented approach to software development. In particular, it believes that object-oriented techniques are essential in the design of solutions able to deal with the complexities of systems management, and it is using them in the development of its open systems technologies.

Systems management applications must provide the control necessary for

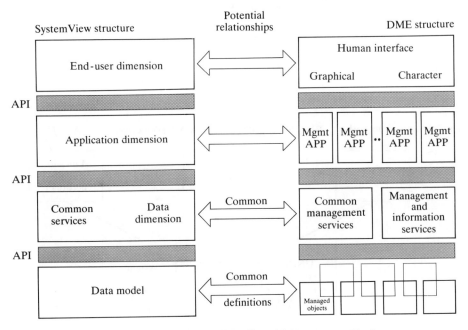

Figure 9.25.   SystemView and the OSF's Distributed Management Environment.

managing multivendor systems and must be able to be extended for future needs. They must therefore be modular in design and incorporate standard interfaces and methodologies. The OSF is working closely with the OMG on standards for object-oriented programming, as are most of its members, including IBM.

9.23   Distributed or centralized control

In considering the design of enterprise networks, corporate IT strategists and MIS departments are often caught between two seemingly opposing sets of forces. One argues for fully distributed solutions, with all systems on the network considered equals or peers. The other argues for some kind of central control (Fig. 9.26).

Supporting the cause of fully distributed computing are the inexorable forces of hardware price/performance and the enormous numbers of PCs; the increasing demands of users for faster delivery of solutions; the continuing demand for easier access to information; and the general demands of the global, distributed market-place. Against full distribution and for some sort of centralized control are: the problems of developing and managing distributed solutions; the specialized knowledge and skills needed to develop them; the lack of standard methods and technologies appropriate for full distribution; the diversity of the platforms present

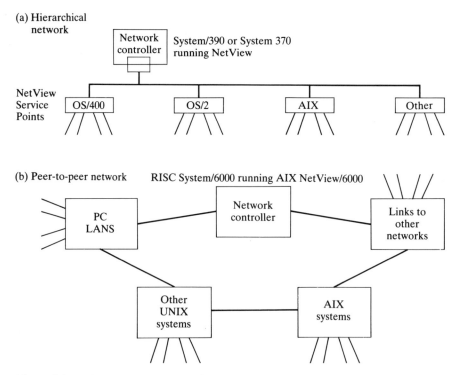

Figure 9.26.   Central and distributed network control.

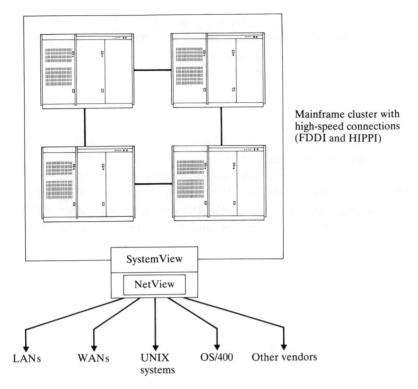

Mainframe cluster with
high-speed connections
(FDDI and HIPPI)

SystemView

NetView

LANs   WANs   UNIX   OS/400   Other vendors
                systems

Figure 9.27.   Central management from IBM.

in the networks; and the need to impose standards on the corporate data. Most user organizations opt for a combination of the two approaches.

IBM dominates in the mainframe world and has an understanding of the needs of large organizations developed through many years' experience. It is natural that it supports the cause of central control of distributed systems from the mainframe, where most of today's system management tools were developed. As a result, many of the products that it produces for management of distributed computing appear first in the IBM mainframe environment (Fig. 9.27).

Studies show that many MIS managers are in sympathy with this approach, particularly since the responsibility of efficient running of the system will probably fall on them. They are accustomed to managing in the mainframe environment and have knowledge and experience of the tools that exist to help in the tasks.

In spite of the attractions of centralized control, IBM must also support the concept of distributed management, since many users, particularly those standardizing on high-performance UNIX systems, are beginning to demand it. IBM is therefore opening up its mainframe network management products so that they may, in certain circumstances, be run on systems considered peers with other systems residing on the network. It is therefore porting many of them to the AIX environment.

When customers want distributed management, it is clearly in IBM's best interests to provide it. But since users are accustomed to a high degree of service and support from IBM, it must also be able to provide the management services and products that such users will need.

9.24   Summary

In this chapter we have reviewed IBM's strategy and products for open communications, networking, distributed computing and network and systems management. The technologies being developed within the Open Software Foundation (OSF) particularly the Distributed Computing Environment (DCE) and the Distributed Management Environment (DME), are vital components of IBM's overall strategy for distributed computing, and it is contributing some of its own technologies and resources to them.

Whereas most of its networking products originated in and for the SNA and SAA environments, IBM has extended them to support OSI, SNA and TCP/IP networks. Other popular network technologies, specifically NetWare from Novell, have been incorporated into a strategy which enables the management of extensive multivendor networks. As in other parts of its open systems strategy, IBM is working with many partners in order to meet customer requirements as quickly and efficiently as possible.

Although the word 'open' has not been used until recently, it is clear that IBM has been behaving and operating in a way which fits with the open systems movement for a very long time. It has licensed many of its technologies to other vendors, and published many of the specifications for, and interfaces to, its proprietary technologies. This has allowed other vendors to build products that are compatible and interoperable with those from IBM. While the technologies were initially developed within IBM, many of them have been submitted for incorporation into international standards, or have become *de facto* standards through market uptake. In this sense, IBM has always been an 'open systems' company.

Because it must protect the interests of both its customers and its shareholders, IBM usually moves with caution. The installed base of its proprietary technologies is huge, and any moves it makes must always bear the installed base and its associated investments in mind.

Nevertheless, we have seen that IBM is moving rapidly to address user requirements for a high degree of multivendor interconnection and interoperability. It is doing this by opening up its previously proprietary world to other vendors, and expanding its services to support their products along with its own. The incremental approach taken is a pragmatic one, and suits the needs of its major customers as much as it suits IBM.

In the next chapter, we will describe how the various parts of the open systems puzzle are being put together to provide solutions for some specific real-world problems. In the process, we will see that the drive is on for even more standards, particularly for some emerging technologies that are expected to change the face of computing dramatically. Without agreed standards, many of the problems of application seem insurmountable; with them, we will see that we can change the world.

10
Open applications

10.1   Introduction

In previous chapters we reviewed the development of open systems concepts and technologies and related these to IBM's open systems strategy and products. The requirement to integrate software and hardware components from many vendors in an infrastructure that can support distributed computing applications is a driving force for open systems. IBM's open enterprise strategy is completely in line with the needs of its users in this regard.

In this chapter we describe some emerging open systems applications, and indicate IBM's contributions to their development. We will see that, as applications widen in scope, standards interfaces for more components of the underlying systems are needed. This will continue as new technologies emerge and are integrated into the environment.

IBM's application offerings span both the SAA and AIX families. They are designed to enable an enterprise to develop a competitive edge through the efficient and innovative use of information. As the examples presented will show, IBM's emphasis is on the business needs of its customers. In order to satisfy these, it is developing innovative ways to incorporate new technologies into its open systems solutions, balancing the desire to retain competitive advantage for itself with the market demand for conformance to standards.

10.2   The open infrastructure

IBM plans to provide the ability to integrate information, applications and business processes, both within and beyond the enterprise. In order to do so, it is moving all its products towards support of an open architecture with specific functionality (Fig. 10.1). This requires the development and integration of a number of key technologies, a major task which is being undertaken with the help of many partners (Fig. 10.2).

Once having established the open systems infrastructure, IBM intends to help customers build enterprise-wide applications. It will do this first by providing a range of application development tools, in association with its partners, and second

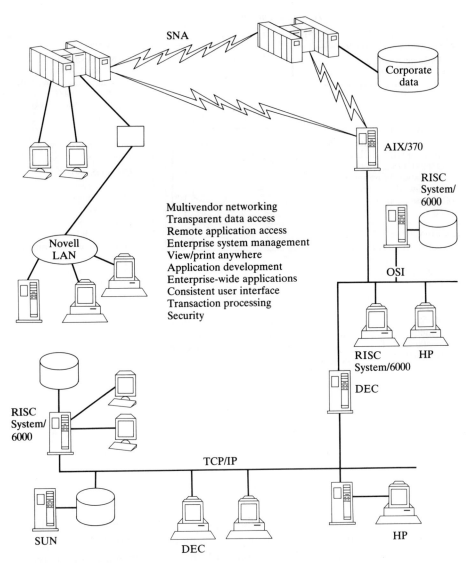

Multivendor networking
Transparent data access
Remote application access
Enterprise system management
View/print anywhere
Application development
Enterprise-wide applications
Consistent user interface
Transaction processing
Security

Figure 10.1.   IBM's open systems infrastructure.

by providing specific products and services targeted to particular application
needs.

10.3   Open application development

As part of its open applications programme, IBM provides an application development capability which is consistent across its own platforms, but allows applications to be generated for execution on a variety of other vendor platforms (Fig.
10.3). Within the programme, it provides a consistent set of compilers for the most

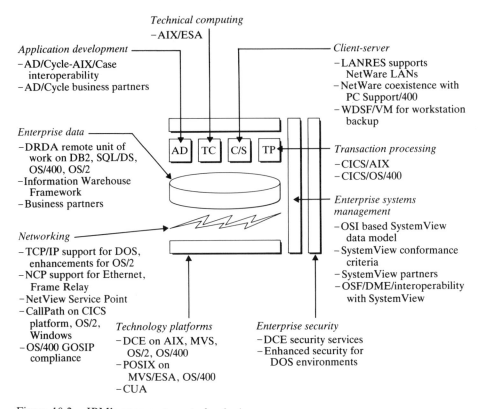

Technical computing
− AIX/ESA

Application development
− AD/Cycle-AIX/Case
  interoperability
− AD/Cycle business partners

Client-server
− LANRES supports
  NetWare LANs
− NetWare coexistence with
  PC Support/400
− WDSF/VM for workstation
  backup

Enterprise data
− DRDA remote unit of
  work on DB2, SQL/DS,
  OS/400, OS/2
− Information Warehouse
  Framework
− Business partners

Transaction processing
− CICS/AIX
− CICS/OS/400

*Enterprise systems
management*
− OSI based SystemView
  data model
− SystemView conformance
  criteria
− SystemView partners
− OSF/DME/interoperability
  with SystemView

Networking
− TCP/IP support for DOS,
  enhancements for OS/2
− NCP support for Ethernet,
  Frame Relay
− NetView Service Point
− CallPath on CICS
  platform, OS/2,
  Windows
− OS/400 GOSIP
  compliance

Technology platforms
− DCE on AIX, MVS,
  OS/2, OS/400
− POSIX on
  MVS/ESA, OS/400
− CUA

Enterprise security
− DCE security services
− Enhanced security for
  DOS environments

Figure 10.2. IBM's open systems technologies.

commonly used third-generation languages in both the SAA and AIX environments, all conformant to ANSI standards.

Under SAA, the Common Programming Interface (CPI) elements provide a consistent interface to system services for application developers. Many of these are based on open standards. Those developed by IBM are defined in published reference manuals and available through licensing arrangements.

IBM is working with worldwide standards bodies to increase the degree of commonality between SAA and AIX. It acknowledges that software developers should be able to choose the development platform and have this independent of the target platform, if they so desire. As a result, the programme takes into account that deployment may be on non-IBM machines.

AD/Cycle supports the entire development process within SAA; AIX CASE does the same for the AIX environment. Developers need a consistent CASE solution across the AIX and SAA platforms, which must provide common tools, interchange of tool data and a consistent set of platform services. AD/Cycle and AIX CASE have a high degree of commonality and interoperability, and this will increase over time.

The repository manager provides a comprehensive mechanism to manage the

Requirement: To provide for consistent application development across
platforms with execution on a variety of platforms

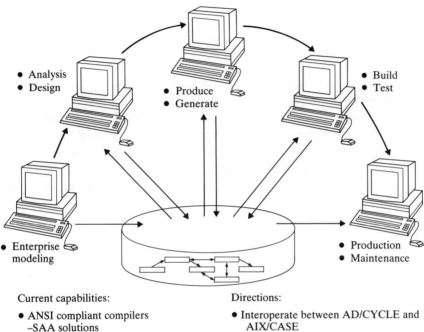

- Analysis
- Design

- Produce
- Generate

- Build
- Test

- Enterprise
  modeling

- Production
- Maintenance

Current capabilities:

- ANSI compliant compilers
  - SAA solutions
    - AD/CYCLE
    - Common programming interfaces
    - Repository manager
- AIX/CASE

Directions:

- Interoperate between AD/CYCLE and AIX/CASE
- IBM CASE solutions converged
- Raise level of AD interface

Figure 10.3. Open application development.

various entities needed in a development program, beginning with the business
model itself. It was originally developed to run on the mainframe under MVS and
to be accessible from OS/2 workstations. An equivalent to it will also be supported
for the AIX family.

As standards emerge, IBM will implement them as appropriate for itself and its
customers. For example, the CASE tools will eventually conform to the Portable
Common Tools Environment (PCTE) and the Open Repository proposed by the
European Computer Manufacturers' Association (ECMA), of which IBM is a
member. As always, there will be no blanket acceptance of the standard proposed.

IBM's own product developments and the needs of its customers often require that the standard is enhanced for practical use in the commercial environment.

10.4   International applications

Open systems implies portability and interoperability of products across system and enterprise boundaries. Multinational companies no longer confine their activities to a single country; many of them span the globe. Portability and interoperability must therefore also work across international borders.

Integration of systems and software across country borders may require cooperation between governments, since these often control their local major carriers of information and impose regulations that are specific to the territory.

The use of computers is spreading to the most remote corners of the earth. Since most of the world's population speak languages other than English, products must be designed for the international marketplace (internationalization), available in many languages (translation), and adaptable to local customs and practises (localization).

IBM's open enterprise strategy includes a full internationalization and localization programme for all of the products involved. It is based on the following requirements

- Interfaces that can be easily translated into any written language
- Functions that can be easily customized for any culture
- The ability to support multiple languages on a single system at the same time
- The support of diverse data types, including double-byte character sets.

IBM is committed to the enablement of its products for National Language Support (NLS), including multibyte support for Asian languages. It also supports Character Data Representation Architecture (CDRA) to enable data to be related to multiple keyboard types, and Unicode, the new 16-bit character standard that encodes most of the approximately 27 000 characters used in the modern world. Unicode has been under development for several years, supported by a consortium of major manufacturers including IBM, Apple and Sun Microsystems.

10.5   Open enterprise applications

Having established the open systems architecture that defines an infrastructure on which distributed applications can be built, IBM uses it to provide products and services for specific application needs. Some of the most important of these are considered here.

Open transaction management

Transaction-processing applications are at the heart of many businesses and are usually 'mission critical' in the sense that the business depends on them for its success or even its survival. The costs to the business if the applications break down can be huge. Such applications are therefore not tampered with unless there are overriding commercial reasons to do so.

Typical transaction-processing applications are found in banking (automated teller machines, for example), reservation systems, retail catalog sales and insurance claims processing.

IBM's CICS and IMS products have provided very effective transaction management solutions to IBM customers for many years, running on proprietary mainframe systems. These will continue to be developed and supported by IBM. Customers who are comfortable in that environment have no need to change for change's sake, especially if it is to move into an environment where the systems management tools are not mature.

In order to get maximum performance from the machines on which they run, many commercial transaction-processing applications in use today were written in assembler language and customized. Such applications are not easily portable to a new environment. The costs of moving them, and the risks to the business when doing so, may well negate the price advantages that seem to be available on newer, high-performance UNIX systems.

Many heavy users of transaction-processing applications today are retaining them in the mainframe environment while developing new applications on UNIX systems or for the distributed environment. Their objective is to balance the best of the proprietary and open worlds through a transitional period that is expected to last 20 years or more. In the meantime, achieving a high level of interoperability between the systems in use is the top priority.

Increasingly, there is a demand to process transactions with integrity across distributed heterogeneous systems as easily as they are processed today on single systems. IBM's CICS is the most widely used transaction-processing monitor in the information-processing industry, and there are more than 100 000 CICS programmers in the world. Companies that have made large investments in CICS skills and applications may well wish to carry these into the future. Distributed transaction processing incorporating CICS will clearly be attractive to them.

IBM's Enterprise Transaction Management

Enterprise Transaction Management (ETM) is IBM's solution to the problem of evolving today's transaction processing solutions to the open distributed computing environment of the future (Fig. 10.4).

ETM is more than an enabling technology; it is a complete business solution for all sizes of enterprises. It is built in an evolutionary manner on IBM's family of transaction-processing products to ensure that customers' investments are protected as much as possible while the benefits of new technologies are introduced. IBM aims to produce the broadest range of transaction connectivity in

Requirement: To provide OLTP access and functions across the open enterprise

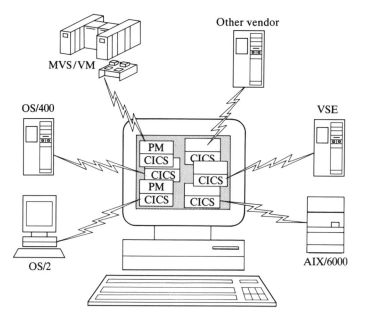

Current capabilities: Directions:

● CICS family   ● CICS for AIX, OS/400
  –CICS common API   ● CICS on other vendor platforms
  –Direct SQL standard
    database interface support
  –Resource manager interface

Figure 10.4.   IBM's enterprise transaction management.

the industry, supporting all the important network protocols including both industry and international standards (Fig. 10.5).

The demand for open transaction-processing solutions encompasses both UNIX and non-UNIX systems. IBM's UNIX (AIX and OSF/1) transaction-processing offerings will conform to the X/Open Distributed Transaction Processing (DTP) standards, which themselves will conform to the international POSIX standards. These products will include a CICS Transaction Processing Monitor (TPM) which will use the transaction-processing core services developed by Transarc Corporation for the OSF's Distributed Computing Environment (DCE).

IBM will continue to support and enhance its non-UNIX transaction-processing environments with their existing and familiar APIs, products and concepts, while

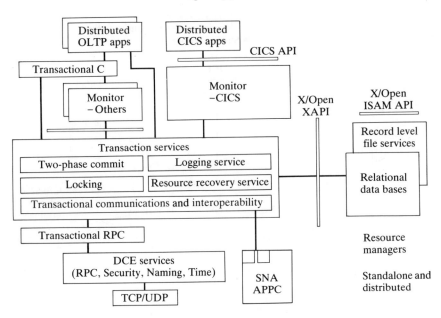

Figure 10.5. IBM's transaction processing components.

at the same time providing enhanced interoperability with both UNIX and non-UNIX systems. This will allow customers to leverage today's applications, data and skills into the new environments.

CICS will be available on an increasing number of platforms. IBM has stated its long-term commitment to the CICS Application Programming Interface (API) and Inter System Communications (ISC) facilities. This means that investments made in CICS will continue to be long-term and secure on both supplier and user sides.

IBM will make the CICS API and ISC facilities available consistently across the SAA and AIX platforms. To enable application portability and allow greater vendor interoperability, it has documented a major subset of the CICS API and the standard ISC formats and protocols. These will be common across all of the platforms on which CICS is provided. CICS then provides standard interfaces to enable other products to connect and interoperate with it.

Distributed TP applications will be able to operate over Token Ring and Ethernet local area networks, as well as wide area networks utilizing various transport protocols including SNA, OSI and TCP/IP. Transactions will be able to be routed over a variety of networks without any impact to applications (Fig. 10.6).

The three principal inter-process communications paradigms—conversation, call and message—will be supported across all environments, allowing applications to be constructed using any and all of these models as appropriate. These mechanisms will be implemented in conformance with accepted industry standards such as the Common Programming Interface for Communications (CPI-C), OSI-TP for conversations, and the OSF DCE RPC for call.

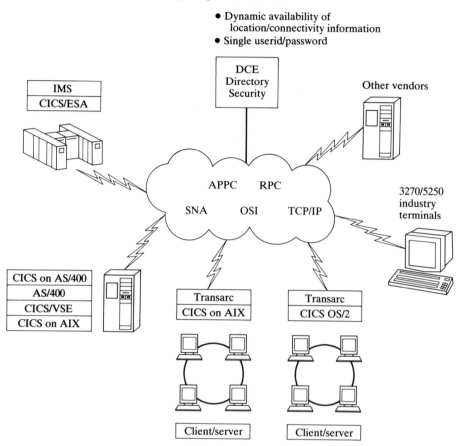

Figure 10.6.   Directions for enterprise transaction management.

IBM will also provide a CICS TPM, including the API and connectivity options, on other key vendor platforms. It plans to open up CICS itself by accepting industry participation in the definition and control of the very important CICS application interfaces and connectivity facilities.

There is no doubt that IBM intends to maintain its position as a leader in transaction-processing applications and to earn recognition as the leader in distributed transaction processing for the open enterprise. Enterprise Transaction Management is the framework through which it plans to achieve this.

10.6   Electronic information networks

An electronic market is the critical mass of network connections required in order that an entire industry or cross-industry business community may do business electronically. Participation in an electronic market can give significant competitive advantage to businesses that want to streamline business processes, strengthen

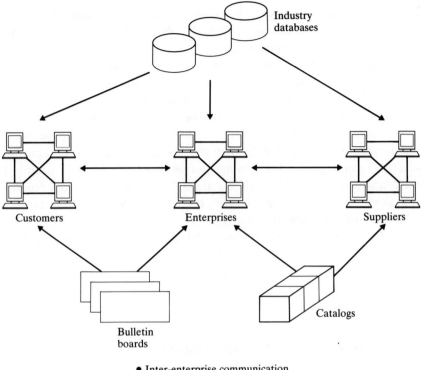

- Inter-enterprise communication
- Value-added applications
  - Interactive
  - Electronic mail
  - EDI
- Connectivity and industry standards
  - X.25
  - X.400
  - ANSI X12
  - EDIFACT

Figure 10.7.   Electronic markets.

trading relationships, improve controls and reach new markets. Electronic markets (Fig. 10.7) are emerging as some of the most exciting markets of the 1990s.

Participants in an electronic market are likely to use computer systems from a wide variety of vendor, be connected over a number of different networks using various network protocols and require access to many databases and data structures. Electronic markets cannot realistically be implemented without extensive use of internationally agreed open standards for the interfaces to their components.

10.7   Electronic Data Interchange (EDI)

Electronic Data Interchange (EDI) is the computer-to-computer exchange of information between firms engaged in transacting business—the electronic trading partners. Its implementation tends to be industry-specific, since standards for data descriptions have to be agreed across industry sectors, for example, banking, aerospace, insurance, or government agencies.

EDI applications involve communications between often incompatible systems, across many network technologies. Their successful implementation depends on the interoperability of the various technological components, and on agreement between the participants on the standards to be used for data descriptions.

IBM has a generic set of products for the implementation of EDI applications, and also targets these to particular industry sectors. Its Expedite family of products, for example, provides translation and networking facilities for electronic data interfacing across the MVS, OS/400 and OS/2 platforms. As its AIX product line continues to penetrate commercial markets, IBM can be expected to provide similar EDI products for the AIX family.

The IBM data interchange family supports data exchange between entities which use national EDI standards, such as the US ANSI X12, as well as international EDI standards, such as the UN EDIFACT and European ODETTE. EDI standards other than these are also supported, provided that they follow the ANSI X12 or UN EDIFACT syntax.

10.8   The IBM Information Network (IBM IN)

The IBM Information Network (IBM IN) is a comprehensive international value-added network which provides networking and remote computing services, electronic mail and electronic data interchange (EDI) services, interactive access to databases, and integrated industry applications. IBM IN supports international standards such as OSI, X.25 and the X.400 messaging standards and customers with 3270 terminals can access business data residing on systems that support X.25.

The IBM IN has agreements for standard electronic mail (OSI X.400) network connections with AT&T, BT Tymnet, GE Information Services, MCI Communications Corporation, Netherlands PTT, US Sprint, and Western Union Corporation. IBM IN participates in an OSI X.500 Directory Forum with other major messaging service providers to help realize the practical implementation of a global directory. This is the essential component that allows users and programs to locate and describe people, places, applications and services that participate in the distributed computing environment. The work is closely coordinated with the directory service of the OSF DCE.

Insurance industry applications of IBM IN

In the insurance industry, independent agents do business with a variety of companies in order to find the best insurance solution for their customers. To do so in the past, they were often forced to deal with an almost infinite variety of terminal and communication requirements. Direct agents having on-line access to data held at their company's home office had a distinct competitive advantage over the independent agents.

In order to overcome this, the independent agents and the insurance companies formed a consortium, the Insurance Value-Added Network Service (IVANS), a prime example of an electronic market. IBM IN provides the majority of the infrastructure used by member agents to communicate electronically with the companies they represent. Today, IVANS has approximately 12 000 independent agents, 150 insurance companies and 50 information service providers, all participating in this electronic insurance market.

The London Insurance Market (LIM), a large insurance community that includes Lloyd's of London, is using IBM IN to run its LIMNET data network. LIMNET annually handles insurance business worth many billions of dollars. LIM needed to update and improve the efficiency of its administrative processes, reducing the paperwork involved. Using IBM IN, LIMNET has tied together LIM's more than 1000 organizations, allowing swift interactive communication among brokers, underwriters and clients.

Retail applications of IBM IN

Many department stores are faced with the challenge of responding quickly to customer demand by keeping the right number of items in stock when and where they are needed.

A US department store chain has taken a leadership position by implementing company-to-company electronic mail, EDI and interactive applications to support a quick-response strategy. Bar coding on the merchandise allows retailers to track inventory at the point-of-sale and order merchandise by specific style, color and size rather than in the previously ordered mixed lots.

The retailer is using electronic mail to communicate with trading partners, electronic merchandise catalogs using Universal Product Code (UPC) data and EDI for ordering and invoicing. The use of standards together with electronic communications has helped this company resolve business transactions quickly and productively. Meanwhile it has gained a competitive advantage by being able to put goods that consumers want on its shelves while the demand is high, and has reduced the wastage from surplus inventory.

10.9   Computer Integrated Manufacturing (CIM)

Industrial enterprises have been particular advocates of the use for standards that enable interoperability of systems used within and across enterprises. This is because they have long recognized the benefits that could accrue from integration of the information and processes on which they depend—for example, in just-in-time manufacturing, the industrial equivalent of the retail example described above, or in working electronically with subcontractors. This general area is known as 'computer integrated manufacturing' (CIM).

The key industrial sector standards include:

- Computer-integrated manufacturing—open systems architecture (CIM–OSA) standards and computer-aided acquisition and logistics support (CALS) standards
- Data and process modelling standards (IDEF0 and IDEF1x)
- Initial graphics exchange specification (IGES) and the evolving product data exchange standard (PDES) using the standard for the exchange of product (STEP) model data
- Electronic data interchange (EDI) standards agreed between trading partners
- Structured query language (SQL) standards for data access
- Networking standards such as Token-Ring and Ethernet, together with protocol standards such as TCP/IP, OSI and the manufacturing automation protocol (MAP)
- Engineering programmers hierarchical interactive graphics standard (PHIGS).

Figure 10.8.   Key industrial standards.

The definition and implementation of industry standards is essential for CIM, and there are many standards that are relevant (Fig. 10.8). IBM has a strong business directed at manufacturing applications. It has long been a leader in standards activity in the industrial sector, participates actively in the standards committees and implements the standards across its enabling product set.

IBM's CIM Architecture

In 1989, IBM announced its computer integrated manufacturing (CIM) architecture, an evolving collection of open software interfaces, functions and components (Fig. 10.9). This defines the IBM strategy for integrating CIM application solutions in a consistent and open manner. It addresses the industrial customer's need for the integration of information, applications and business processes in a multivendor environment.

IBM's CIM architecture conforms to key industry standards and provides layered software with enabling services for interoperability and integration. APIs and product interfaces are openly defined and published, allowing application developers, system integrators and customers to access IBM application data for solution integration. Interface products provide bridges between IBM applications and other IBM or non-IBM applications.

Tools are provided for managing distributed data across host environments, distributed workstations and desktops, and to manage unique control devices. The solutions accommodate a variety of data types, including alphanumeric data, graphics, image, and long-string data—for example CAD drawings and process recipes. A wide variety of networks are supported, including IBM, *de facto* and industry standard LANs and WANs. In keeping with its endorsement of the OSF DCE, IBM will evolve its industrial products to utilize those elements of DCE that are appropriate for industrial applications.

10.10   Integration of voice and data

Until recently, data networks have been the norm in the information systems industry. In the future, these are likely to be replaced by integrated voice and data

Requirement: To provide the ability to integrate information, applications, and business processes, both within and beyond an industrial enterprise

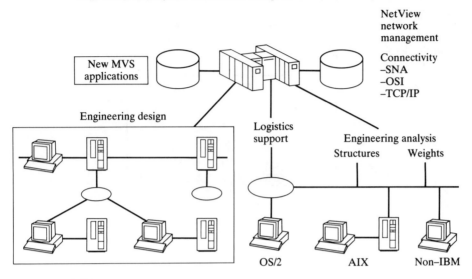

Current capabilities:

- IBM data interchange family
  –National EDI standards
  –International EDI standards

- IBM CIM architecture
  –CIM–OSA, CALS
  –IDEF0, IDEF1X
  –IGES, PDES, STEP
  –EDI
  –SQL, IRDS
  –IEEE 802.X, TCP/IP, MAP
  –PHIGS
- Published APIs

Figure 10.9.   IBM's computer integrated manufacturing architecture.

networks, with image and video being added as network performance develops to support them.

The telephone has become the input/output device of choice for convenient access to services. It is available almost everywhere, provides faster access to services than transactions by mail, and can reduce the cost of conducting business. Telemarketing is replacing face-to-face business transactions for many companies, particularly in the USA, where the relatively low cost of telecommunications services has been a key driver. There the proliferation of the 800 number services, the availability of unlimited local calls for residential subscribers, and the low cost of telephone sets have all played their parts. Similar trends for telecommunications services in other countries are being experienced, especially with the move towards deregulation of the telephone companies.

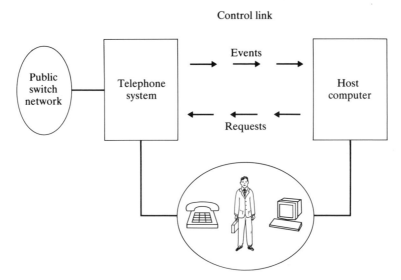

Figure 10.10.   Voice/data applications.

Increased use of the telephone to deliver a broader spectrum of services has led to the need for efficient ways of handling telephone transactions. These can provide opportunities for businesses to offer new services for expanded hours and at affordable costs.

Integrated voice and data applications

The key resources for offering a telephone service are the telephone agents, the telephone system and the information system (Fig. 10.10). The agent typically has a telephone set and a terminal and integrates the activities taking place on the telephone system with those on the computer system. For example, the agent may retrieve the computer records for the customer associated with a particular call.

Providing solutions that automatically integrate telephone and data processes can reduce the amount of time a business transaction needs and reduce the chance of error in the process. Automating some aspects through a voice-processing function can relieve agents from routine tasks, allowing them to become more specialized. Integrated solutions can provide the ability to create new services and enhance existing ones, resulting in increased revenue potential and service differentiation for competitive advantage.

Integrating voice and data

Telephone switches are not designed for general-purpose applications and it is not usually practical for users to program them. Instead, a control link from a telephone system to a computer can allow a host application to have access to the telephone functions of a switch, allowing for the creation of integrated voice–data applications.

Integrated Services Digital Network (ISDN) can deliver network information, such as the caller's ID number, to the end-user. This can be used in applications such as the 911 emergency service in the USA, which uses a link to provide network information to the host, automatically integrating an incoming call with the address at which the calling telephone is located. Voice messaging is another example of special-purpose switch-to-computer links.

Many switch vendors are implementing switch-to-computer links. These are generally bi-directional and allow requests to be passed from the host to the switch and event messages to go from the switch to the host. These links allow for application level interactions between a host application and the switch call-processing program.

An application can request telephone functions from the switch on behalf of a station—for example, it might request the switch to dial a number or transfer a call on behalf of one station to another station. The application may also ask for information from the telephone system, such as the status of a station or the length of a queue. Network information, such as automatic number identification (ANI), dialled number identification services (DNIS) and station and trunk identification from PBXs, allows applications to retrieve relevant customer records and invoke the appropriate data processes.

Standards for voice/data applications

For implementation of voice/data applications, diverse technologies must be integrated, which once again requires agreement on standard interfaces. Interest in developing standards comes from many groups, including computer vendors, switch vendors, telecommunications carriers and application providers.

There are two important standards emerging: the European computer telephony applications (ECTA) standard from ECMA and the switch to computer application interface (SCAI) standard from ANSI, together covering a broad set of call control functions. As with other standards, individual vendors are likely to develop supersets of the defined standards in order to differentiate their products by offering a superior service to their customers.

Applications of the switch-to-host control link

An application developer can use the functions of a switch-to-host control link to achieve several call control capabilities. Examples are:

- *Intelligent answering*—The application uses information about an incoming call automatically to select an appropriate screen of information to present to the service agent.
- *Intelligent dialling*—An application automatically dials, detects that someone

has answered, and passes only the successful connections to an available agent. Agents then spend their time providing service, not dialling and discarding no-answers and busy responses.

- *Personal telephony*—Users invoke phone functions from a terminal screen. Automated dialling, call logging, and integration with directories and other electronic mail services can be implemented.
- *Coordinated voice/data transfer and consultation*—An application automatically transfers database records along with a transferred call.
- *Intelligent routing*—The application uses information about a call, or about the status of service agents, to route an incoming call in a way that improves the level of service.

Open systems requirements for voice/data applications

From the application's point of view, the services of the switch-to-host control link need to meet several open systems requirements:

- *Independence of the switch link*—The application should work the same way on a wide array of switches, regardless of the differences among the protocols and transport mechanisms of the corresponding switch-to-host control links. A business with multivendor switches should not have to change its PBXs, nor develop the same application several times in order to accommodate each switch.
- *Independence of the computer systems*—A customer with multiple computer systems should be able to install the same integrated voice/data application on different computer systems without the need for redevelopment of the application.
- *Comprehensive telephony functions*—The set of telephony functions accessible to the application should be comprehensive enough to support a broad range of requirements. Applications should be able to make use of newly added functions with minimum development effort.
- *Support of standards*—As standards for the switch-to-host control link evolve, the integrated voice/data applications should require little or no change to accommodate them.

Application programming interfaces

Integrated voice/data applications should be developed using an API to access the services of telephony systems through program calls that are consistent across different computer systems. These should support a comprehensive set of telephony functions and be easily extensible. This would shield the application developer from the specifics of the underlying switch-to-host control link and would help meet the open applications requirements listed above.

Implementing such an API requires the development of two subsystems:

- Telephony subsystem, which supports the telephony program calls in the computer system, providing the application with a unified model for all telephony systems, and shields the application developer from the differences in computer systems.
- Link subsystem, which maps the unified view of the telephony systems as seen by the application to the switch-specific control link functions and protocols. Development of this subsystem requires cooperation between computer vendors and telephony system vendors.

Several computer vendors have developed telephony APIs and the corresponding subsystems to meet the above criteria. These include IBM, DEC, HP, Stratus and Wang. The IBM system is CallPath.

The IBM CallPath Services

The IBM CallPath Services architecture and product family implement a consistent telephone API (CallPath Services API) and underlying telephony and link subsystems meeting the open voice/data applications requirements. These run in the MVS/CICS, OS/400 and OS/2 environments and will be ported to AIX. IBM, its customers, and many third-party partners use this API to develop integrated voice/data applications.

10.11   Multimedia applications

Integrated systems built on open technologies bring information from around the world onto the desktop. At present, most of this information is received by users in the form of text on ASCII terminals, although graphical images are beginning to make an impact.

The amount of information available to a typical user is enormous. It is currently unfiltered, often unstructured and usually not prioritized. The availability of electronic mail, together with automatic dialling and faxing systems, means that it is easy to be swamped in a surfeit of potentially useful information that there is no time to absorb.

Studies show that people retain about 20 per cent of what they hear, 40 per cent of what they see and hear, and 75 per cent of what they see, hear and do. The conclusion is that information must be sorted, applications written that allow it to be prioritized, and technologies of imaging, touch, sound and video brought into the user interface.

In the near future, these 'multimedia' technologies will be incorporated into the 'window into information' that will be the access point onto open integrated information networks (Fig. 10.11). Multimedia will then be an important aspect of computing across a broad aspect of uses. This will include systems ranging from standalone desktop personal computers to networked workgroups, as well as

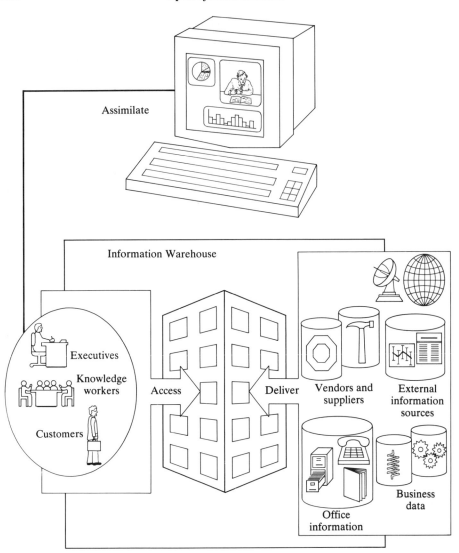

Figure 10.11.   Accessing and assimilating information.

industrial, marketing and public-access kiosk information systems. These systems will span a wide range of requirements, function and price (Fig. 10.12).

To help accelerate the delivery of these technologies to the marketplace, IBM has proposed the definition of the Standard Multimedia System (SMS). Its purpose is to create a base-level definition of function that many vendors can provide, and which software providers and customers can assume is available on any platform that meets the standard. Uptake of SMS will help multimedia developers sell in volume, and in so doing will encourage a wide variety of important new applications to emerge.

Examples

1992 Olympic Games: Used a touch screen system that provided historical and biographical information for Olympic events, linked to real-time updates on results. Over 1000 workstations in 40 venues supported journalists in 4 languages

Car dealers in Japan: The Yanase Hitouch System allows comparison shopping among 700 car models, including crash tests in full-motion video

IBM Educational Systems: More than one-third of IBM's internal education is done using multimedia systems, reducing expenses on travel and hotels. Touch-based screens give immediate access to data which can be delivered in video clips, where appropriate.

Figure 10.12.   Multimedia access to information.

The SMS standard provides an open architecture based on three important concepts:

- A powerful, functional base for multimedia hardware and software
- A set of options that enable maximum flexibility, while preserving compatibility with existing applications and enablers
- File standards, programming interfaces and data compression standards across all hardware and software platforms.

SMS spans the multiple operating environments of OS/2, MS Windows, and AIX. While several of the key technologies were originally developed by IBM—including the graphics and digital signal-processing capabilities—IBM is making these technologies available to the industry as a whole. This will help promote compatibility across applications, and will provide rapid access to new IBM technology, including future versions of these processes.

IBM's own multimedia system, the Audio Visual Connection (AVC), is designed to capture images from video and floppy-disk cameras, video disk players, video tape, scanner files or a large number of PC graphics packages. It is a combination of software and PS2 adaptor cards that seamlessly integrates images and sound with media productions and presentation capabilities. IBM has taken all the common elements of multimedia and offered them in an integrated package with authoring tools.

Because video requires huge amounts of storage—20 Mbytes per second—compression techniques are required. IBM has a strategic relationship with Intel for the development and exploitation of Intel's Digital Video Interactive (DVI) technology, including the development of add-in products for PCs to allow full-motion video to be processed on a PC.

Multimedia applications for the desktop, providing the window onto complex data sources, are expected to show phenomenal growth in the next decade. These applications must be able to interoperate with other software components and hardware devices on the network. They will be built with the object-oriented standards emerging from the Object Management Forum (OMF). International standards for the interfaces to all the multimedia components must be developed and agreed and must be integrated with other standards developments.

IBM's work with Intel, along with its development work with Apple, is designed to define and promote the multimedia technologies that are developed within the partnerships. The technologies will be licensed to other vendors, and the interfaces will be published. In this way, IBM expects to be able to define market standards for emerging technologies faster than can be achieved through the formal process.

10.12   Summary

In this chapter we have described some of the application areas in which the concepts and technologies of open systems are essential. All have the characteristic that several technologies must be integrated, and these may come from any of a number of vendors. The integration can take place efficiently only if the individual components are built to standard interfaces. This means that standard interfaces must be defined and supported by groups of vendors.

IBM has a consistent approach to all the application areas covered. It is focused on providing appropriate and high-quality, technically superior solutions; providing an upgrade path from present to future systems; helping its customers preserve investments made to date; maintaining a competitive edge over other vendors; working with other vendors to define and promote standards; and retaining a loyal customer base through an understanding of the real-world problems.

In the next chapter we will consider how an enterprise can set about implementing an open systems strategy. We have already seen that the major problems concern migration from the systems of today to the open architecture required for the future. Concentration in the chapter will therefore be on the services that IBM is building up in order to help the migration and integration process.

11
Implementing open systems

11.1 Introduction

In reviewing the evolution of enterprise systems, we saw that early centralized systems were usually sold bundled with software and services, and were supported by experts located centrally within the enterprise. As systems became distributed and hardware commoditized, vendors unbundled the hardware, software and service components. This enabled them to compete on hardware pricing and helped to identify the value-added services.

When PCs were personal systems sitting on the desks of individuals, support requirements were not perceived to be high. But when large numbers of distributed PCs began to be connected over local area networks, communicate with the mainframe and link to outside services, technical problems started to increase. Internal support resources, which previously had been centralized, have often been distributed to the machines, and are either duplicated or stretched thin in the process.

While the purchaser of open DOS and UNIX systems may not see the need to pay for support services that were previously regarded as 'free' from the hardware vendor, margins on commodity hardware no longer allow the vendor to supply them as part of the system purchase. Furthermore, as networks are made up of systems and components from many vendors, it is often not clear which vendor should supply the necessary support. The problems created by the desire to integrate systems on networks are increasing, and the burden of solving them has started to fall back to the user.

When an enterprise decides to design and manage fully integrated open information systems, the need for professional services and support can reach a critical level. The choices for the enterprise are to develop the required integration and management skills in-house, contract them from an outside supplier, or apply a judicious mixture of the two. In any case, there are likely to be substantial associated costs.

In this chapter, we discuss some of the practical issues of open systems implementation, and the basic principles to be considered by organizations preparing to make the move to an open architecture. We describe IBM's approach to open systems implementation, highlighting the nature and range of the support services that it offers. In the process, some of the problem areas are mentioned.

11.2   Preparing for the open environment

The computer industry as a whole is moving slowly but surely to open systems. In consequence, every user organization will eventually find itself moving that way too. The sooner this is recognized by users, and the appropriate procurement guidelines agreed and set, the easier the implementation will be.

There are a number of steps that should be taken when preparing for the open environment (Fig. 11.1). The most important ones concern the general problems of how to relate the business strategy to the information systems strategy, and how to manage the change process. In principle these are exactly the same issues that must be addressed when making any major changes to the internal information systems. The major issues specific to the open systems implementation strategy relate to the procurement policies that need to be adopted in operating a multi-vendor open purchasing strategy, and the details of the particular open systems technologies chosen.

At the start a detailed assessment must be made of the current information systems environment, from the central mainframes to the PCs in the user departments. This should include a description of their hardware and software capabilities and an assessment of user requirements for information and capability in the future.

The needs of the enterprise as a whole should be identified. This will include making an analysis of which departments should be integrated with which, and in what order of priority. The requirements for inter-enterprise integration must also be identified. The decisions here clearly relate to the objectives of the business as a whole.

- Assess current environment
  - Needs
  - Capabilities
- Define enterprise information systems strategy and objectives
  - Intra-enterprise
  - Inter-enterprise
- Establish guidelines and standards
  - Platforms
  - Communications
  - Data
  - User interface
  - Software products
- Develop an implementation plan

Figure 11.1.   Preparing for an open environment.

Guidelines on the components to be used in the implementation must be established and agreed, and the commitment of appropriate individuals secured. This means agreement on the nature of the platforms, the communications technologies, the user interface standards, and the data standards.

Some organizations carry the level of standardization a step further, down to the database management products to be used across the enterprise and sometimes even to the actual applications themselves. For example, a particular word processor or spreadsheet might be adopted everywhere in the enterprise. Though unpopular with those people who have developed familiarity with a product that is not chosen, standardizing at the application level can provide a very high degree of portability of people, skills, documents and other information to the enterprise.

The business plan for the enterprise, taken together with the complete assessment of resources, needs and suitable technologies can be used to provide the overall strategy for the integrated information infrastructure for the business.

11.3   Some of the problems

Although the steps described above may sound straightforward, for most enterprises they are not.

The distributed purchasing of PCs and networks which has taken place over the last decade has allowed many systems to build up without much central knowledge or control. While standards may have been set for hardware purchases, they have not usually been set for software. Many users have been able to buy whatever they wanted from within their own budgets. In the process they have built up a large reservoir of skills which few enterprises are able to track. As a result, many enterprises do not know the full extent of their information systems assets, whether in hardware, in software or in skills.

Few companies have imposed data standards, and there are now contradictions and redundancies in the total enterprise data. People resist changing the names or shorthand with which they are accustomed, and on which their own applications probably rely. Getting agreement on data standards, and ensuring that they are adhered to, can be very difficult.

The overall business strategy is not always clearly defined, and, when it is, it is often not closely tied to the information systems strategy. Too many organizations still regard their information systems as a service function and not as an active component of revenue generation. Tying the business strategy to the information systems strategy requires a model of the enterprise. Building the model and evolving it over time requires sophisticated and specialized skills of a kind which few organizations have, or want, in-house.

The technologies are changing constantly and quickly. Open systems requires the adoption and use of mainstream standards. Identifying what these are is a time-consuming job and understanding the implications of the individual vendors' enhancements is very difficult technically. There are few sources of independent advice.

This leads to the logical conclusion that most enterprises embarking on an integrated open systems strategy will need experienced and professional help as they are moved from the old environment to the new.

Whence should they seek it? The answer is from a company that has a deep understanding of both the starting position and the desired ending position. That company should have sufficient breadth of resources to handle the complexity of the implementation issues, a strong quality focus, standards-conforming products and a good reputation for support. For many organizations, particularly those which start with a large installed base of IBM systems, or have IBM mainframes at their heart, this could well be IBM itself.

11.4   An open-minded approach

Over the last several years IBM has undergone many changes in the way in which it conducts its business. It describes the outcome of these as its new, 'open-minded' approach. IBM is making a positive effort to provide customers with more creative solutions and services to meet their business requirements. This attitude is reflected throughout the organization, supported by many public statements and confirmed by major customers.

The support structure is focused on delivering integrated solutions to identified problems. In particular, the open-minded marketing and services organization is fully prepared to support enterprises in building multivendor information systems based on the principles of 'What you have is what we will support,' and 'What you need is what we will help you to get.' This is a revolutionary change for IBM.

11.5   Basic principles

IBM's open systems strategy, reflected in its products development and service offerings, is based on the pragmatic needs of commercial users. These have been identified through extensive studies of user requirements undertaken by X/Open, the User Alliance for Open Systems (UAOS), Uniforum and many others, as well as by IBM itself.

Among the most important of the guiding principles for users that have emerged from the research are (Fig. 11.2):

- Extend functionality of present systems
- Increase choice through standards-conformant products
- Facilitate integration through connectivity standards
- Make sure supplier can provide proper support services

Figure 11.2.   The basic principles.

- Plan to extend the functionality of the installed systems. Build on existing IT investments as much as possible, and add state-of-the-art function only when and where needed.
- Increase the choice for new solutions in the future by selecting products that incorporate IT standards as much as possible today.
- Facilitate an integrated structure through standards-based connectivity and interoperability options.
- Ensure that the chosen supplier can provide the required level of support and skills.

11.6   Open Systems Services

IBM's Open Systems Services have been designed to address all the issues of open systems implementation. They include: defining strategy, planning, design, implementation, operation and evaluation services (Fig. 11.3), and are offered as individual services or as integrated sets.

The creation of an information system strategy involves translating business requirements into technical directions (Fig. 11.4). The planning phase which follows leads to the proper definition of system requirements. The requirements phase is followed by the design phase, where particular technologies are applied. The solution is then implemented, tested and integrated into the information system and business environments, after which follows the operational stage.

IBM has services targeted to each and all of these phases, independent of whether the implementation involves IBM equipment or not. Among the particular services offered are the following (Fig. 11.5):

- Network custom services, which are a set of networking services including

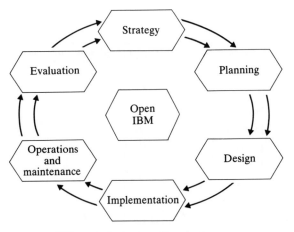

'What you have, we will support.
What you need, we will help you to get.'

Figure 11.3.   Open systems services.

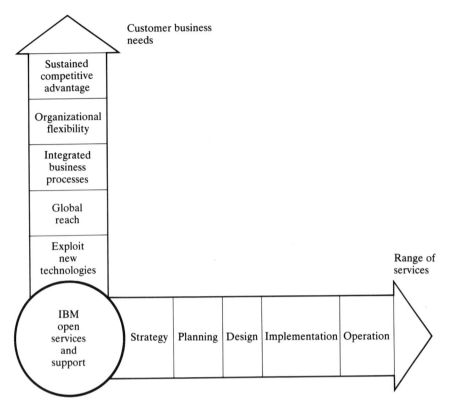

Figure 11.4.   Open services and support.

Service offerings	Strategy	Planning	Design	Implementation	Operations
Network Custom Services	✓	✓	✓	✓	✓
Professional Services	✓	✓	✓	✓	✓
Information Network Services			✓	✓	✓
Enterprise Alliance		✓	✓		
Multivendor Client Services		✓	✓	✓	
Design Assessment			✓	✓	✓
Network Solutions Lab	✓	✓	✓		
Software Excel		✓		✓	✓
End user Support					✓
Site Services	✓	✓	✓	✓	
Customer Solutions Center		✓	✓	✓	
Business Recovery	✓	✓	✓	✓	
NetView Extra		✓	✓	✓	
Multivendor Maintenance		✓			✓
Systems Operations	✓	✓	✓	✓	✓

Figure 11.5.   Open enterprise services.

consulting, planning, design, implementation and operation in support of IBM and multivendor environments.

- Professional services, which are a set of skills and resources providing services that range from general assistance on technical tasks, installing and customizing software products, managing and developing major customer applications, or acting as prime contractor in the delivery of major business applications.
- IBM Information Network (IIN) services, described in Chapter 10, based on a state-of-the-art communications network that includes electronic mail and EDI, managing the customer's network, and linking heterogeneous networks of customers and suppliers to enable the exchange of business information.
- Enterprise alliance, which provides an integrated solution for multivendor connectivity, data access and presentation.
- Multivendor client services, which provide a solution for a client wishing to integrate IBM systems or networks into an existing or new multivendor environment. The solution may include custom hardware and software integration services.
- Design assessment, in which a group of IBM technical professionals assists the client in identifying and resolving design issues in the pre-production and post-production phases of the project development cycle, and provides recommendations on tuning, capacity and availability aspects of the application in multivendor environments.
- SoftwareExcel, which is an umbrella of software services that provide support for systems management. Services include electronic connections to the IBM Support Center, software customization, upgrade planning, problem prevention, exception problem management, migration assistance, complete systems package installations and support for IBM and non-IBM software.
- Network solutions development services, which offer a testbed facility for the development and testing of network connectivity solutions, including the integration of IBM and other networks based on open protocols.
- Customer solution centers, which provide subsystems integration services for IBM mid-range customers and customizes hardware and software into a total systems package that is tested as a whole before delivery.
- Business recovery services, which offer a complete backup and recovery service for the customer's information systems environment, including recovery plan assessment and testing.
- NetView extra, which offers customers simple ways to acquire network management functions, including pre-installation planning, installation, tailoring, on-site customer training and expanded support.
- Multivendor maintenance services, which provide a single point of contact for servicing all the customer's IBM and non-IBM equipment.
- Systems operations services, which provide effective management and operation of all or part of a customer's information system operations in an IBM or multivendor environment.

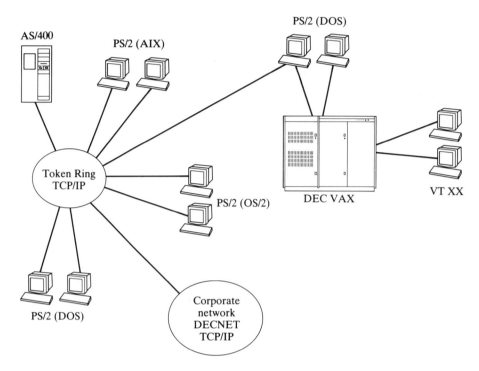

Example of customer requirements:
● Equal access for PC to AS/400 and VAX
● File access between systems
● Build backbone network
● Maintain existing investments

Figure 11.6.   The IBM Multivendor coexistence center.

● End user support, where IBM serves as the customer's end-user help desk for
  hardware and software.
● Site services, which provide connectivity, relocation, site planning and data
  center services.

11.7   Integrating multivendor systems

IBM has set up a number of centers installed with equipment from many vendors
in order to help customers solve their particular integration problems. In these, it
is often possible to duplicate the customer's environment and show a working
model of the proposed solution.

   The IBM Multivendor Coexistence Center (Fig. 11.6) has Apple, Bull, DEC,
Honeywell, HP, Sun, Unisys, Wang and other systems installed alongside the IBM
systems. Using the Center, the customer's environment is able to be simulated and
tested.

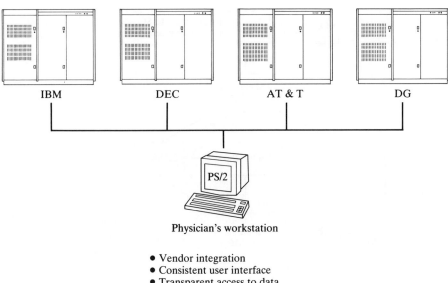

Figure 11.7. Example of multivendor integration.

Typical examples of IBM integration solutions are:

- A bank holding company that provides back office services to 300 small rural banks had a range of non-IBM mainframes, ATMs and personal computers and wanted to integrate them into one extended enterprise-wide information system backed by an IBM 3090 mainframe. To protect the investments already made as much as possible, IBM's professional services organization integrated the systems into a single SNA network, writing customized software to adapt Burroughs, Diebold, Stratus and other non-IBM hardware and software products into the backbone network.
- The Memorial Sloan-Kettering Cancer Center in New York City has become one of the most advanced health care institutions in the world for the application of information technology. Recently, it had the problem of integrating information from four mainframe vendors—IBM, DEC, AT&T and DG— and providing them in one integrated user interface on a single workstation for the physicians' use. The historic solution involved multiple display/keyboards and a clipboard in the hands of the doctor, and was time-consuming and open to transcription errors. The IBM approach was to overcome the problems of connectivity, data access and presentation with a single OS/2-based technology (Fig. 11.7). The functional working prototype was delivered in just four weeks at a fixed price agreed at the start, and the solution is now being implemented across the whole hospital.

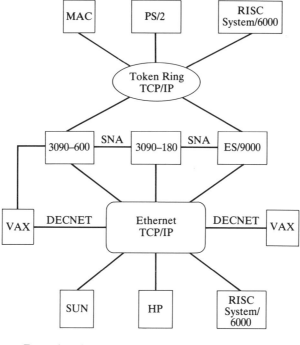

Figure 11.8. IBM Engineering/Scientific National Support Center.

11.8   The engineering/scientific support center

The IBM engineering/scientific support center (Fig. 11.8) has been in place since 1986 to help customers develop complex engineering and scientific solutions. These generally require a wide range of processing capabilities, from high-function workstations to supercomputers, and typically require a multivendor, multiproto-col environment.

Utilizing the multivendor configuration shown and an extensive complement of software from partners, the focus of the center is to provide support across multiple industries for applications and disciplines including structural analysis, fluid dynamics, computational chemistry, technical documentation and scientific vis-ualization.

11.9   Enterprise modelling

The concept of enterprise information modelling (Fig. 11.9) is critical to IBM's approach to the implementation of integrated information systems. This concept is used in AD/Cycle and AIX CASE, SystemView and NetView, and in the

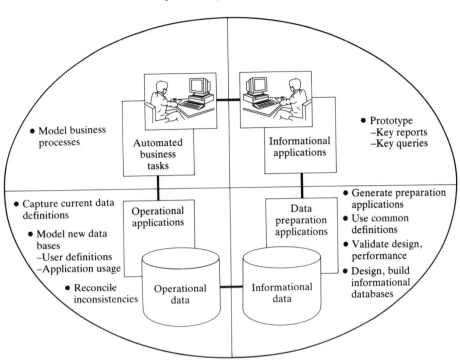

Figure 11.9. Model-driven development.

Information Warehouse. It is also used by IBM in applications such as computer integrated manufacturing (CIM).

Modelling enables the essential characteristics of an enterprise to be captured in a repository (Fig. 11.10); thereafter, this can be held within the distributed system and used for the integration of any and all enterprise-wide applications. The critical aspects of the enterprise that must be captured are:

- What the business does
- What data it needs to do it
- When and where this is required
- How the systems support the processes.

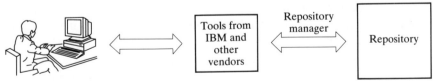

- Enterprise models
- Data definitions
- Application development methodology

Figure 11.10. The open repository.

Today's problem	IBM solution
	(AD/Cycle, AIX CASE and partners)
Business requisites—who should have what information and where?	Enterprise modelling and repository
What applications are needed to do what? How can users input to the process?	Phototyping and design tools
How can code be standardized and easily maintained?	Code generators
How can the testing process be speeded up?	Automated testing
How can data redundancy be avoided?	Repository
How to implement version and change control?	Application development platform
How to produce standard user interface across applications?	SAA/AIX development tools
How to monitor and control the development process?	Repository

Figure 11.11.   Open software development. (*Source*: Computer Technology Research Group)

Building enterprise models is a highly specialized task that requires an intimate understanding of the business, its objectives, its current systems and the technologies that might give improvements for the future. It can be done only in very close cooperation between the enterprise and a trusted service supplier.

IBM has developed tools and high-level consultancy services to help organizations build suitable models (Fig. 11.11). It is working with many partners to define open interfaces at various levels so that a wide selection of compatible products and services can be developed by other vendors in the marketplace. Since it is the basis for integrating applications across the enterprise, the model must be exhaustively tested. Any errors in it may be reflected in the applications that use it.

11.10   Open structured programming

Today, the mainframe contains the enterprise data that many critical applications use. These applications often date back a long time, and have been added to over the years. On average, 80 per cent of the work of MIS departments consists of maintaining the code within them.

Because of its history, this code tends to be unstructured, built by many people over the years, and difficult to maintain. For many organizations, a big attraction of the move to open systems is that it provides an opportunity to rewrite the code, using modern structured programming techniques and object-oriented technologies.

With modular programming, the job of the corporate programmer becomes one of 'gluing' components together rather than of coding from the raw state. Any programming that is done needs to be approached through a set of rules that requires strict adherence to standards so that the systems become easier to maintain in the future. Software development environments like AD/Cycle and AIX CASE should be used for systems development whenever possible.

11.11   Today's transaction-processing applications

Transaction processing applications are at the heart of many service businesses. They are found in banking, reservation systems, retail sales and trading. Many of them are mission-critical in the sense that the business relies heavily on them, and they must run with guaranteed minimum response times around the clock. A good example of such a system is an airline reservation system.

Most transaction-processing systems of any size today run in the IBM proprietary mainframe environments. Many of them meet the descriptions of the applications described above—they are old and built with out-dated technologies, have been added to over time by many different people, are not very well documented and are extremely difficult to maintain. The desire of many organizations is to rewrite them with new software technologies, and to run them in the environment that is most suitable for the present and future needs of the company.

11.12   Rightsizing

Choosing the 'right' environment is also known as 'rightsizing'. The organization must examine its overall information system requirements and make certain decisions about the resources it will need to support its goals into the next century (Fig. 11.12). This will be part of the enterprise modelling activity. In the process, it will make decisions about what applications will run where, and what data and other services will be held on which machines.

Sometimes this will mean that applications will be rewritten and moved off (ported from) the traditional mainframe and onto high-performance RISC UNIX systems. At other times it will mean that the software will be rewritten to conform to modern standards, but will still run in the existing mainframe environment. Which method is used will depend on the needs and resources of the business and what is right for the application and the time.

11.13   Outsourcing

Distributed applications are inherently harder to manage than those that are centrally controlled. Communication interfaces between the hardware and software have to be maintained along with the application. A multivendor network adds yet another dimension to the problem.

IBM is working actively with many partners to provide tools and services for the management of distributed systems made up of SAA, AIX, UNIX and other systems, based on standard interfaces. It has set up new initiatives to help customers design and test multivendor network configurations.

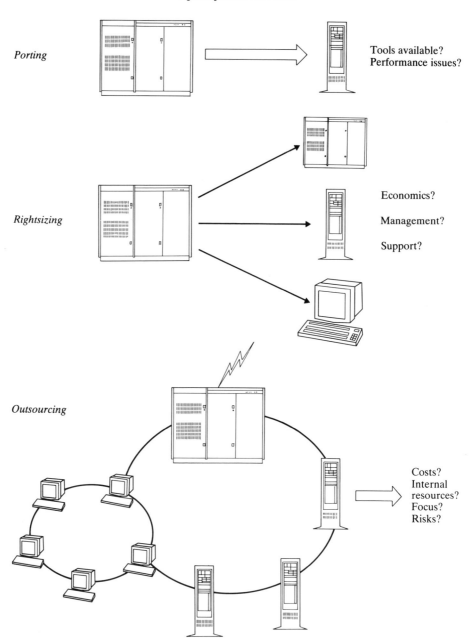

Porting

Rightsizing

Outsourcing

Tools available?
Performance issues?

Economics?

Management?

Support?

Costs?
Internal
resources?
Focus?
Risks?

Figure 11.12.   Porting, rightsizing and outsourcing.

Many organizations have recognized that specialized resource commitments are
needed to manage their distributed environments and that these are outside the
scope of activities that they wish to handle internally. They are therefore 'outsourcing' the management of the corporate network to third parties. This means that the

outside company is contracted to manage the network as if it were the owner, designing, managing and updating it as the client requires. The client can then concentrate its attention and resources on its core activities.

IBM is already a leading supplier of outsourcing services, and is actively growing this part of its business. Since many of the organizations have IBM mainframes that they wish to integrate into the distributed environment, IBM is often the logical choice.

11.14   The role of the mainframe

Open systems has sometimes been interpreted to mean the end of the mainframe. This is far from the truth. Hundreds of millions of dollars have been invested in building today's mainframe applications. While it may make sense for some organizations to move from the mainframe to a completely distributed network, most large organizations prefer a route to open systems that integrates the mainframe into the distributed computing environment. This can be facilitated if the mainframe environment becomes more 'open' through conformance to industry standard interfaces.

This is the basis of IBM's approach. It has made it easier to integrate the mainframe into a distributed environment by making MVS, its mainframe operating system, conformant to the first of the POSIX standards, and by offering AIX/ESA, a full UNIX implementation, as an alternative. IBM supplied the first of its MVS POSIX systems to the US space administration, NASA, which required POSIX conformance as a matter of policy, and the systems management characteristics of MVS for practicality.

The IT equivalent of the sportsman's adage 'Don't change a winning game' is not to throw out systems that continue to provide, a good service to the enterprise. The mainframe has proved its worth in many applications, but the new UNIX systems clearly have a price/performance advantage in many situations. Offloading some software systems from the mainframe onto these new machines will help at both ends. The ported programs will run faster and the mainframe will too. Coexistence is the name of the game.

Open systems will not mean the demise of the mainframes in the foreseeable future. Instead, the mainframe will open up through conformance to standards, and will continue to serve the enterprise in whatever capacity makes sense. Mainframe hardware technology will evolve along with the rest of the industry. Technical advantages which the mainframe currently has will be transposed to the UNIX environment and vice-versa. Working together is the way to go forward to the twenty-first century.

11.15   UNIX on the mainframe

AIX/ESA is a native implementation of IBM's AIX on the ESA architecture, unlike the previously available AIX/370, which ran under VM.

AIX/ESA allows UNIX to be used in conjunction with the capabilities of the mainframe—large and fast disks, the very high-speed ESCON data channel, dynamic control and connection, high-speed peripherals, and interfaces to commercial applications. AIX/ESA includes support for large single image processors, large real and virtual memory, large address space and IBM's supercomputing facilities. AIX users will be able to access files created by current mainframe applications.

AIX/ESA offers support for Sun's Network File System (NFS), Network Computing System (NCS), Documenter's Workbench and HP's SoftBench for AIX CASE. As with all other AIX systems, it will comply with the OSF DCE and with OSI standards.

AIX/ESA will meet the same standards and have the same commands and libraries as AIX for the RISC System/6000, although the kernels will be different, at least for a time. (AIX/ESA uses the OSF/1 Mach kernel, while AIX for the RISC System/6000 uses that of UNIX.) The high degree of compatibility between the two systems will mean that mainframe software can be developed on the RISC System/6000. AIX/ESA is targeted to technical users, large-volume file server needs and interactive campus use.

RISC System/6000 systems can be connected directly to the mainframe through the high-speed ESCON channel interface. This is much faster than either Token Ring or Ethernet connections. ESCON connections will offer RISC System/6000 computers fast access to mainframe storage and will greatly enhance the distributed computing environment. ESCON interfaces for other vendors' systems are also available.

The use of channel interfaces implies acceptance of central control, whereas distributed computing normally regards all computers as peers on the network. Thus, connecting RISC System/6000s directly, while increasing the speed of access, maintains control at the mainframe level.

Applications

There are more than 3500 applications listed as available in the 1992 IBM AIX applications software catalog. Even so, this is an underestimate of the number actually available.

Many of the products listed are databases, 4GLs and other development tools, themselves having many hundreds of applications written on them as a base. Furthermore, many applications software suppliers now take it for granted that potential purchasers will know that they have UNIX and AIX versions, and so do not bother to enter them into catalogs. With every manufacturer now supplying UNIX systems, there are few software suppliers that have not moved their application products onto UNIX platforms in general, and AIX in particular.

All the major PC suppliers now have UNIX products and many of the mainframe suppliers do too. The last companies to move have been the large suppliers of IBM mainframe management tools. Secure in the high margins they have been able to realize on their mainframe products, they have only recently realized that they must move to UNIX if they are to retain market share. The fact that they have been slow to recognize the opportunity in the UNIX market has been unfortunate, since the professional systems management tools they supply have been noticeably absent in many UNIX implementations. However, they are all moving rapidly to change this situation.

Skills

The only way to obtain the skillsets needed to deal with the UNIX and open systems environment is to take the necessary training and liaise closely with organizations that can provide up-to-date and independent information.

The skills that are most useful are 'bridging' skills—those that bridge across the currently used proprietary environment and the proposed open environment. These are best acquired from an organization that has in-depth knowledge of both sides of the bridge, rather than from one that knows only the new. Integration, migration and networking knowledge needs to be acquired along with specific UNIX knowledge.

Services

Services in the UNIX environment are available at a cost. The margins on UNIX hardware systems are too low to support the levels of service that organizations are accustomed to receiving apparently free-of-charge in the proprietary world. While users have gained in one respect through the price/performance advantages of UNIX hardware, they may not necessarily have gained when all the associated costs of ownership are taken into account.

IBM has implemented a wide range of services (Fig. 11.13) designed to help organizations implement open systems strategies by whatever definition makes most sense for a particular customer. This covers multivendor installations and ranges through the business as well as the technical issues. In particular, it offers management of change through professional services.

11.16   Using the mainframe as data server

Although database management systems from independent vendors have been available in the IBM-compatible mainframe environment for many years, IBM's DB/2 is the leading proprietary database in use on mainframes, and it is the only one whose user base is growing. As a result, many vendors of UNIX and DOS-based database management front ends are concentrating their efforts on linking to DB/2.

Cooperative client/server processing with the mainframe as server makes sense

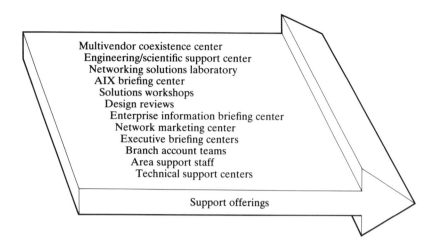

Figure 11.13. Open enterprise support.

for applications where there is a relatively small amount of database access required—for example, in decision support applications which require data to be downloaded from the mainframe and manipulated at the workstation. There are four main benefits from such an approach as well as reduced load (Fig. 11.14):

Cost

The costs of adding a client/server network are much lower than adding a mainframe with the equivalent amount of processing power. By offloading appropriate tasks from the mainframe to the client/server network, the mainframe can be freed for tasks that require its power. This can postpone the day that the mainframe needs to be upgraded or replaced.

Productivity

Productivity increases and training costs decrease when the easy-to-use graphical interface on a workstation replaces that of the 3270 interface of the mainframe database. The data is easier to comprehend, and several applications can be accessed at once with results compared in different windows.

Tools

Workstations and PCs generally have better tools and applications available than those on the mainframe. Spreadsheets and word processors are much more sophisticated, for example. Data can be presented and used in ways that are impossible today using the mainframe environment alone.

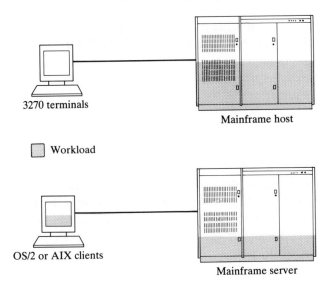

3270 terminals

Mainframe host

Workload

OS/2 or AIX clients

Mainframe server

- Reduced load on mainframe
- Lower costs
- Improved productivity
- Better tools
- Higher performance

Figure 11.14.   The mainframe as data server.

Performance

Local processing can improve system responsiveness for many applications. Some applications currently running on the mainframe do not need its massive power. Other applications do not need frequent access to the database. Putting the applications on the workstation front-end can provide faster response times for the users.

In spite of the advantages, there can be problems using the mainframe as a data server in a client/server environment. For example, although there is an industry standard for structured query language (SQL), no two vendors implement it in quite the same way. This complicates the communications between software on the workstations and the mainframe database. The same applies to application development languages. Although there are some agreed international standards, they are not yet well enough defined or used. In consequence, the level of interoperability that the user and application requires does not come automatically, and some customized work is usually required for implementation.

IBM developed the technology on which the SQL standards are now based. It has developed technologies for distributed database management and made these available to other vendors. IBM owns the DB/2 database on the mainframe. IBM has a full set of services designed to help customers implement client/server multivendor-distributed systems. It has developed the Information Warehouse Framework for integrating enterprise information. Clearly, it has the tools and skills needed to help enterprises implement client/server applications that use the mainframe as data server.

11.17   Centralized management of data

The primary danger of distributed systems is that data in different parts of the organization becomes inconsistent. Keeping a master set in a central location, probably on the mainframe today, and accessing it from workstations solves this problem. The in-house MIS specialists must then control access to the corporate data, and require that standard security and integrity features be included in applications that access it.

No two organizations are alike in their data management needs, and some will reject the centralized approach to data control. Even when this is the case, policies for controlling the access, security and integrity of the data must be imposed on the network.

11.18   UNIX for the corporate user

In spite of the rapid growth of the installed UNIX base, discussion continues on the relative strengths and weaknesses of UNIX in the corporate environment (Fig. 11.15). According to the results of a survey of corporate users reported in *IBM System User* (February 1992), the most commonly expressed concerns that MIS departments have concerning the use of UNIX in the enterprise are:

- *Management*—How good is the service and support for UNIX systems? What

---

Advantages
- Hardware price/performance is better
- Cost of ownership is usually lower
- Cost of software licenses is usually lower
- Openness offers some portability of applications
- There is a fast-growing software library available
- Some limited hardware vendor independence exists
- Long-term and strategic advantages

Disadvantages
- Poor system management tools—for example, automated operations, monitoring, performance and capacity management
- Relatively immature network management
- Not yet fully supported by IBM's SystemView and AD/Cycle
- Less effective for transaction processing
- Still lacking in commercial software, especially at the high end
- Can be difficult to get disaster recovery support
- Many standards are still evolving
- Migration costs are high and support resources scarce

Figure 11.15.   UNIX pros and cons: the corporate user.

about the reliability, availability and serviceability (RAS) factors? Are they as good as in the proprietary environments?

- *Transaction processing*—Is transaction processing possible on UNIX? If so, what are the problems of managing and developing TP applications in that environment? How can applications be migrated from other environments? Is IBM's CICS available on UNIX systems? If not, will it be? When?
- *Applications*—Can applications be ported to the UNIX environment or must they be rewritten? What tools are available to help in the process?
- *Skills*—How easy is it to acquire the skills required for the UNIX environment? Where do we get them from?
- *Management of Change*—What issues must we deal with when changing over from another environment? How do we manage the change process?
- *Services*—Who is going to help us?

Each of these issues is addressed below:

Management of UNIX systems

With the high margins that were once built into systems pricing, vendors were able to offer a great deal of bundled service and support. In the highly competitive UNIX and open systems market, hardware is becoming a commodity and must be priced accordingly. Margins on hardware are too low to support the level of services that most users need. As a result, users now find that they must either do more for themselves or buy services from a supplier that they trust to do the job properly for, or with, them.

Until the management tools—operational, debugging, performance tuning, distribution, asset managers—that have evolved to a high degree of sophistication over many years on the mainframe have their equivalent in the UNIX environment, the support burden on UNIX systems will remain high. Users must either carry this themselves or else subcontract it out.

UNIX systems apparently have much better price/performance ratios than proprietary systems. Although it is true that technology has improved the basic ratio, there have been few studies made of the true costs when lifetime costs of software, service and support are taken into account. Because they are no longer paying the vendor directly for these, the real costs are not always being seen by the users. Service and support requirements have not been removed by moving to the new environment; in fact, they may have increased. Employees distributed within the organization may have assumed the support burden, carrying hidden costs by decreasing their productivity in the process.

Transaction processing and UNIX

Although some relatively small TP applications have been moved onto high-performance RISC machines, UNIX as supplied on most systems is not yet considered to have the facilities required for the support of large mission-critical applications. This is changing slowly as the robustness needed by these applications is added to the UNIX environment. Many of the enhancements which IBM has made to UNIX in its AIX products are in support of commercial customers' requirements, and AIX/ESA is an example of a commercially acceptable TP UNIX environment, available for the mainframe.

Migrating CICS applications to UNIX

Transaction processing applications have been built predominantly with IBM's customer information control system (CICS), a family of products specifically designed for such applications. CICS is installed in 99 of IBM's top 100 accounts, and in 490 of its top 550 accounts. Worldwide, there are about 22 000 CICS installations and 3 million application programs, most of which are written in Cobol.

In order to migrate large TP applications to high-performance UNIX machines, many technical issues need to be addressed.The applications are usually large and critical to the establishment, and so the migration path must be carefully prepared. The UNIX development environment is on the whole powerful and flexible, but certain tools which are common in the mainframe environment are not available on all UNIX systems. UNIX text editors, for example, do not have the functionality of most mainframe editors, and UNIX systems do not often have the sophisticated system management tools that mainframe users expect.

IBM supplies virtually the full CICS environment under OS/2, and a subset under DOS. It offers a full implementation for AIX on the RISC System/6000, and has licensed this to other UNIX vendors. For distributed TP applications, IBM will supply the transaction toolkit provided by Transarc to the OSF as part of DCE (Appendix 1).

A company wishing to rewrite mainframe applications to new software development standards and either run them on the mainframe in the present environment or migrate them to a RISC UNIX environment would be well advised to consult IBM through one of its service offerings. No other company has greater experience of transaction processing applications, nor the support services already set up to aid in the transition.

11.19   Distributed systems and distributed support

When personal computers first appeared on the desktop, they required little in the way of professional support. Users were able to source the packaged software that they wanted, read the manual or take a basic training course, and load and run the applications. When customization was required, they either learned to do it for themselves or put the job in the queue at the central facility.

As loads built up and waiting times stretched out to months and even years,

• Security	• Cost control	• Software distribution
• Backup	• Asset management	• Updates
• Disaster recovery	• Supplies	• Integration
• Help desk	• Performance	• Storage management
• Integrity	• Training	

Figure 11.16.   Services and skills.

departments started to build up their own development, maintenance and support staff. This not only meant that costs and skills were duplicated several times across the organization, it also meant that many people were being distracted from their primary jobs.

The problems intensified when the PCs began to be connected over local area networks, to the departmental minis, to the mainframe and to external systems. Issues such as security, backup policies, disaster recovery, help desks, data integrity, systems management, supplies, performance, software updates and so on, all began to grow in importance (Fig. 11.16). Whereas the MIS department was full of people trained to handle these, the individual departments generally were not.

The need for more in-depth, and expensive, expertise grows with the complexity of the networks. The support costs of each individual department are probably less than the costs of a central support group, but it is no longer clear whether that can be said for the sum of the costs of all the separate groups (Fig. 11.17). Furthermore, it is essential to handle some of the issues, for example security and network management, centrally on behalf of all the components attached to the network.

Some local area networks today remain under departmental control, but most do not. Planning, setting of standards, overall design, software development, security and overall management are returning to central control, with only some routine operations remaining in the department. The wide area networks and external connections, such as those required for EDI applications, were not distributed. They have always been acknowledged to require highly specialized designers and operators.

The swing away from centralized control to distributed and back again has followed the evolution of the systems themselves. Most organizations recognize that they must find ways of balancing the freedom of the users with the needs of the enterprise as a whole.

As recognition grows of the importance of distributed networks and the data they contain, issues such as integrity, reliability, availability and security become a high-level concern. The vital corporate information must be protected in the best possible way. At the same time, it is a characteristic of the 1990s that more and more companies are returning to their core businesses. The overall trend is away from anything that detracts from the mainstream activity of the individual, department, division or company.

The result is that the function of looking after the information network is

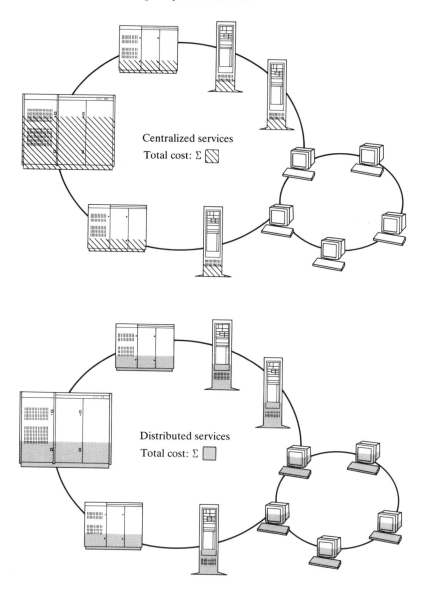

Question: Which is greater, Σ ⬜ or Σ ⬜ ?

Figure 11.17.   Centralized and distributed services.

increasingly outsourced—by the department to the central organization and by the
enterprise to an external company. This may appear expensive, but at least the
enterprise has the comfort of knowing exactly what the costs are, and is relieved
of the burden of managing the systems people, since these are usually transferred
to the outsourcing company as part of the management contract.

11.20   Resource implications

The major accumulated investment in enterprise information systems lies in the customized applications software that has been built up over the years, and in the know-how of the people who develop, maintain and use it. When making the move to open systems, preserving as much of the software investment as possible is a high priority. So also should be preserving the know-how of the people. The move to open systems can make obsolete knowledge that has taken many years to build up, and this can create problems for the people involved.

In the open world, the skills required may be different from those needed previously. For example, when software components are interoperable, the relevant components for a particular solution need to be identified and linked together, possibly with a customized software layer on top. This contrasts with the previous situation, when most software was built from scratch, with teams of programmers required for the task. This may imply reductions in staff, and retraining of those remaining.

In the new world of integrated information systems, it will be important for MIS managers to understand the priorities of the business and help to design information systems based on them. This may mean that the MIS Manager is trained in business rather than technology. Many enterprises have already recognized this, and have reorganized responsibilities accordingly.

While some organizations find that they can move virtually overnight to a new open systems strategy, most companies of any size find themselves embarking on a 5-, 10- or even 25-year plan to do so. The timing depends on the analysis of the advantages, tempered by a calculation of the costs. When and how to make the move will always depend on the starting position, and there are no hard and fast rules that can be applied.

11.21   Summary

In this chapter, we have considered the service and support requirements for implementing open systems. We have seen that these range from the highest levels of management consulting to the nuts and bolts of software development and support. As the systems become more complicated, each level of the implementation plan must be carefully integrated with the others.

IBM's consultancy and support services closely follow the identified needs in the user base. They are based on in-depth analyses of user problems and requirements. At the heart of the methodology is the information model, on which the IBM frameworks—AD/Cycle and AIX/CASE, SystemView and NetView, Information Warehouse—are based.

As with IBM's product strategy, the service offerings are designed to support multivendor environments, and enable other suppliers to work in close cooperation with IBM.

Although the cost savings in moving to an open systems strategy can appear at first sight to be considerable, there are many hidden costs to be considered. These relate to the costs of retraining and redistributing people and to general costs associated with the change process. IBM has professional services that can help to identify and minimize these. Many organizations are deciding to outsource the management of the corporate network in order to concentrate on their core businesses. IBM is a key player in this area, and its outsourcing business is growing fast.

In the final chapter we will finish with a brief summary and draw some conclusions. These will relate particularly to IBM and its present and future position in the open systems marketplace.

12
Summary and conclusions

12.1   Introduction

This book has been presented from the practical viewpoint of potential open systems users interested in understanding IBM's position in the open systems market. It has tried to give a fair representation of the major issues which users today must face. The mainstream activities of the computer industry as a whole have been related to user problems, and the particular approach taken by IBM has been described wherever possible. This final chapter summarizes the material presented, and draws some conclusions.

12.2   Open systems summarized

Open systems is that concept of computing that is based on and responsive to the growing requirements of enterprises for integrated information systems. It is the information systems infrastructure that allows integrated systems to be implemented across a multivendor and multinational environment.

Today, when new systems below the mainframe level are purchased, proprietary operating systems are being rejected in favor of standard environments implemented with the UNIX, DOS/Windows or OS/2 operating systems. The only exception to this trend is demonstrated by the phenomenal uptake of IBM's AS/400 systems, which are in any case closely integrated into IBM's overall strategy for the open enterprise.

Economics dictate that many of the systems in use today, particularly those at the high end that are running customized transaction processing applications, cannot be replaced for many years. The integration strategy of computer vendors must therefore allow for the new open technologies as well as the proprietary systems in use in critical applications. The Open Software Foundation (OSF) has taken a leadership position in its approach to the integration problem through its Distributed Computing Environment (DCE) and associated Distributed Management Environment (DME). The DCE and DME will be adopted by most of the world's hardware and software vendors.

Opening up systems architectures allows discrete islands of computing to be

235

Open systems requirements must provide the ability to:

- Interface between systems from multiple vendors
- Share and access information from multiple sources
- Share and access system resources, such as applications and print capabilities
- Protect investments in application development.

Open systems must provide portability across the enterprise, including the capability to:

- Develop and deploy new applications across heterogeneous system platforms
- Utilize consistent skills across disparate systems
- Minimize training requirements as users move to new applications and system environments.

Figure 12.1. Open systems summary.

integrated into an enterprise-wide information infrastructure that allows systems to interoperate (Fig. 12.1). By facilitating portability and interoperability both within and among enterprises, an open system protects users' present and future investments.

The open systems movement is driven by the urgent need in the user base for information systems that will support the enterprise into the twenty-first century. A strong desire to use information more efficiently within and across businesses requires the integration of multivendor hardware and software. This in turn requires the specification of standard interfaces for the components, and their adherence in products from many vendors.

Standards can be set only by companies working cooperatively to define them, followed by agreement of the vendors to conform to them. This applies to today's technologies and to those that will emerge in the future. In open systems, we are seeing the beginning of the end of the use of proprietary technologies in the computer industry, and with it the end of the associated proprietary thinking.

12.3   Open systems into the twenty-first century

The increasing availability of personal computers and workstations, departmental minis and the mainframe, linked on high-performance networks, is dramatically changing the way information is accessed, assimilated, processed and used. Many people no longer work as individuals. Instead workgroups form and re-form as people work together, often electronically, to perform and manage those tasks appropriate to the group. Organizations become flatter and more open in nature as a level of management previously needed to control and disseminate information disappears.

New technologies will be embedded in the workstation in order to make information more easily accessible to the user. These include the multimedia technologies of voice, touch and video, as well as new input devices based on handwriting recognition and voice. A higher level of interaction with the computer will develop from virtual reality technologies.

New methods for describing and assimilating information will evolve, requiring the cooperative input of researchers in psychology and human perception. New

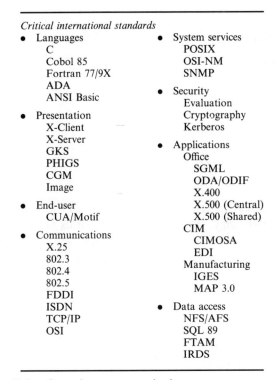

Critical international standards

- Languages
  - C
  - Cobol 85
  - Fortran 77/9X
  - ADA
  - ANSI Basic
- Presentation
  - X-Client
  - X-Server
  - GKS
  - PHIGS
  - CGM
  - Image
- End-user
  - CUA/Motif
- Communications
  - X.25
  - 802.3
  - 802.4
  - 802.5
  - FDDI
  - ISDN
  - TCP/IP
  - OSI

- System services
  - POSIX
  - OSI-NM
  - SNMP
- Security
  - Evaluation
  - Cryptography
  - Kerberos
- Applications
  - Office
    - SGML
    - ODA/ODIF
    - X.400
    - X.500 (Central)
    - X.500 (Shared)
  - CIM
    - CIMOSA
    - EDI
  - Manufacturing
    - IGES
    - MAP 3.0
- Data access
  - NFS/AFS
  - SQL 89
  - FTAM
  - IRDS

Figure 12.2. Commitment to standards.

devices will emerge for the desktop, office, home and in transit. Cellular communication will allow identified access to the network from anywhere in the world.

Before these systems can become a reality, the infrastructure issues must be addressed. Early definition of, and adherence to, standards for interfaces to the components is required, and cooperative methods for addressing these areas more efficiently must continue to be developed.

Full interoperability of present and future hardware and software components of global networked systems is the ultimate goal, closely followed by innovative applications which can take advantage of the underlying technology for the full benefit of the users.

12.4   IBM's open systems strategy summarized

To provide customers with the ability to implement an information infrastructure that supports the open enterprise through:

- Commitment to standards (Fig. 12.2)
- Superior technology and innovation, interoperability architectures, frameworks and infrastructure products (Figs 12.3 and 12.4)
- Extensive services and support (Fig. 12.5).

(IBM, 1992)

- Open networking
- Enterprise data: database
- Enterprise data: file
- Enterprise data: print
- Enterprise security
- Client/server computing
- Enterprise system management
- Consistent graphical user interface
- Transaction processing
- Enterprise application development
- Enterprise application solutions

Figure 12.3.   Infrastructure products.

IBM qualifies as a leading open systems company under most of the definitions of open systems that are accepted today. It has licensed many of its technologies to and from other companies; it has published interfaces to many of its own proprietary technologies, enabling other vendors to produce compatible products; it dedicates huge resources to standards-setting activities and makes many of its own technologies available to the standards bodies. Its products are increasingly designed to work together with products from other vendors, both those based on UNIX and those that are proprietary to the vendor.

IBM is the world's largest systems integrator. It is now expanding its services to include all those which implementation of an open systems strategy requires. Management of the change process is always difficult, and organizations will undoubtedly need and seek the kind of help that IBM offers.

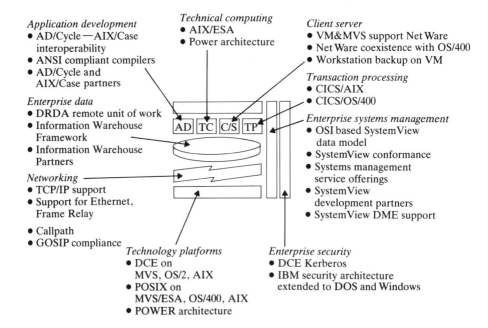

Figure 12.4.   Open system products.

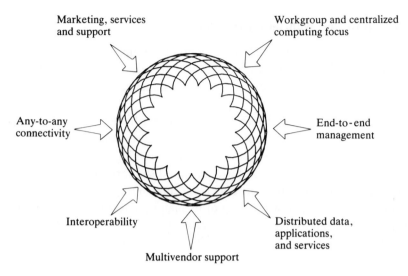

Figure 12.5. Enterprise integration.

IBM's roadmap to open systems (Fig. 12.6) is based on its vision of becoming the market's 'open vendor of choice'. There is no doubt that, with the strategy it now has in place, it has the potential to achieve that vision. But there are some challenges to overcome on the way, not the least of which requires educating the market, internally and externally, on what it is doing and why.

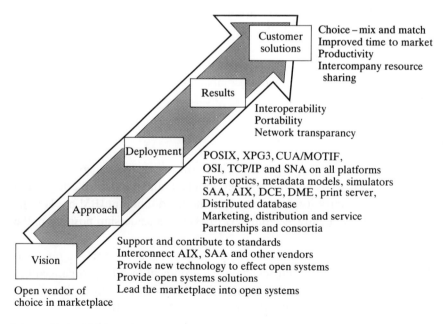

Figure 12.6. IBM roadmap to open systems.

12.5   Into the twenty-first century

For the foreseeable future, IBM must continue to support both its SAA and AIX product lines while continually increasing interoperability between them. While it does so, the two product lines will often be in direct competition. This will tend to confuse the market.

Support of the SAA and AIX families places a huge burden on the company. Not only must it continue parallel research and development work, but it must also spend on parallel promotional, educational and training activities. It must continue to maintain its high reputation for quality and support, even when competing in a marketplace that may not yet value them enough to pay a premium for them. It must learn to cooperate with many of its major competitors and yet continue to compete with them as aggressively as possible.

IBM is not alone in having to deal with problems created by the market's move to open systems. Almost all other vendors are in similar positions, if not on the same scale. Some vendors will survive the challenges; others will not, and further consolidation can be expected as a result. Open systems will not be firmly established in practise until well into the twenty-first century—it will take large enterprises many years to implement the necessary changes, both technical and organizational.

The focus for new technologies into the twenty-first century will be on making the access to information easier for more people. This means using new technologies—incorporating sound, voice, video, touch, pen input, handwriting recognition—on the desktop, in public-access points, within portable devices and in the home, in ways that today can be only guessed at. What is certain is that the software will be object-oriented, the platforms and networks will be very high-performance, and the infrastructure required to support the information flow will be extremely complex. The partnerships that IBM is developing, particularly that with Apple, can be expected to put both companies at the forefront of the application of these new technologies.

12.6   Conclusion

After examining the evidence presented in IBM's open systems strategy, investigating its current and planned product development and service offerings, and analysing its new organizational structure, no one can doubt that IBM has laid the foundations that should allow it ultimately to assume a leadership position in the open systems market.

Will it do so without some setbacks along the way? Probably not. A strategy so complex, implemented in a rapidly changing environment by a huge organization, is unlikely to be carried out to perfection. But the evidence shows that if any company can come close to doing this it is most likely to be IBM.

12.7   The last word: British Airways sums it up

British Airways (BA) Pensions Fund Trustees Limited is run as two divisions. The first is principally in charge of administration of pension benefits and looks after 120 000 lives. Some 30 000 pensioners are dependent on the company for their income; this represents a payroll of almost $200 million a year. On average, staff write to and see more than 1000 members a week. The second division is an in-house invested fund of the order of $7000 billion. Support comes from in-house finance and IT departments.

In 1985 these systems ran in a difficult and unwieldy mainframe environment, and needed to be reviewed. The objectives were defined to be: enhancement of customer services achieved through systems chosen for speed, accuracy and flexibility; and homogeneity across the company's divisions, balanced with the need to be cost-effective.

In 1988 the decision was taken to move to a distributed approach based on PCs and minicomputers, and to use as much as possible off-the-shelf products that would be integrated in-house. The way in which the products would be used was the important factor—not the technology itself. Specific hardware and software policies were not the driving factors. The decisions taken were always to be based on the needs of the pensions business itself.

The critical requirement was seen as the need to move around the company's most important asset—information. This strategy led to consideration of local area networks in a Token Ring environment, which allowed the use of TCP/IP.

The decision to use IBM equipment was based on the flexibility of the product range, particularly in the networking arena, the price/performance of the RISC System/6000 systems, the ability to have UNIX and AS/400 systems coexist on the same network, the availability of the applications software for the front and back office investment management requirements on the chosen systems, and the high level of expertise of the IBM reseller partner, with whom BA has worked for many years.

Although the systems have been supplied by a single vendor—IBM—it was not part of BA's defined strategy to go with a single supplier. The process was completely open, and many vendors' products were considered. The only constraint was that the systems must run on the Token Ring network and that all the applications must interface easily.

The front and back office systems are running on the AS/400, where appropriate software already existed. The pensions benefits system, which now runs on an RISC System/6000, supports 40 users and very large volumes of data—more than two Gbytes—which needed external updating from the mainframe. The IBM UNIX platforms were chosen because the RISC System/6000 was deemed '[to have] twice as much memory, two and a half times as much disk, went twice as fast as its nearest competitor—and was cheaper', according to the company that supplied it. It was also known to be easily upgradable for the future, and to inter-operate with the AS/400s on the network.

The BA Pensions open systems strategy has enabled it to automate connections to external agencies such as bankers and brokers using a number of different platforms.

With the new systems now in place, the business decision-making is considerably accelerated. Information which previously took a month to prepare in the form of reports is now available on-line. Staff numbers have been reduced, the business is almost wholly automated, and the incremental costs of change in the future should be minimal. The annual IT budget has been reduced by half, and the payback on capital expenditure has taken less than two years. The smooth installation process and the lack of problems in implementation is credited in large part to the in-depth communications skills of the external supplier and integrator.

According to BA Pensions' systems development manager, 'We have invested in a competitive, broad-based open architecture which will enable us to respond to change wherever it may originate and to meet those changed needs quickly and at minimal cost.'

That's what open systems with IBM is all about.

Appendix 1
Open standards organizations

Contents

1. Introduction
2. OSI Standards Organizations

   - OSINET
   - COS
   - SPAG
   - NMF

3. Object Management Group (OMG)
4. Open Software Foundation (OSF)
5. X/Open Company Limited
6. User Alliance for Open Systems (UAOS)

A.1   Introduction

There are many organizations in the world dedicated to the identification, specification, testing and promotion of standards, and IBM is active in most of them. Gray (1991) describes in detail the activities of the most important; additional information can be obtained through the contacts/addresses listed in Appendix 3.

In order to help the understanding of material presented in the main text, some key organizations are described briefly here. The activities of the Open Software Foundation (OSF) are particularly relevant to IBM's open systems strategy.

A.2   OSI standards organizations

There are many organizations around the world dedicated to the definition and support of OSI standards. IBM is actively involved in most of them.

OSINET

OSINET is an international corporation composed of potential users and suppliers of OSI products whose object is to foster the development, promotion and deployment of OSI through activities relating to interoperation tests and testing. IBM is a member of OSINET and chairs the Steering Committee.

COS

The Corporation for Open Systems (COS) is a USA-based consortium of vendors and users whose mission is to promote the development and use of OSI-conforming products and to verify standards conformance through testing and branding. IBM is a member of COS and participates fully in all activities, including the testing service.

COS acts as the administrative umbrella for the MAP Users Group and the User Alliance for Open Systems (UAOS), and provides management of the OSINET Corporation.

The European equivalent of COS is the Standards Promotion and Application Group (SPAG), based in Brussels and responsible for the concept of profiles. In Japan, the equivalent body is the Japanese Conference for the Promotion of Open Systems (POSI).

COS, SPAG and POSI work closely together, with all three organizations working to define profiles relevant to the application needs of their geographical area, as well as testing standards conformance and testing interoperability of products.

SPAG

In 1992 SPAG officially launched its Process to Support Interoperability (PSI). This is a full service, open to all suppliers of open communications products. It provides vendors with a multivendor quality code of conduct for the successful development, implementation, testing and demonstration of interoperability. IBM was one of the first companies to submit products to this process.

NMF

The OSI Network Management Forum (NMF) is an open consortium of telecommunications and computer vendors, service providers and users worldwide. Its goal is to accelerate the availability of products that utilize international standards for interconnection of network management systems in multivendor voice and data networks. It was formed in 1988, and has over 100 members in more than 17 countries.

The NMF executes specific work programs in both technical and marketing areas. The primary technical work involves the specifications for open network management to be used by the members in their own products and services. The NMF publishes specifications and conformance testing tools, while the marketing work focuses primarily on user education.

IBM is a member of the NMF and participates actively in all aspects of its work.

A.3 The Object Management Group

The Object Management Group (OMG) is an international organization of more than 150 companies involved in systems and software development, as well as many software users. It was formed to help find ways to reduce the complexity, lower costs and hasten the introduction of new software applications.

The OMG plans to achieve this through the introduction of an architectural framework with supporting detailed interface specifications. These specifications will drive the industry towards interoperable reusable portable software components based on standard object-oriented interfaces. The adoption of this framework should make it possible to develop a heterogeneous applications environment across all major hardware and operating systems.

A major goal is to define a living and evolving standard. It should have realized parts so that application developers can deliver applications incorporating off-the-shelf components for common facilities like object storage, class structure, peripheral interface and user interface. The function of the OMG is to promulgate the standard specifications throughout the international industry and to foster the development of tools and software components compliant with the standards.

IBM is a member of the OMG and participates fully in all of its activities.

A.4 The Open Software Foundation (OSF)

The Open Software Foundation (OSF) is a not-for-profit research and development organization set up to develop and deliver an open software environment based on standards for the benefit of the information-processing industry. OSF solicits technologies from the industry-at-large, and delivers its technology in source code form. Headquartered in the USA, OSF has more than 300 members around the world and offices in four countries. IBM was a charter member of OSF.

The OSF utilizes an innovative open process called its Request For Technology (RFT) procedure to address some key open computing requirements. Through this process, OSF solicits and evaluates technology from the worldwide computer industry as well as educational institutions, government agencies and end-users. Through a collection of open systems technologies, OSF enables users to mix and match software and hardware from several suppliers in a virtually seamless environment.

OSF's vendor neutral software environment consists of several offerings, all based on relevant industry standards. The foundation is the OSF/1 operating system. Layered on this foundation are the OSF Distributed Computing Environment (DCE), an integrated set of technologies that lets users access diverse network resources, and the Motif graphical user interface, which gives applications a common look and feel on all classes of systems, from desktop to mainframe. DCE and Motif can be layered on OSF/1 as well as other operating systems, including UNIX.

The operating system OSF/1

An operating system which is based on UNIX, as is the case for OSF/1, has two main components—the kernel, which is the part that is closest to the hardware, and the system commands and utilities. The kernel for OSF/1 came from Transarc, while the commands and utilities came from IBM's AIX.

AIX/ESA is IBM's first complete implementation of OSF/1. Eventually, OSF/1 will be supported across all the AIX family.

The Motif graphical user interface

Through its first RFT, OSF addressed one of the computing industry's most pressing problems—that of portability of people through a standard graphical user interface to software applications.

The Motif graphical user interface has been widely accepted by end-users, system vendors and application developers. One year after its release, it was already available on more than 120 hardware platforms and 42 operating systems.

Motif provides a three-dimensional environment based on a widely accepted standard, the X Window system developed by the Massachussetts Institute of Technology (MIT). Motif simplifies user interaction with computers by reducing complex commands to easily recognizable pictures or icons for manipulating both local and remote applications as well as data.

IBM's CUA for SAA significantly influenced the development of Motif, and considerable similarity exists between them. IBM will provide OSF/Motif on both SAA and AIX workstations, and Motif on all AIX systems. IBM is working with the OSF to analyse the differences between CUA and Motif, and a common style guide is emerging from this work.

Prerequisites for Motif

AIXwindows is the IBM implementation of the OSF/Motif interface definition, is built upon code licensed from OSF. The license allows OSF code to be built into a product and then remarketed.

Motif, and therefore AIXwindows, is dependent on the transport (remote interface) facilities and constructs of the X Windows system from MIT. Here also a licensing agreement is in place to allow relicense of the code from MIT. In a similar manner, TCP/IP is a prerequisite to X Windows, which until recently has been most often built on a UNIX (or AIX) platform.

Distributed Computing Environment (DCE)

DCE is a comprehensive, integrated set of services that supports the development, use and maintenance of distributed applications. The availability of a uniform set of services anywhere in the network enables applications effectively to harness the power that tends to lie unused in many networks.

Technology for the DCE was supplied principally by IBM, Hewlett-Packard, Locus, Transarc and DEC. It is estimated that the investment by the industry in DCE so far is more than \$100 million and that it incorporates more than three-quarters of a million lines of code. IBM has made a major commitment to the DCE technology and is acting as integrator of the various technologies.

The motivation behind DCE is in line with that behind most open systems development:

- To allow application integration by retaining the same notions of users and groups within all applications. This means, for example, that a user could use the same password for all applications on the network;
- To provide a high level of availability of systems, so that if one crashes, the job is automatically moved to another;
- To allow geographically distributed computing, within and across enterprises, with sharing of resources, including data, between users and applications;
- To allow for incremental growth on the networks, while preserving investments made in the installed base;
- To avoid duplication of programming efforts, and therefore costs, by sharing code—for security, directory services time services, and so on—across applications.

The DCE services, which incorporate standards wherever possible, are organized into two categories:

Fundamental distributed services

These provide tools for software developers to create the end-user services needed for distributed computing. They include:

- Remote procedure call (RPC)
- Naming service, which provides a global directory service for every cell on the network, to be based on X.500
- Time service, which keeps all the clocks on the network in synchronization
- Security service, which manages the passwords and authentication of communicating parties
- Threads service, which allows concurrent work to take place within a process, and is necessary for parallel processing to take place either within a system or across systems.

Data-sharing services

These provide end-users with capabilities built upon the fundamental distributed services. These services require no programming on the part of the end-user and facilitate better use of information. They include:

- Distributed file system, which allows transparent, wide-area file access
- Diskless support
- MS-DOS file and printer support services.

Architecture Neutral Distribution Format (ANDF)

ANDF is a compiler intermediate language technology that enables developers to develop and distribute their applications in a form that can be installed and run on diverse open systems architectures. This technology, a hardware independent software distribution format, provides a consistent development and distribution environment for multiple platforms.

DCE, Transarc and IBM

Transarc, which supplied some of the technology for the DCE (the distributed file service and the local file system), has produced a developer's kit for DCE to help developers design or port products to the DCE definitions. It has also extended the DCE to support distributed transaction processing. IBM is a major shareholder in Transarc, and works closely with it.

Distributed Management Environment (DME)

The OSF has recognized the importance to users of being able to manage an assortment of distributed systems coherently, and is working to provide a Distributed Management Environment (DME) that will provide a uniform framework for the efficient, cost-effective management of open systems.The resultant technologies will work across multiple platforms and will include applications for accounting, backup, restoration and licensing of management.

IBM plans to support the DME in future system management products for the AIX environment. Where appropriate, the SystemView definition will include interoperability features between AIX systems management and the SystemView standards, interfaces and protocols. These will allow operators to extend their SystemView management capabilities into AIX environments. SystemView itself will interoperate with DME systems.

A.5   X/Open Company Limited

X/Open Company Limited was founded in 1984. It was set up as an international, non-profit organization by a group of major manufacturers 'to facilitate, guide and manage the process that will allow commercial and government users, software vendors, standards organizations and systems makers to solve the information technology dilemmas caused by incompatibilities in their systems and software components'. IBM is a corporate member of X/Open.

Since its formation, X/Open has led the information technology's movement to a vendor-independent, common computing environment that allows optimum and economic use of information. Its common applications environment (CAE) for open systems is based on formal *de jure* and widely accepted *de facto* standards, and is supported by organizations around the world.

The scope and focus of the CAE are shaped to a large degree by open systems user requirements as identified through the X/Open Xtra process and published in the X/Open Open Systems Directive. Within the scope of the CAE development program, the technical working groups of X/Open develop the appropriate interface definitions for the CAE, based on standards and emerging standards.

Since the CAE is based on standards, it contains a superset of the POSIX standards and incorporates the OSI standards. It also incorporates the OSF's DCE and DME frameworks.

The CAE is published in the *X/Open Portability Guides* (XPG), and products that have been proven to conform to XPG standards can use the XPG brand. Many of IBM's AIX products are so branded.

The X/Open User Council

The X/Open User Council consists of representatives from a number of large user organizations and provides cross-industry and user input to the development of open systems infrastructures defined within X/Open. User council members are instrumental in driving the Xtra process, designed to identify and prioritize user requirements within the open systems infrastructure.

A.6   User Alliance for Open Systems

The User Alliance for Open Systems (UAOS) is a group of companies from the manufacturing, process and aerospace industries that have banded together to provide a single voice to channel users' open systems requirements back to the computer industry, including the standards-setting bodies. Members include American Airlines, Boeing and Du Pont. UAOS is now affiliated with COS as a requirements generating body.

Appendix 2
Glossary

The computer industry is full of jargon and abbreviations, and it has been impossible to write this book without using them. As much as possible, their use has been kept to a minimum.

The following is a list of abbreviations used in the main text, with a brief explanation of each of them. When the text itself does not contain sufficient information on a point of particular interest, Appendix 3 and/or the Bibliography should be able to provide it.

386

Intel microprocessor used in PCs.

486

Intel microprocessor used in PCs; the next generation after the 386.

4GL

Fourth-generation language.

6150

IBM RISC processor used in the first IBM UNIX systems known by the same number, also known as the IBM RT.

8080

Early Intel microprocessor, used in early PCs.

88K

Motorola 88000 RISC microprocessor.

88open

A consortium of companies and individuals dedicated to creating a multivendor, open computing environment, based on the Motorola 88000 RISC processor family.

A/UX

Apple's version of UNIX.

ABI

Application binary interface.

ACE

Advanced computer environment, based on the MIPS processors.

AD/Cycle

IBM's CASE strategy for its SAA family.

AES
Application environment specification, from the OSF.

AIX
Advanced interactive executive, IBM's implementation of UNIX.

AIX/370
IBM's implementation of AIX for its mainframe 370 family.

AIX PS/2
IBM's implementation of AIX for its personal PS/2 family.

AIX/6000
IBM's implementation of AIX for its RISC System/6000 family.

AIX/CASE
IBM's CASE strategy for its AIX family.

AIXwindows
IBM's implementation of X Windows for AIX.

ANDF
Architecture neutral distribution format, the OSF technology for software distribution from a single version, independent of target processor.

ANI
Automatic number identification.

ANSI
American national standards institute.

ANSI X12
US EDI standards committee.

API
Application programming interface, a standard interface between an application and a set of services.

APPC
Advanced program-to-program communications.

AppleTalk
Proprietary networking technology from Apple Computer.

APPN
Advanced peer-to-peer networking.

AS/400
IBM's mid-range family of systems based on proprietary technology.

AVC
Audio visual connection, IBM's multimedia system.

BISON
The original name of X/Open, formed from the initials of the founder members.

BSD
Berkeley software distribution, one of the early and popular UNIX versions, now merged into UNIX System V.4.

CA
> Computer Automation Inc., one of the world's largest software companies.

CAD
> Computer-aided design.

CAE
> Common applications environment, specified by X/Open.

CallPath
> IBM's technology for voice/data applications.

CAIS
> Common APSE Interface Set, a CASE technology.

CASE
> Computer-aided software engineering.

CCITT
> International consultative committee for telegraph and telecommunications.

CCS
> Common communications support, part of IBM's SAA.

CICS
> IBM's customer information control system, a *de facto* standard for transaction processing applications.

CIM
> Computer integrated manufacturing.

CMIP
> OSI's common management information protocol.

CMIS
> Common management information service.

COS
> Corporation for open systems, an association of suppliers and users that promotes open systems in general, and OSI in particular.

CP/M
> Digital Research's control program/monitor, first of the microcomputer portable operating systems.

CPI
> Common programming interface, part of IBM's SAA.

CPI-C
> Common programming interface—conversational mode.

CRDA
> Character data representation architecture.

CSP
> IBM's cross system product for developing client/server implementations.

CUA
> Common user access, part of IBM's SAA.

CUA 91

CUA with object-oriented enhancements.

DB/2

An IBM proprietary database product.

DBMS

Database management system.

DCA

Document control architecture.

DCE

OSF's distributed computing environment.

DEC

Digital Equipment Corporation.

DECNET

Proprietary network technology from DEC.

DG

Data General.

DME

OSF's distributed management environment.

DNIS

Dialled number identification services.

DOS

Microsoft's disk operating system for PCs.

DP

Data processing.

DRDA

IBM's distributed relational database architecture.

DTP

X/Open's distributed transaction processing standards.

DVI

Intel's digital video interactive technology.

ECMA

European computer manufacturers' association, a consortium of computer vendors that provide input to various standards bodies.

ECTA

European computer telephony applications standard from ECMA.

EDA/SQL

Enterprise data access/structured query language, developed by Information Builders to provide access to many different data types.

EDI

Electronic data interchange.

EDIFACT

A UN proposed EDI standard under development within ISO.

ES/9000

    The IBM family of mainframe enterprise systems.

ESA

    IBM's enterprise systems architecture.

ESA/370

    IBM's mainframe 370 enterprise system architecture.

ESCON

    IBM's high speed data communications channel for mainframe and RISC System/ 6000 connections.

ESPRIT

    European strategic program for research in information technology.

Ethernet

    Standard local area network technology using CSMA/CD techniques.

ETM

    IBM's enterprise transaction management technology.

FAP

    Formats and protocols.

FDDI

    Fiber distributed data interface, an ANSI standard for transmission over fiber optic cable.

FIPS

    The US federal information processing standard.

Gosip

    Government open systems interconnection profile.

Harmonization

    A process which ensures the compatibility of standards.

HP

    Hewlett-Packard.

IBM

    International Business Machines.

IEEE

    The US Institute of Electrical and Electronics Engineers, reponsible for the POSIX work.

IIN

    IBM Information Network.

IIS

    Integrated information systems.

IMS/ESA

    IBM's information management systems for the enterprise system architecture.

Information Warehouse

    IBM's structure for integrating information sources across an enterprise.

INX/IPX

Novell's network protocols for the linking of PCs and servers onto local area networks.

IS

Information strategy.

ISC

Inter-system communications in CICS.

ISDN

Integrated service digital network, an evolving CCITT standard for the integration of voice, data and images over a network.

ISO

International standards organization.

IT

Information technology.

IVANS

Insurance value-added network services.

Kaleida

An independent company formed by IBM and Apple to develop and promote multimedia technologies.

Kerberos

A security technology developed within MIT and incorporated in OSF's DCE.

LAN

Local area network.

LIM

London insurance market.

LIMNET

LIM's data network.

LU 6.2

IBM's standard SNA communications technology for peer-to-peer communications.

Mac

Popular personal computer from Apple, incorporating a proprietary and user-friendly graphical interface.

MAN

Metropolitan area network.

MAP

Manufacturing automation protocols.

MAXM

Multivendor expert manager for telecommunications devices offered by IBM through an alliance with International Telemanagement.

MIS

Management information systems.

MIT
> Massachusetts Institute of Technology.

MITI
> An association of Japanese companies concerned with standards.

Motif
> The *de facto* standard graphical user interface supplied by OSF.

MQI
> Message queue interface.

MS-DOS
> Microsoft's standard disk operating system for Intel-based PCs.

MSA
> Management Sciences of America, a mainframe software company.

Multimedia
> The combination of sound, vision, video and touch on the desktop.

MVS/ESA
> The IBM operating system which dominates in the large mainframe environment.

MVS
> The IBM mainframe operating system for the 370 architecture.

NCS
> Network computing system.

NetView
> IBM's network management technology.

NetWare
> A LAN operating system developed by Novell and now an industry standard.

NFS
> Network file system, developed by Sun Microsystems for file transfer between UNIX systems, and now an industry standard.

NLS
> National language support.

NMF
> Network management forum, a consortium of vendors and users formed to define network management standards.

Odette
> A European EDI standard.

OEM
> Original equipment manufacturer, a company that buys component technologies from others and assembles them into products of its own.

OMG
> Object management group, a consortium of vendors and users set up to define standards for object-oriented programming.

OpenView
> Hewlett-Packard technology licensed to IBM and used in IBM's NetView/6000 .

OS/400

 IBM's operating system for its AS/400 family.

OS/2

 IBM's operating system for the PS/2 family under SAA.

OS/2 DBM

 IBM's database management system for OS/2.

OSE

 Open systems environment, as defined by the IEEE in POSIX.

OSF

 Open Software Foundation.

OSF/1

 The operating system developed by OSF as an alternative to UNIX.

OSI

 Open systems interconnection, the international standards for communications.

OSINET

 International corporation composed of users and suppliers of OSI products.

PABX

 Private automatic branch exchange.

PC

 Personal computer, usually referring to those compatible with IBM PCs.

PC-DOS

 Microsoft's MS-DOS operating system as licensed to IBM.

PCTE

 Portable common tool environment, proposed by ECMA as part of the emerging ISO standards for open software development.

PM

 Presentation Manager, the graphical user interface developed by IBM and used in OS/2.

POSC

 Petrochemical Open Systems Group.

POSIX

 Portable operating system interface, defined within the US IEEE before submission to ISO.

PowerOpen

 The computing environment that will result from the IBM/Apple/Motorola alliance.

PowerPC

 The family of single chip RISC microprocessors that will result from the IBM/Apple/Motorola alliance.

Profiles

 Groups of OSI standards tailored to meet specific application requirements.

PS/2
> IBM's Personal Systems family, part of the SAA line.

PSI
> Process to support interoperability, from SPAG.

RAS
> Reliability, availability and serviceability.

R & D
> Research and development.

RDA
> Relational database architecture, a standard proposed by SAG.

Repository Manager
> Software to manage the information model of the enterprise, particularly to allow tools from several vendors to work together.

Repository
> The information model of an enterprise.

RFC
> Requests for comment, part of the process prior to ISO authorization of a standard.

RFS
> Remote file sharing.

RFT
> Request for technology, part of the OSF process.

RISC
> Reduced instruction set computer.

RISC System/6000
> IBM's family of systems based on its own RISC processor.

RPC
> Remote procedure call, a mechanism to allow a program on one system to cause a procedure to be carried out on another.

RPI
> OSI's remote programming interface.

RT
> Shorthand form used to refer to IBM's first RISC technology UNIX system (also known as the 6150).

S/400
> The system built by Itautec of Brazil from IBM's AS/400 components.

SAA
> IBM's Systems Application Architecture.

SAG
> SQL Access Group, formed to define standards for data access.

SCO
> Santa Cruz Operation, suppliers of a packaged version of UNIX, originally called Xenix, now incorporated into UNIX System V.4.

SIGMA

A Japanese consortium sponsored by MITI and concerned with standards.

SMIT

IBM's systems management interface tool for AIX.

SMS

Standard multimedia system, as defined by IBM.

SMTP

Simple mail transfer protocol, standard on UNIX systems.

SNA

IBM's *de facto* standard wide-area Systems Network Architecture.

SNA/DS

SNA/distribution services.

SNMP

Simple network management protocol in TCP/IP.

Softbench

Hewlett-Packard's CASE technology, which has been licensed to IBM, among others.

SPA

IBM's standards program authority, the person responsible for the technical direction of standards activities in a particular area.

SPAG

European standards promotion and application group.

SQL/DS

IBM technology for distributed SQL.

SQL

IBM's structured query language, a database query language that is now an international standard.

STARS

Software technology for adaptable and reliable systems.

System V

The standard version of UNIX as supplied by the UNIX Systems Laboratory, and incorporating both BSD and Xenix versions.

SystemView

IBM's technology for systems and network management.

Taligent

An independent company formed by IBM and Apple to develop and market a new software platform using object-oriented technology.

TCOS

The US IEEE's technical committee on open systems.

TCP/IP

Transmission control protocol/internet protocol, developed by the US Department of Defense for standard networking, and now widely used, especially in UNIX networks.

TIRS

The Integrated Reasoning Shell, one of IBM's software development tools.

Token Ring

A standard LAN technology.

TOP

Technical and office protocols.

TP

Transaction processing.

TPM

Transaction processing monitor.

UAOS

User alliance for open systems.

/usr/group

Previous name for Uniforum.

UI

UNIX International, a non-profit organization responsible for directing the further development of UNIX.

Unicode

New 16-bit character standard.

Uniforum

A non-profit international organization which disseminates information on open systems.

UNIX

The operating system originally developed within AT & T and now licensed to most computer manufacturers.

USL

UNIX System Laboratory, the company formed by AT & T to further develop the UNIX operating system.

VAR

Value-added reseller.

VM/ESA

An IBM mainframe operating system for ESA.

VM

An IBM mainframe operating system.

VMS

DEC's proprietary operating system for its VAX family.

VSE

An IBM mainframe operating system.

WAN

Wide area networks.

Windows

A graphical user interface developed by MicroSoft for PCs as an upgrade path to DOS.

X/Open

An international non-profit organization, owned by a consortium of the world's largest computer manufacturers, set up to define, promote and supply open systems technologies.

X Windows

A network transparent window system developed at MIT and now embedded into most vendors' UNIX systems.

X.21

The CCITT standard for communication between devices in a circuit-switched network.

X.25

The CCITT standard for communication in packet-switched networks.

X.400

OSI's mail and message interchange.

X.500

OSI's directory services.

Xenix

The version of UNIX originally supplied by Microsoft, and later offered as a packaged product by SCO.

XPG

X/Open portability guide, the specifications for the components of open systems, based on a mixture of public and *de facto* standards.

Xtra

The X/Open process for identifying the needs of the users in the open systems environment.

Z80

Zilog's 8-bit microprocessor on which many microcomputers using CP/M were based.

Appendix 3
Standards organizations

COS

Corporation for Open Systems
1750 Old Meadow Road, Suite 400, McLean, VA 22101, USA
Tel: 1 703 883 2700
Fax: 1 703 848 4572

ECMA

European Computer Manufacturers' Association
114 Rue du Rhone, CH-1204 Geneva, Switzerland
Tel: 41 22 735 36 34
Fax: 41 22 786 52 31

IAUG

International AIX Users' Group
Suite 300, 9050 Capital of Texas Highway N, Austin, TX 78759, USA
Tel: 1 512 795 2016
Fax: 1 512 343 9650

OMG

Object Management Group
Framingham Corporate Center, 492 Old Connecticut Path, Framingham, MA 01701, USA
Tel: 1 508 820 4300
Fax: 1 508 820 4303

OSF

Open Software Foundation
11 Cambridge Center, Cambridge, MA 02142, USA
Tel: 1 617 621 7300
Fax: 1 617 621 0631

SPAG

Standards Promotion and Applications Group
Avenue Loiuse 149, Box 7, 1050-Brussels, Belgium
Tel: 3 22 535 0811
Fax: 3 22 537 2440

UAOS

User Alliance for Open Systems; *see* COS

UI

Unix International
Waterview Corporate Center, 20 Waterview Boulevard, Parsippany, NJ 07054, USA
Tel: 1 201 263 8400
Fax: 1 201 263 8401

Unicode Consortium

1965 Charleston Road, Mountain View, CA 94943, USA
Tel: 1 415 961 4189
Fax: 1 415 966 1637

Uniforum Association

2910 Tasman Drive, Suite 201, Santa Clara, CA 95054, USA
Tel: 1 408 986 8840
Fax: 1 408 986 1645

X/Open Company Limited

Apex Plaza, Forbury Road, Reading RG1 1AX, UK
Tel: 44 734 508 311
Fax: 44 734 500110

1010 El Camino Real, Suite 380, Menlo Park, CA 94025, USA
Tel: 1 415 323 7992
Fax: 1 415 323 8204

Bibliography

AIX Reports and Newsletters (1991, 1992). International Technology Group, 330 Distel Circle, Suite 125, Los Altos, CA 94022-1433, USA.

Earl, Michael J. (1989). *Management Strategies for Information Technology*, Prentice-Hall, Englewood Cliffs, NJ.

Gray, Pamela A. (1991). *Open Systems—A Business Strategy for the 1990s*, McGraw-Hill, London.

IBM's AD/Cycle and Repository, IBM's NetView and others (1991, 1992). Reports from Computer Technology Research Corporation, 16 East Elliott Street, Charleston, SC 29401-2573, USA.

The World of Standards: An Open System Reference Guide (1991). 88open Consortium Limited, 100 Homeland Court, Suite 800, San Jose, CA 95112, USA.

Index

PATRON CHARGED ITEMS

Patron: Sanjay Arun Khobragade
Patron ID: 60179600599916018
Patron Grp: Graduate Assistant

Title/Item ID	Due Date	Status
AS/400 client/server systems : business applications and solutio 39346007064613	1/13/2004 02:00 AM	Charged 1/1/200
CICS programmer's desk reference / Doug Lowe. 39346005674488	1/13/2004 02:00 AM	Charged 1/1/200
Client/server strategies : implementations in the IBM environme 39346006622015	1/13/2004 02:00 AM	Charged 1/1/200
From Beirut to Jerusalem / Thomas L. Friedman. 39346005852589	11/13/2003 11:59 PM	Charged /14/200
Guide to SAS/DB2 / Diane E. Brown. 39346006521233	1/13/2004 02:00 AM	Charged 1/1/200
Mutual funds : analysis, allocation, and performance evaluation / 39346006804431	1/13/2004 02:00 AM	Charged 1/1/200
Mutual funds on the net : making money online / Paul B. Farrell. 39346007161146	1/13/2004 02:00 AM	Charged 1/1/200
Open systems and IBM : integration and convergence / Pamela 39346006342168	1/13/2004 02:00 AM	Charged 1/1/200
Oracle, a beginner's guide / Michael Abbey, Michael J. Corey ; [	11/20/2003 11:59 PM	Charged /21/200